"Life for Singaporeans
is not complete
without shopping!"

Prime Minister Goh Chok Tong,
National Day Rally Speech, 1996

Life is Not Complete Without Shopping

Consumption Culture in Singapore

CHUA BENG HUAT

National University of Singapore

SINGAPORE UNIVERSITY PRESS
NATIONAL UNIVERSITY OF SINGAPORE

© 2003   Singapore University Press
NUS Publishing
Yusof Ishak House
31 Lower Kent Ridge Road
Singapore 119078

Fax: (65) 6774-0652
E-mail: supbooks@nus.edu.sg
Website: http://www.nus.edu.sg/npu

ISBN 9971-69-272-4 (Paper)

Typeset by: Scientifik Graphics (Singapore) Pte Ltd
Printed by: Photoplates Pte Ltd

Contents

Preface

The life of a consumer object is very short. It is meant to be so in order to keep the factory that produces it working, workers employed, its consumers happy (but not for long), and the economy moving. This brevity of existence is a constraint on critical analysis of any consumer object, singularly or in constellation as a trend or a lifestyle. The problem is that by the time the analyst figures out the critical angle for commentary, the object in question would have already been consumed and committed to the trash-heap. Consumed and rejected, or unsold and rejected, either way it is discarded. It no longer sits on the display shelf because it has become old and unfashionable. Or having served its fashionable time as a trendy consumable, it has been left behind, not to be used again, but to embody specific memories of its once trendy owner. Ironically, if the item were kept long enough, it might become a 'classic'. It might find another day to display its glory in the symbolic world of consumption as 'retro' or 'antique', with a monetary value disproportionate to its original price or utility. This enhanced monetary value derives from the fact that the once-unremarkable mass-produced object has now become rare and singular, having withstood the passing of time. In general, however, the brevity of life of a consumer object and of a consumer trend makes it unavoidable that all published materials on consumer products and trends are by definition 'historical'.

Given this 'historical' character, many of the Singaporean readers of the essays in this collection may recall fondly the objects and trends discussed, attaching a piece of private memory to them. For others the objects and trends will be met for the first time, and the behaviours relative to the objects will appear strange and even incredible; readers may be incredulous at their ancestors' strange appearances and the behaviours that were determined by the consumer objects. Recall here the experience of looking at old photographs, even one's very own, and getting a sense of this strangeness at the kind of clothes worn by those in the photographs.

The actual reaction of an individual will depend on the age of the reader. Regardless of generational location, reading about these objects and trends should be pleasurable to a Singaporean.

From a sociological perspective, the brevity of life of consumer objects demands that the analysis of such objects be placed within larger theoretical and substantive concerns which go beyond fascination with specific short-lived items. Each item selected for analytic attention should address some of the following questions: of cultural penetration from outside; of individual and collective identity constructions through the use of consumer goods; of the symbolic and cultural capital that is inscribed on consumer objects; their use to signify class distinctions; and of the place of consumerism not only in economic stability but also the political legitimacy of the ruling government. Obviously, this slate of macro-sociological concerns cannot and will not be carried by every item of consumption. Neither is there a specific item that is so strategic that all the macro concerns are inscribed upon it. In practice, different objects can be used strategically to illuminate aspects of the macro concerns and, hopefully, in a collection of analysis of different objects over a period of time, as in this collection, many of the larger social issues would have been given due analytic attention.

In this collection of essays which deals specifically with the culture of consumption in Singapore, the following issues have been examined. First, eschewing the prevailing belief in the distinctiveness and separateness of cultural practices of the three visible races, this study looks at the complexities of consumption practices shared within each generation, and differing across generations, cutting across all racial groups as seen particularly in the adornment of self. The analysis of actual practices in cultural boundary crossings in food consumption also breaks down the seeming isolation of Malay/Muslims imposed by religious injunctions. Second, sociological interest and public interest in consumption coincide in their mutual concern with 'excess', which expresses itself in terms of moral critique of 'individualism', 'materialism' and 'class competition'. These three concepts and their manifestations in consumption practices are embedded in the concept of lifestyles: display of class status through the consumption and ostentatious display of specific consumer items, such as cars, houses and items of bodily adornment including (but not confined to) designer clothes. These issues are examined in terms of the differential demands and stresses on Singaporean families in the lower-income strata and the middle class. Third, on the issue of Singaporean 'identity', the conventional search for some specific characteristic that is entirely Singaporean is conceptually misplaced. Singaporean identity claims emerge, indirectly through the ways Singaporeans interpret cultural products that are imported from elsewhere, especially television programmes and films. Here, the 'Chinese-ness' of Chinese-Singaporeans relative to Chinese in other locations where ethnic Chinese are demographically predominant, such as Taiwan and Hong Kong, provides insights to certain aspects of the Singaporean identity. Finally, fragments of the Singaporean identity also emerge in the way Singaporean cultural producers project and represent Singaporeans to themselves and, of course, to others. In the latter case, the tendency of middle-class producers to focus on the underside of the widely-accepted economically triumphal success story of Singapore comes through as a critique of the existing social order. However, the class position of these cultural producers is also simultaneously exposed: Their representation of life among those who have fallen through the net of the success story, is little more than putting into visual clarity the written texts of the daily reportage of the official construction of failure.

This collection of essays, therefore, has several levels of intellectual investment: the essays mark the different moments in the history of the culture of consumption in Singapore, as the society emerges out of economic underdevelopment and material deprivation. They analyse different social issues and disrupt conventional, therefore comfortable, assumptions held by a majority of Singaporeans about race, class and individual and collective identities, assumptions that are often officially circulated so as to be used as the basis of public discourse and policies. Finally, they are concerned with the private desires, memories, and other sentiments that consumers have for specific objects. Accordingly, the essays afford different readings and they are arranged for different reading interests. Professional readers can decide for themselves how they want to read the book. My concern here is with readers who do not want to be bothered with the sociological issues. For you, my advice is to skip Chapter 2 and read the rest of the individual chapters, each one dealing with specific instances of consumption, depending on which object and/or instance interests you at any different sitting. My hope is that for Singaporeans, each of these instances will be filled with the pleasures of self-recognition as individuals and as a people, as Singaporeans. That would be 'empirical' evidence enough for the observations that I have made in the text.

April 2003
Singapore

Acknowledgements

The editorial work for this book would not have been possible without leave from teaching duties granted by the Faculty of Arts and Social Sciences at the National University of Singapore for me to take up the inaugural Distinguished Visiting Scholar fellowship at the Carolina Asia Center, University of North Carolina at Chapel Hill. I am grateful to the generosity of both institutions. At the personal level, I would like to thank Lily Kong, Dean of the Faculty at NUS and Steven Levine, Interim Director of the Center, one for granting me leave and the other for making me feel at home. At UNC, Don Nonini and the other Asianists in the various departments, including James Peacock, Judith Farquhar, Peter Coclanis, Tony Day and Sarah Weiss, had not only help me with the necessities that enabled me to work productively but also with enjoyable dinners and intellectual company.

Most of the essays in this collection have been previously published for different occasions, different places and different audiences, over more than a decade. The permission of the various editors and publishers to reproduce the material, in whole or in part, are gratefully acknowledged: A longer version of Chapter 2 was previously published as 'World Cities, Globalisation and the Spread of Consumerism: A view from Singapore' in *Urban Studies*, volume 35 (1998); Chapter 3 first appeared in the *UTS Review*, volume 5 (1999); Chapter 4 combines the previously published 'Steps to Becoming a Fashion Consumer in Singapore', *Asia Pacific Journal of Management*, volume 7 (1990) and 'Shopping for Women's Fashion in Singapore', in Rob Shields (ed.), *Lifestyle Shopping: the subject of consumption* (London and New York: Routledge, 1992); Chapter 5 was first published in *Postcolonial Studies*, volume 3 (2000); Chapter 6 was first published in David Y.H. Wu and Tan Chee-beng (eds.), *Changing Chinese Foodways in Asia* (Hong Kong: The Chinese University Press, 2001); Chapter 7 first appeared in Chua Beng Huat (ed.), *Consumption in Asia: Lifestyles and Identities* (London and New York: Routledge,

2000); Chapter 8 was previously published in Eyal Ben-Ari and John Clammer (eds.), *Japan in Singapore: Cultural occurences and cultural flows* (London: Routledge/Curzon, 2000). Chapter 10 was previously published in *Inter-Asia Cultural Studies*, volume 4 (2003). The original versions of Chapters 5 and 10 can be accessed at <http://www.tandf.co.uk>.

INTRODUCTION

1

Framing Singapore's Consumption Culture

The People's Action Party (PAP) that has governed Singapore without break since 1959 is driven by pursuit of national economic growth. And its record has been nothing short of impressive. This is its 'performance' principle and singular claim to legitimacy to rule. It will go to all lengths, including curtailing conventional democratic rights and practices, to 'deliver the goods' to the people. In this sense, the PAP is singularly motivated to improve the material life of Singaporeans through expansion of material consumption. The country did not become independent until 1965, and the first generation of Singaporeans suffered material deprivations during economically underdeveloped colonial days. They responded to the government's drive with an equally single-minded determination, and subsequent generations kept up this effort, in employment, education and other forms of skills upgrading. After forty years of undisrupted PAP rule, consumption levels of Singaporeans have expanded across the entire society in tandem with economic development.

Singapore now shows evidence of a consumer culture comparable to that of advanced developed nations. All the major fast food chains are here; all the major fashion names are here; all the luxury cars can be seen on the roads, with the exception of those from American manufacturers, who stubbornly refuse to build right-hand drive vehicles; Singaporeans from all income groups travel, the difference between individual travellers is one of distance, destination and frequency. The proportion of disposable income spent on food has been increasing because of the tendency to eat outside the home. The multitude of activities — shopping, entertainment, transformation of oneself — and the endless stream of new and improved products of consumption — from small items such as soap to big ticket items like cars and houses — constitute an expanding part of the local culture of everyday life. The insertion of aggregated consumption activities and commodities into everyday life allows us to speak, appropriately, of an emergence of a consumer culture or of consumerism as a culture among Singaporeans.

The activities that support the endless stream of products and services that constantly vie for consumer attention are such a large part of the economy and society that it is impossible to conceptualise and analyse them as a whole: the constant research to find new products or improve on existing products to gain new markets or expand existing share; the dissemination of knowledge of these products through different modes and media of propagation — print and televisual advertisements, home sales parties, hand leaflets and miniature promotional items; the circuit from production to distribution to finally ending up in the hands of the consumers; the speed of use-by dates and the replacement of commodities; each one of these processes is a very large area of socioeconomic activity that can be investigated in its own right. Consequently, as a field of social commentary and academic research, it is both conceptually and substantively impossible to examine this consumerism-as-culture as a coherent and integrated object, at least not without excessive generalisation or serious distortion. The totality of consumerism as culture is an abstraction that can only be examined in fragments. This collection of analyses of different instances of consumption practices and different objects of desire of Singaporeans is a reflection of this methodological constraint.

A second methodological constraint, following from the short shelf-life of commodities, is that the objects of analysis and commentary are likely to disappear even before the ink is dried on the writing. Furthermore, given the vast universe of possible objects of consumption, the readers of the analysis may not even be familiar with the objects that engage the commentator. Given the fleeting character of the life of commodities, analysis of such objects and their consumption should strive to disclose how these practices reflect underlying social, economic, political and cultural relations of the location of consumption; this is what each chapter in this book will attempt to do.

In this brief introduction, I would like to sketch out three features — globalisation of commodities, social class and domestic economy — which taken together broadly define the loosely organised parameters within which Singaporeans are transformed into, and sustain themselves as, consumers.

Globalisation of Commodities

Singapore exports almost everything it produces, imports almost everything Singaporeans consume. This is but a condition of the globalisation of commodity distribution and consumption. Within global capitalism few consumer products are produced exclusively for local markets. Contrary to conventional belief, successful globally distributed products, recognised by their brand names, are significantly 'un-nationalistic' in their production and marketing strategies. Products can be produced anywhere, as long as production cost is low and quality control, specified by the brand-owners, is high. Brand-owners are quick to erase the national origins of their business, unless it is advantageous to sell the origins as icons of desire; to be 'global' is to be 'everywhere' and not from a specific 'somewhere'. For example, take McDonald's hamburgers. Their reach as a 'global' product is reflected in the possibly apocryphal story of an Asian child arriving in Los Angeles, remarking to his parents, "Look, they have McDonald's here too!"

Secondly, to be globally successful a commodity must attempt to insinuate itself as much as possible into the local cultural context, into the daily life of the people in its market destination; at its most extreme, to be 'indigenised'. Otherwise, it will always be in the realm of the consumption of the 'exotic', which is singularised and an occasional thing: meaning, low volume sales. Take for example a t-shirt, whether from *Hot Tuna* or *Nike*, and a batik shirt from Indonesia; the t-shirt is an everyday thing everywhere, the brands are add-ons, whereas the batik shirt, outside Indonesia or in a stretch perhaps, outside Southeast Asia, is exotic and is worn only occasionally, almost ceremonially. The difference in quantum of sales between t-shirts and batik shirts can be readily imagined.

Another mode of 'indigenising' an imported commodity is to re-configure the similarities in the lifestyles of its consumers in the different locations of the world and rearticulate it as a product of a 'cosmopolitan' culture, through its marketing strategies, particularly in and through its advertising images; advertisements partake in the very construction of the idea and image of the 'cosmopolitan'. The idea of the 'cosmopolitan' refers positively to no specific geographical site in particular, and thus belongs everywhere in the cosmos. As tailoring of marketing strategies to the cultural specificities of each market location is expensive, the cosmopolitan strategy may be preferred. Both marketing strategies are to be found in Singapore.

An example of indigenisation in Singapore is, not surprisingly, McDonald's. In a political/ideological space that is infused with cultural anti-Americanism such as Singapore, McDonald's sells itself through inserting its products into a representation of Singaporean everyday life in its advertisements on local television. As shown in Chapter 6, within a space of one minute or less, McDonald's advertisements insert their products into the 'daily routine' of Singaporeans of all ages, rather than transporting Singaporean consumers to an 'American' space for the consumption of 'American' culture. In this manner, McDonald's attempts to insert a foreign food item as local fare.

The idea of cosmopolitanism needs to be examined within the Singapore context.[1] The ideological/moral discourse in Singapore has always pitched reinvented good and wholesome 'Asian' cultures and values against a homogenised, bad and decadent 'Western' culture.[2] The highest crescendo was probably reached during the early to mid-1990s, when the rise of capitalism in Asia seemed miraculously unstoppable and sustainable. It has since subsided very noticeably but is unlikely to be erased completely, and continues to maintain a low-grade rumble. In this East/West discourse, consumerism is often seen as part of the 'westoxification' of Singaporeans and a new infection of the young. The below thirty-year-olds are the prime target of moral criticism. For young working adults, without families of their own, the body is both a medium for symbolic display of achievement and a machine for ingestion. The very visibility of a young person, all togged-out in brand-name clothes, drinking wine and eating Italian food, *al fresco*, is an easy target of moral reproach, by his/her seniors, for being 'Westernised'. This reproach signifies a fear of consumerism by investing too much credence in the common sense conception that 'one is what one consumes'.

It might be a truism that a person constructs a self-image with the objects consumed. Precisely because a self-image is a construction a consumer need not be, indeed often is not, committed in any depth to a particular image as an essential identity. Indeed, a most important feature of consumerism is that 'identity' is an occasional thing; it can be readily changed with changing fads, changing seasons and changing occasions, at a moment's pleasure. Quick image/identity change is the very ideological and practical centre of consumerism, otherwise shopping malls would not be the space of fantasy, of chimera. Consumer culture is playful, or put negatively, superficial. Absence of deep commitment to any particular image/identity underlines the idea of consumer sovereignty in consumerism as culture. Given this, the fear of deracination of the Singaporean through consumerism seems unfounded.

The apprehension may be said to result from an intentional exaggeration of the commitment of Singaporeans to a reinvented 'Asian' cultural identity. Against the exaggerations, I will merely mention that in a single unremarkable day, there are more noodles consumed by Singaporeans than all the fast-food hamburgers and fried chicken, put together. In this context, the food habits of Singaporeans remain largely intact and globalised fast-foods remain occasional things, even if they are consumed with relatively high frequency by some. Nevertheless, the reinvented 'Asian' identity has stirred cultural and sentimental resonance among some segments of the population. The most visible effect is to be found in women's clothes. As analysed in Chapter 5, one should note here the re-emergence of the *cheongsam* as formal dress for Chinese women, particularly on occasions of social and political consequence during the period of triumphal rise of capital in the early 1990s. Also noticeable is the apparently more permanent discarding of the *kebaya* among Malay women with the intensification of religiosity since the late 1970s. That men do not similarly wear their respective ethnic costumes, except on ritual occasions, should not be surprising because, as in all patriarchal societies, in Singapore women are the bearer of tradition and suppression.

However, in the larger arena of fashion, the sense of the 'cosmopolitan' prevails. It moves away from neo-colonial anxieties of cultural imperialism which imagine the Singaporean cultural space as thoroughly penetrated and dominated by the West, demanding a defensive cultural politics that privileges reinvented local values. Examining the clothing practices of different segments of Singaporeans (Chapter 5) as part of the larger consumer cosmos, we find firstly, as Singapore receives cultural flows from the outside world, different segments of the population select different reference points from this global flow, disrupting the simplistic idea of a singular dominant 'western' cultural imperialism penetrating every community on the island. Secondly, looking at cuisine practices,

Singaporeans contribute directly to the idea of the 'cosmopolitan' when elements of Singaporean cultural practices are taken up by others, including tourists, who come into contact with Singapore and Singaporeans (Chapter 7).

Consumption and Social Class

Improvements in material life can never be evenly distributed in capitalist economies. Inequalities are defining characteristics of capitalist economies, producing different social strata, which interact with different identity markers, such as race and religion, to create complex subjectivities. Under conditions of general expansion of consumption for all but the very poor, intensification of inequalities may be and, indeed has been, submerged. It has been intensifying nonetheless and the politics of inequality has become part of Singapore's public sphere since the early 1990s at least.

Public discussions of increasingly visible differences in ability to meet rising costs of living in a developed consumer society led to the convening of two cost review committees by the government, in 1991 and 1995. In his National Day Rally speeches, in 1995 and 1996, the Prime Minister warned that income inequalities will get worse in the future. He counselled individual citizens not to engage in the 'politics of envy' by comparing themselves with others who are making perceivably far greater economic advances. Finally, in his 1999 National Day Rally speech, he divided the nation into the 'cosmopolitans' — techno-savvy individuals and investment bankers, residing in high-price private properties who are globally marketable and important to national economic expansion — and the 'heartlanders', such as bus drivers and factory workers, who live in public housing estates and constitute the majority of the nation's core population. This signalling is evidence of the expanding social consequences of income inequalities. Ideologically, the emerging inequalities are also veiled by two concepts that organise Singapore society; namely, the idea of 'meritocracy' and the idea of race.

To deflect possible politicisation of inequalities into class politics the idea of 'meritocracy' has been deeply and repetitively inscribed on the social body. 'Meritocracy' as an idea admits of the presence of inequalities, not only in income but also other opportunities including comparative advantages in consumption. It suppresses the idea that such inequalities are in part systemic and social-structurally determined, displacing the cause of inequalities onto individual efforts: one reaps the benefits of one's natural endowments in intelligence and one's labour, thus individualising success and failure. During the years of rapid economic growth, there had been a very high rate of upward mobility across the entire population. However, quietly, a class structure that is more determining of individual's long-term achievements has emerged. Going forward, occupationally and socially, intra-class recruitment will be more pronounced and class closure will become more noticeable. The window of upward mobility will narrow and the likelihood of the emergence of a permanent underclass will increase. As social class structure rigidifies, official efforts to insist on the ideology of 'meritocracy' may intensify but the determining effects of class differences will increasingly erode the 'reality' of meritocracy for many, if not most.

Secondly, the idea and practice of Singapore as a 'multiracial' society also helps to contain possible politicisation of inequality. The poor, the middle class and the rich of each race are supposedly 'integrated' as a social unity through their presumed shared 'traditional' culture; each racial group is presumed to be integrated vertically. This idea is behind the setting up of 'community self-help' organisations, such as the Singapore Indian Development Agency (SINDA) and Chinese Development Assistance Committee (CDAC), where working individuals contribute to the needy of each one's respective racial group. Additionally, each racial group has been encouraged to look at year-on-year economic improvements only with reference to their own past rather than to compare themselves across racial divisions, in order to reduce the likelihood of the emergence of class-based political alliances. Again, the persuasiveness of vertical race-based integration will likely be increasingly tested as income inequalities are made visible by differences in consumption.

Significantly, official ability to reduce class awareness is constantly being undermined by consumer culture. Consumerism is by its character always ostentatious. It thrives on display of differences. An overt expression of social class is, of course, the ability to consume. The differential ability to consume constantly disrupts the surface calm in daily life, bringing about the 'return of the repressed' class awareness. For example, shown in Chapter 3, a salesgirl in a high-priced boutique is reminded daily of how 'meagre' is her wage when she serves other women who spend several times more than her monthly earnings on a dress. Awareness of such disparities not only affects the relatively 'have-nots' but also impacts the attitude of the 'haves'. Here, the politics of envy meets politics of discrimination in everyday life. Two debates on lifestyles can be provided as evidence of each of these tendencies.

First is in the area of housing. Singaporeans are among the best housed people in the world. Ironically, this has given rise to an area in which class differences can be best displayed. For many in the emerging middle-class, breaking away from the masses in public housing estates is more important than the economic consequences of a rationally unsound decision to purchase a substantially smaller flat in a 99-year leasehold condominium in a location poorly serviced by public transportation and other daily necessities, but one built by a private developer. The result is often over-consumption of housing at the expense of other aspects of daily life.

Even the self-proclaimed 'tough' PAP government has succumbed to the pressure of the desire of the middle-class to segregate itself from the 'toiling' masses, by introducing a category of publicly-subsidised housing, the 'executive condominiums'. These are meant for those in the middle class who cannot afford to purchase similar accommodations in the private sector. Giving in to such pressure did not endear the government to public housing residents, who viewed this as pandering to a group that considers itself to be above them. The government has, perhaps unwittingly, contributed to public demarcation, expression, and indeed, the politicisation of class differences through its housing programme.[3]

The second instance is to be found in the discursive emergence of the figure of 'Ah Beng' and his female counter-part 'Ah Lian' in the public sphere. Deriving their names from the Chinese linguistic practice of abbreviating a full given name to Ah 'X' these two figures emerged around the mid-1980s. They represent, for the English-speaking middle-class, caricatures of youth who are working class or otherwise failures in the competitive education system and market economy. Beng and Lian stand as the 'Other' of the self-appointed sophisticated English-speaking cosmopolitans. In the mid-1980s, the signature of the figure 'Ah Beng' was the particular sartorial configuration of working-class males: the quintessential item of clothes was a multi-pleated, wide-hip, shiny polyester pair of trousers made by local tailors, with the end of a big brush comb protruding prominently from the back hip-pocket. The female 'Ah Lian' was a more complex figure to caricature. Her image was generally centred on 'over-the-top' clothing configurations that feature too-bright shiny tops and dresses and patent shoes. 'Loud' would be a key word in this caricature. In contrast to the British fashion scene, where working class youth are firmly grounded in their street fashion and where street styles are often appropriated and normalised by upmarket fashion designers to present on the catwalk, the fashion sense of the working class in Singapore remains in the realm of 'bad taste' to the young English-speaking middle class. The two discursively generated figures of 'Ah Beng' and 'Ah Lian' have become icons of everything that is 'gauche' in consumption and working class individuals' by definition poor attempts at 'sophistication'.

By the mid-1990s, these figures had become progressively entrenched in public discourse, through repetition in popular culture, in magazines and television programmes. The English television sitcom *Phua Chu Kang* continued with the caricature. Phua is the character of a small time contractor who is poorly educated in English, overly laden with gold jewellery, with long finger nails on his baby fingers for digging the nose and ears, a head of big permed dyed black hair and a huge prominent black mole on his cheek. He lives in a house that "looks like Haw Par Villa" because of the number of cheap ceramic animals that clutter up the sitting room. On the other hand, on the Chinese television programme *City Beat*, its youthful presenters began to wear Beng and Lian clothes, appropriating the caricature as self-identity. The popularity of these programmes also caused a change among some in the young English-speaking middle class. Media personalities began to claim a 'little bit' of Beng or Lian in themselves. For these figures, it became 'cool' to speak Beng and Lian talk and Singlish became a self-appropriated identity marker, standing for being Singaporean. Concurrently, Chinese languages other than Mandarin also made their appearance on the big screen; the effects of which are analysed in Chapters 10 and 11. All this popular cultural celebration led to panic in the government. Starting in 1999 Singlish was successively condemned by different cabinet ministers, culminating in its being mentioned as a serious issue by the Prime Minister in his 1999 National Day Rally speech. Mediacorp Television was to send the character Phua to night school in the following season, to learn proper English. It should be noted that these discursive social political biographies of Ah Beng and Ah Lian in Singaporean popular culture and their differentiated appropriations by both English-speaking middle-class youth and their Chinese-educated counterparts does not erase the class differences between the two groups of youth; differences that will tax government's ability to maintain a balance in allocation of public resources to different consumption groups, so as to garner mass loyalty from all citizens. Meanwhile, the socially-disadvantaged position of poor-English or non-English speakers has become a familiar theme in Singapore-produced films, as shown in the last two chapters in this book.

Consumption and Domestic Economy

The expansion of consumerism is, of course, both a cause and an effect of the construction of shopping spaces and facilities. The rapid expansion of spaces for consumption — entertainment, fashion and food — in Singapore since the late 1960s has been phenomenal. Since the mid-1980s, Singapore often appears as one continuous shopping centre to foreign visitors; shopping and food register deeply in the memory of all who visit. This development was tied to the development of tourism as a national industry. In the heady days of the bubble economy of the 1980s, Japanese tourists flush with high-value yen arrived in droves and bought up-market consumer items, less pricey in Singapore than in Japan. The same shops also served local Singaporeans with high disposable incomes. The rapid expansion of the retail consumer sector not only encouraged the expansion of local department stores, such as Metro and Tangs, but also brought in foreign chains, Isetan from Japan and Printemps and Galleries Lafayette from Paris. The illustrious example that best embodied the intensity of consumption expansion was Metro. Beginning as a modest shop in High Street in the late 1950s, it kept pace with the development of Orchard Road as a tourist belt and by the mid-1980s, had five large anchor stores in the Orchard and Scotts Roads area.[4]

Through the 1980s, it would appear that there was no saturation point in the expansion of consumption and thus shopping malls; developers of retail spaces were quick to point out that the exit of one retailer often heralded the entrance of another, often bigger one paying higher rents. New developments kept coming on stream. Two notable developments were Marina South and the rezoning of four of the town centres in newly-established public housing estates as 'regional' town centres. The latter have extended commercial spaces intended to relieve congestion in the tourist belt of Orchard Road to Marina South. As a result, retailers have had to establish outlets in these regional centres to maintain their respective market shares, incurring added operational costs without corresponding expansion in profits. The apparently unstoppable expansion of retail space faced an abrupt reckoning in the mid-1990s, when the retail sector went into a sustained downturn, several years before the Asian economic crisis of 1997.

Within a short period of two years, the retail sector contracted radically. From 1994 onwards, Metro began to close its stores, leaving only one outlet in Orchard Road, switching its business interests into property development. In 1996 it closed all three of its K-Mart stores, a partnership with the American chain, after very hefty losses in two years of operation. Lane Crawford, among the first overseas ventures by the very successful Hong Kong up-market department store, folded after barely three years of operation. Galleries Lafayette finally closed its doors in 1996, after having already radically downsized earlier, following the footsteps of Printemps, another French department store. Finally, C K Tang, a local family-based store, also downsized. In addition to these failures were those of small businesses that are more difficult to track and seldom register in public awareness. The economic outlook for the retail sector continued to be grim, even as other sectors in the economy affected by the 1997 crisis regained stability in late 1999. By 2000, the Singapore economy was heading towards a sustained downturn, facing structural unemployment for the first time in four decades.

Significantly, the pre-1997 decline in the retail sector happened within an expanding economy. Thus the reasons for the prolonged decline in the retail sector must be accounted for in the shifts in expenditure among Singaporeans. First, and perhaps the most obvious, is market size. The limited size of the market was mismatched with an oversupply of retail space. The expansion of the regional centres with goods that were previously sold in the tourist belt largely reduced sales from the downtown stores by siphoning off customers rather than adding new ones. Second, the high costs of the three big ticket items — houses, cars and domestic maids — drastically reduce the level of disposable income to be spent in other areas of consumption. Thirdly, in an intensely competitive environment, much disposable income is spent on education. This includes educational enrichment for children, such as private tuition, upgrading skills and educational training for adults and high-cost tertiary education overseas for those not admitted to local universities. These priorities in expenditure impose severe limits on other outlets for household and individual consumption. Finally, the appreciation of the Singapore dollar and higher retail prices relative to the region worked in tandem to encourage Singaporeans to shop overseas, particularly in neighbouring countries. Malaysia, Thailand and before the regional crisis, even Indonesia, were aggressively developing their own retail sectors. Added to all these domestic reasons, the bursting of the bubble and the subsequent sustained downturn of the Japanese economy, throughout the 1990s, was a fatal blow to the retail sector, from which it is yet to recover.

Within the general decline, two exceptions deserve attention. First, as to be expected, the very high end of the consumption sector is less vulnerable to economic fluctuations. For example, Mercedes continue to be among the best selling cars and the *haute couture* end of the fashion market continues to thrive. As analysed in Chapter 4, contrary to popular assumption, the latter establishments do not depend on the tourist trade but cater to a small coterie of wealthy locals who, in the words of an ex-proprietress of women's wear, are "unemployed or self-employed". Second, the only department store to buck the downturn was Robinson's, which has redirected its market focus to the lower middle segment of local consumers, where the proverbial 'value-for-money' approach rules. Other than these instances, an industrial shakeout will likely continue until a balance between consumption and service is reached, with a substantial reduction of both spaces and retail establishments.

Conclusion

These three features — globalisation of commodities, economic inequality and the general state of the national economy — determine the development of consumerism as a significant part of the culture of everyday life of Singaporeans. In terms of commodities, the items analysed in this collection of essays will have, inevitably, passed quickly into historical interest, replaced by a constant and successive stream of new products coming on to the market, transforming existing consumer tastes and converting and creating their own consumers. For as long as we have capitalism, this is an endless spiral, as the realisation of profit for the next cycle of investment and production comes from the destruction of the commodity through consumption. In this spiral of birth and death of consumer items, the consumption patterns of Singaporeans will be increasingly cosmopolitan, determined by and fitting into the global marketing strategies of producers of consumer goods. However, this does not mean that Singaporeans, along with other consumers in the rest of the world, will be dragged into a 'homogenised' global consumer culture. Local cultural practices will continue to absorb these products into their own idiom. Cultural differences between localities will continue to be noticeable. Cultural imperialism is less likely than the constant 'indigenisation of the imported' in Singapore, as elsewhere.

Within the local culture arena, display of class differences through different consumption patterns will inevitably intensify. No serious political consequences need be drawn from this, even if there might be an increase in class consciousness and some political realignment along class lines. Such differences have been the nature of things in advanced capitalist societies in Western Europe and North America without political incident. In Singapore, the unlikeliness of the eruption of class conflict is further reinforced by government's successful effort to maintain a relatively high level of the basic standard of living for the entire population through its efficacious provision of collective consumption goods, such as public housing, health care, transportation and education. The overwhelming majority of the population who lives in public housing estates shares homogenous daily household routines which reduce the visibility of class differences.

Looking at mounting personal debt in developed countries, the Singapore government appeared to be determined to control consumer credit and debt to relatively manageable margins. Measures here included strict policing of bank loans for consumer goods and controls of credit card issuing and credit limits. However, success proved to be short-lived, if not illusory. Such controls could not single-handedly buck the logic of capitalism, which is the interminable expansion of consumerism at the cost of everything else. Witness here the destruction of the environment and the destruction of values of thrift to save capitalism from itself by encouraging consumption; the propensity to spend, conceptualised as the consumer confidence index, is now a standard measure of the health of an economy. Thus, at the beginning of the twenty-first century, having arrived at developed economy status, the Singapore government found itself changing its relatively draconian regulations on consumer loans. At a point when the economy is facing a sustained downturn and structural unemployment for the first time in its post-colonial history, the government is encouraging consumption of big ticket items. In early 2002, it lifted stringent regulations on loans for properties and cars, making ownership much easier. The government stated that this was a response to public criticism of it being a 'nanny' state, and that it is time that Singaporeans as consumers learn to live with the risks of their private decisions. The question is whether the PAP government has finally taken an about turn on its commitment never to seek popularity over prudence or has it simply, unavoidably, given in to the logic of continuous expansion of consumption as the growth point of capitalism.

Notes

1. The term 'cosmopolitanism' is used differently here from its recent use by Prime Minister, Goh Chok Tong. The latter used it to divide the population into two classes with different trajectories in life, while in the context of this essay, every Singaporean, regardless of class, is in principle able to configure him or herself as cosmopolitans through the goods they consume.
2. For an against the grain reading of the Asia values discourse, see Chua (1999).
3. For more details on the debate regarding subsidies on housing see the letters column of *The Straits Times* during the months of August and September 1995. Suffice it to state here that complaints from the middle-class against the one billion dollar per annum subsidy in upgrading of old public housing estates had resulted in the need for the Minister of Finance to clarify that the money would not come from personal income tax revenue. On the other hand, public housing residents' complaint against the subsidy on executive condominiums led the Minister of National Development to ask for clearer direction from the public as to what they would like the government to do regarding the young professionals' housing needs.
4. There were Metro stores at Scotts, Holiday Inn, Lucky Plaza, Far East Plaza and the Paragon; in addition, there were Metro in Marine Parade and Beach Road.

2

The Emerging Culture of Consumption

Life for Singaporeans is not complete without shopping!

This declaration by the Prime Minister of Singapore in his 1996 National Day Rally Speech, the most important address to the nation of the year (*The Straits Times*, 18 August 1996) summarises and signifies the sea-change of living conditions in the island nation since political independence in 1965 — from underdevelopment to affluence, from material deprivation to material excess — brought about by rapid economic development. The economic development initiated in the 1960s was facilitated by the new international division of labour, in which multinationals from the US, Western Europe and Japan were relocating production of consumer goods to inexpensive production platforms in Asia. Since then, Singapore has been able to keep pace with the changes in the global economy, transforming its economic base at different times, and has managed to exit from labour-intensive industrialisation to an increasingly service-based economy. The processes that produced Singapore's economic achievement are nicely summarised: "encouraging higher tech industries; pushing low wage/low tech investment off-shore (e.g. the 'growth triangle' with Southern Malaysia and Indonesia), and promoting the outflow of Singapore capital into low wage economies (most recently China), at the same time working to ensure that regional headquarters and profitable producer services for these activities are located in the republic; and pursuing various 'human resources' options to upgrade the skill level of the Singapore workforce" (Kahn, 1996:62). The resultant rapid economic growth, along with constant upgrading of national education at every level to meet the demands of skills and knowledge in new industries, has provided continuous expansion of wages. In 1977 Singapore reached the second highest per capita income in Asia, at US$30,000.

The expansion of income has primed Singapore for an explosion in consumption, leading to the emergence of a loosely-organised 'culture of consumerism'. Available time and financial capacity to consume leisure have expanded across the board except for, perhaps, the lowest 10 per cent of income-earners. There is a television in practically every home. Locally-produced programmes compete with imports for viewership. In the 1990 national census, it was found that television-watching consumed the greatest proportion of leisure time and 'window-shopping' ranked as the number one leisure activity conducted away from home (Ho and Chua, 1995:40). Expenditure on food has increased because the varieties of food consumed have increased and qualities have improved. The average proportion of expenditure on cooked food — i.e. food purchased in restaurants or from other vendors — as part of total food expenditure per household has also increased very significantly (Chua and Tan, 1995:6). In spite of the multiple layers of taxation that make the prices of cars in Singapore among the highest in the world, approximately 40 per cent of households owned at least one car and the luxurious Mercedes has consistently ranked among the top-selling brands.

The emergence of this consumer culture has been codified locally into an ideological/moral discourse with two explicit dimensions: first, the criticism against the 'excess of affluence'; and secondly, the critique against 'Westernisation' or its variant 'Americanisation'. The conceptualisation of consumer culture as 'excess' recalls the conditions of deprivation, prior to industrialisation, that are still fresh in the collective memories of Singaporeans. It recalls a time when consumption was for utility. The critique against 'Westernisation' locates Singapore as a non-Western Asian culture and points to an awareness of the symbolic significance of consumer goods. The conceptual matrix constituted by these two critiques is the space within which the discourse and issues of consumption and consumerism in Singapore are to be examined in this book.[1]

Singapore as a Modern Space

Before embarking on the analysis of the culture of consumption, it should be noted that the evolution of Singapore into a 'world city' is but its logical unfolding as a modern space. Singapore has always been a modern city.

In this insistence on its 'modern' character, we are reminded of the fact that 'globalisation' of capitalism is far from a new phenomenon or process (Hall, 1991:19).[2] Singapore was born of the modern age of mercantile capitalism; of steamships and telecommunications, essential to international trade between Europe and Asia; of immigrants from East, South and Southeast Asia and from the colonial metropolitan centres of Europe, not exclusively Britain, all in search of economic opportunities and better material life. Singapore has, therefore, always been part of global service capitalism, adhering to the contours of its different phases as evidenced by, historically, the successive layers of investment in its telecommunication system. Had it not been so, Singapore's position as a regional and world city in Southeast Asia would not have been realised with such speed. In this sense, the period of low-tech and labour-intensive industrialisation might be an aberration; it is fast-paced but short-lived in the long period of Singapore's integration into the global economy since its founding in the early nineteenth century.

Given this embeddedness in global capitalism, Singaporeans, even before that name existed to anchor their national identity, have never been strangers to the process of modernisation and have been adaptable to each period of change in the modernisation trajectory. Capitalist modernity as a cultural context has never been an importation of the West imposed upon and destroying an existing 'traditional' culture. Singapore could not have been narrowly defined as a 'traditional' nation; given its multi-racial population since its founding, it has always been impossible to talk about a single 'Singaporean' tradition. Singapore was, thus, never a Third World location, culturally and economically isolated on the periphery of capitalism, rather, its very own historical trajectory has been inextricably tied to global capitalism. It is precisely because of the absence of a pre-colonial traditional or tribal culture that the cultural modernity of capitalism should be emphasised, rather than narrowly conceptualising this modernity as 'Western'. Perhaps, it is this division between modernity of capitalism and the much more specific features of 'Western' modernity that enables the Singaporean government and its people to inhabit a thoroughly capitalist Singapore while espousing anti-Westernism (Ang and Stratton, 1995).

To emphasise Singapore's modernity is not to deny that each of the ethnic groups that constitutes the population does not engage in their respective particularistic cultural practices. Indeed, they do. At a most mundane level, rice and noodles still remain the main staples for Singaporeans, and chopsticks and hands (especially at home) are still the preferred utensils for all, with few exceptions. Asian languages are still spoken at home and are learned in schools. 'Traditional' clothes, like the modified Chinese *samfoo*, Indian *sari* and Malay *baju* are still the daily wear of women in their sixties or older; those who are less than that age are likely to wear contemporary fashion. The point, therefore, is that such culturally specific daily practices have always been mixed with modern attitudes and commodities. The inextricable mingling of ethnic and modern elements is constitutive of the complex of social life of all Singaporeans: neither could be erased.[3] Furthermore, the cultures of the various racial groups and that of capitalist modernity are inscribed on each individual Singaporean. Thus, with the exceptions of the small and disappearing strata of immigrants educated in the classical vernacular traditions of their respective homelands, the cultural composition of each Singaporean has always been multicultural, of varying degrees of hybridity.[4] This is evident in the everyday life-world of street languages where individuals, with varying degrees of competency in various languages, switch and mix codes readily, and in the crossing-over of food practices at home and at eating-places. Ironically, as we shall see, the modernity and cultural hybridity of Singaporeans have been made more problematic by the government's multi-racial policies and its attempts to 'Asianise', or 'self-Orientalise' the population within the current ideological conjuncture through the negative ideological transmutation of the modern component of Singaporean culture to 'Westernisation'.

The Emerging Culture of Consumption

Decades of rapid economic growth, since the early 1960s, have spawned an expanding middle class and, perhaps more importantly, have all but eliminated abject poverty. National economic growth becomes meaningful in the everyday life of its people when it translates into improvement of people's material lives. Evidence of this expansion is everywhere in the island-nation. Prestigious cars are not the only famous goods known to Singaporeans. Almost every international fashion house is represented, from mass market 'diffusion' to the exclusive couture lines of all the well-known designers — Issey Miyaki, Sonia Rykiel, Donna Karan and Gianni Versace, respectively from different fashion centres around the world — to 'no-designer' brand-name sports wear — Nike, Fila — which are conveniently gathered within the island's ubiquitous shopping complexes. Fast-food chains, particularly American ones, with their global reach, are highly visible. McDonald's outlets are found not only in leisure districts, but also in the public housing estates that accommodate more than 80 per cent of the population. Less ubiquitous, but perhaps symbolically more important in signifying the new affluence, are international-chain cafés, such as Starbucks from the US and Dome from Western Australia. Singapore is without doubt a space penetrated by the global marketing strategies of producers of consumer goods. This penetration is, of course, facilitated by a highly-developed telecommunications and information technology infrastructure, and transport facilities that are central to economic development in global capitalism.[5]

Massive improvements in material life and the attendant cultural practices constitute discursively the 'culture of consumption' or 'consumerism'. To emphasise the culture of consumption is to recognise the ways in which consumption ceases to be a simple appropriation of utilities, or use values, and becomes a consumption of signs and images. The emphasis upon the capacity to endlessly reshape the cultural and symbolic aspect of the commodity makes it more appropriate to speak of *commodity-signs* (Featherstone, 1995: 75). However, individuals or groups can reshape symbolic aspects of commodities within a cultural terrain constituted by different relevant agencies and individual consumers. In the case of Singapore, the expansion of consumer culture is subjected to multiple layers of ideological discourse. Each discursive rendering of the symbolic meaning of singular items of consumption, or of loose constellations of items into 'lifestyles', becomes unavoidably embroiled in the politics of experience. At least three strands of the moral/ideological discourse of consumption can be identified: First, there is the general theme of 'excessive' consumption, conceptualised as 'excessive materialism' in society; second is the 'fear' of 'Westernisation/Americanisation', primarily articulated by the PAP government but with deep resonances in society; and, thirdly, the displacement of the two themes onto the young for being 'materialistic/consumerist' and 'Westernised'. The following discussion will take up first the issue of Westernisation, then the discussion of youth, and then the general issue of excessive consumption.

Consumerism as the 'Curse' of Westernisation

The simplistic thesis of cultural imperialism — that the Third World is being 'Americanised' by the inundation of American-produced consumer goods and entertainment products — now has few adherents among academics.[6] However, this has not stopped this thesis from being used in the politics of many locations, because of its utility in generating nationalist sentiments and identities (Classen and Howes, 1996: 179–82). It is a thesis that is often kept alive for this purpose in Singapore.

Part of the official, ideological discourse of the Singapore government on consumerism takes on a particular trope of being 'anti-West' in general and anti-American in particular. While it is substantively true that Singapore is a space well penetrated by American consumer, recreational and entertainment goods, this itself is not new and is not the reason for official anti-Westernism. This is borne out by contrast: Singapore is also, significantly, full of Japanese consumer goods, yet there is no fear of the 'Japanisation' of Singaporeans in the consumer cultural discourse, as there is of Westernisation/Americanisation.[7] The different reception lies in part in the conceptualisation of the 'cultural' contents of the goods imported from the two countries.

In general, the bulk of Japanese exports to the rest of Asia are identified as 'technology' items — for example, household goods such as cars, televisions, refrigerators, radios and other electronic goods. Japanese technological superiority is recognised in these consumer goods. However, they are seen as instruments without 'cultural' substance. For example, as in the case of television or different kinds of audio-receiving or audio-recording instruments, the respective substantive television and music programmes for these instruments, in which cultural content is embedded, are perceived to be dominated, overwhelmingly, by globally-marketed American products.[8] In actuality, Singapore's cultural, particularly entertainment, consumer space is equally penetrated by Hong Kong, Taiwan and to a lesser extent, India. Finally, American television entertainment is also being contested by local television productions.

Indeed, the viewer-ratings of local drama and situation comedies generally exceed those of American imports. That these local programmes are framed within local ideologies and are aimed at contesting American products should not be surprising when one realises that all local television stations are government-owned.

Nevertheless, it is to the 'cultural' content of the American products that the anti-Western and anti-American sentiments are ideologically directed. American mass entertainment programmes are seen as the carriers and harbingers of Western/American 'liberal' values, especially individualism. The programmes are deemed to be reflective of the moral 'laxity' of liberalism, where individual rights and self-interest rule with disastrous consequences, such as high divorce rates, strong legal rights and protection for criminals over the rights of crime victims, and promiscuity in sex and drugs. These themes, common in American films, television programmes and popular music, are read as reflecting the 'reality' that is America — i.e. a place where criminals are turned into folk heroes and promiscuity in sex and drugs is celebrated. Ostensibly, official fear is that liberal individualism will make inroads into the cultural sphere of the local population, supposedly leading them away from local 'traditional' values and undermining local social cohesion. Built into this anti-Westernism is thus not just a discourse of value difference, but of value conflict. It is to this discourse of difference as conflict that we must turn our attention.

That the moral/ideological discourse is directed at 'individualism' is, of course, no accident. The link between individualism and liberal democracy poses an ideological challenge to the semi-democratic polity, fashioned by the unbroken rule of the PAP. In the attempt to preserve the ideological and political systems operant in Singapore, the political differences between Singapore and developed nations are discursively reformulated in terms of the 'Otherness' of the West. This 'othering' creates the space for a discourse of cultural 'difference' between 'Singapore' and the 'West'.

The term 'Singapore' in this discursive difference is further expanded into a more inclusive notion of 'Asia/Asian' by drawing on the convenient fact that the population in Singapore is composed of three different communities — of Chinese, Malays and Indians. At one level, the 'culture' of Singaporeans is thus constructed as being a composite, distilled from the three 'traditions', Sinic, Islamic Malay and Indian. The modernity of the people is discounted in this abstract attribution of 'traditions' and, instead, reinvented 'traditional' Asian values and attitudes are inscribed on them. Thus, a 'traditional' Singapore deemed to be essentially 'Asian' emerges discursively, suppressing and denying Singapore's very modernity, which is displaced as a 'Western' cultural influence. As a 'traditional Asian' space, the community-oriented culture of Singaporeans becomes vulnerable to the 'unhealthy' cultural penetration of the West/America (Chua, 1996). The bridgehead of this 'insidious invasion' is supposedly embedded in the 'Western culture' that is inscribed in consumer products imported from the US.

Again, the ideological/cultural critique of 'Westernisation' can be gleaned from the contrasting total absence of ideological thematisation of the fact that Singapore television, movies and popular music spaces are equally penetrated by Asian producers and products, particularly those from Hong Kong and Taiwan, and increasingly those from Japan. This is an absence that is only intelligible in the official presumption of cultural affinities, if not similarities, between the latter locations, within a discursively mystified 'Asia'. Indeed, there has been an increasingly presence of programmes on television, including music videos, from other parts of Asia, alongside the expansion of local production. The annual Singapore International Film Festival is increasingly a showcase of films from countries in Asia.

This 'Asianisation' of Singapore, as it is elsewhere throughout East and Southeast Asia, has obviously been buoyed by the rise of capital in Asia since the 1960s. This rise of capital has produced a new confidence and has led to a 'search' for cultural explanations for this very capitalist expansion. This reworking of so-called Asian values under conditions of capitalist success has been hailed as portending an age of 'Asian Renaissance' (Ibrahim, 1997). Backed by success in global capitalism, this Asianisation discourse is able to avoid the danger of conceptually reducing the people of Singapore into 'primitives' governed by tradition (Bhaba, 1983). It is the Western modernity of liberalism that is rejected, not the modernity of capitalism. In this sense, the reconfiguration of Asian values in Singapore does not amount to a 'fundamentalism' which often accompanies 'the refusal of modernity' (Hall, 1991: 36). Instead, at its most progressive, it is an attempt to project the reconfigured Asian values as a moral system that will act to alleviate capitalist social inequalities and restrain the rapaciousness of market forces (George Yeo, Minister of Information and the Arts, *The Straits Times*, 21 June 1997).

In the 'demonising' discourse on cultural difference (Mahbubani, 1993), America has a central symbolic place both as a possible place of attraction for populations which are deprived of the freedoms guaranteed by democracy, and as a place of 'moral decadence' for governments who are afraid to institutionalise the same freedoms. 'America' is simultaneously both an object of repulsion and of attraction. Both features can potentially be utilised in the cultural politics of Singapore. A symbolic imaginary America as 'land of the free' may be said to frame some of the consumption practices of young Singaporeans, as will be discussed in the next section.

That the anti-West/anti-American discourse, via the critique of consumerism, is to a certain extent self-serving on the part of local governments in Asia is quite obvious. The conservative values that they juxtapose against liberalism have the potential effect of generating support for the political status quo, which is the desire of governments.[9] However, this official reading is not without positive public resonance — otherwise its ideological efficacy would be very limited indeed.[10] Support for the official critique of emergent 'decadence' in the cultural sphere tends to come from the generations who have just emerged from conditions of economic underdevelopment, while the targets of criticism are the generations that grew up under conditions of relative prosperity.

The Consuming Young

Generally speaking, the period between teenage years and marriage — the period generically known as 'youth', when one belongs to the 'younger generation' — is a window for unlimited consumption for and on the self, constrained only by one's own financial circumstances. Without concerns for 'big' items, like financing the mortgage of a house or the financial burdens of familial concerns, one can freely spend on oneself. In the particular instance of Singapore, where the ownership of a car — because of its exorbitant price — is out of the question for teenagers and early entrants to the workforce, the body has emerged as a primary locus of consumption. Body adornment is its primary modality.

The consumption practices of youth are thus highly visible and therefore an easy target for moral/ideological criticisms. The young are criticised for their lifestyles; togged out in 'designer' or 'brand-name' clothes and accessories and spending comparatively significant sums of money in discos, listening and dancing to Western music and eating at expensive foreign restaurants. In a context where the collective memory of material deprivation in the period before rapid economic growth remains vivid, the younger generations of Singapore are 'children of affluence'. Their highly-visible exposure to and participation in globalised consumerism transforms them into icons of consumer lifestyles which are supposedly inscribed with 'Western/American decadence'.

The cultural/ideological/moral criticism of Westernisation can be best illustrated by examining youth fashion. At the general level of the sociology of fashion, there is an 'adult' puzzle as to why youth dress to 'shock' their elders — without apparent understanding that 'shock' is a mechanism through which teenagers define themselves from their parents, thus acquiring identity as 'youth'. Secondly, parents are generally sceptical regarding youth's claim to 'individuality' through fashion; they point out that the latter in fact wear similar clothes and are thus conforming to a code rather than breaking out with individualising styles. This conventional criticism is similar to that of the social scientist who suggests that, under conditions of mass production, any promises of 'individuality' through the consumption of such products must necessarily be false (Ewen, 1976). Such criticism fails to understand a central characteristic and dynamic of 'fashion': in fashion, consumers' desire to be different is a limited desire — that of individualising within a trend. Fashion is necessarily a trend which is constructed by mass participation; to be 'fashionable' is to be with the trend, with the crowd (Finkelstein, 1996: 82). Few desire to be totally different from others. That would make one 'weird' rather than 'fashionable'. Individuality is expressed through the ways in which fashionable items are configured on one's own body, rather than breaking with the fashionable crowd.

At the level of 'Americanisation', fashionable items are largely derived from styles found in the globalised, popular culture industries — such as television, movies, popular music and direct advertisements. In all these media, the US may be dominant, but it is not exclusive in Singapore. However, American fashion items are easily available in stores that specialise in items that may be called 'American street fashion'. Youth are criticised for 'aping' the 'Americans' in their donning of these items. Consumption of 'American' clothes is actually very selective; while blue jeans (are they still American?) are almost uniform for youth, the hip-hop clothes of Afro-American rap singers go begging for customers, reflecting the 'middle-class' self-image of Singaporean youth.

One reading of this mimicking is that it is symptomatic of the 'cultural' and 'identity' confusion of youth because they have supposedly lost their essential identities as 'Asians'. However, there is little to suggest this supposed confusion outside the fashion sphere. Indeed, the youth of Singapore appear to be very stable and socially responsible — including their attitude towards money, as discussed in the next section. Youth delinquency rates are not particularly high; public order is not routinely disrupted by confused and disgruntled youth. On the other hand, rates of passing stringent examinations in the highly-competitive education system improve year after year.

A contesting interpretation of the fashion consumption of youth, as part of lifestyle, may be offered here. The argument of 'identity confusion' is only intelligible against a background assumption that identity formation and stability are entirely dependent on a notion of unchanging 'traditions'. However, the youth are drawn elsewhere. Youth in Singapore, as in other parts of the world, draw from a globalised 'image bank' projected in the popular mass media of movies, television and music, which in Singapore includes Taiwanese and Hong Kong productions. Indeed, a major teenage phenomenon in Singapore is the 'fandom' of Mandarin and Cantonese pop-singers from Taiwan and Hong Kong (Soh, 1994/95). The reference point for Singapore's youth is, therefore, a global mix of images of youth, rather than merely local cultural images. It is the global rather than the local that provides stability for their identity as 'youth', instead of confusion. However, consumption of global images unavoidably passes through local cultural and political conditions. This by now accepted point will be demonstrated later in the analysis of Singaporean consumption of American media and consumer products.

In the particular instance of Singapore, where the spaces of everyday life are institutionally highly administered within reinvented 'Asian traditions' aimed at eliciting conformity from the population, America has been symbolically transformed in the local ideological mind into an icon of 'freedom' — the land of freedom, where individuality and differences rule and indeed, are celebrated. Selective items of clothes are taken as 'symbols' of the American way of life; the selectivity is itself evidence that 'America' is a symbolic reconfiguration by Singaporeans. The attractiveness of American street fashion is filtered through the suppressed desires of the Singaporeans in question. Within the Singaporean symbolic representation of America, debates on 'Americanisation' in the local cultural sphere have everything to do with ideological contests within Singapore, rather than what is 'really' going on in America. Selective 'American' cultural products are consumed through local semiotics in which the products are used to express resistance to local repressions. The centrality of clothes in this resistance is succinctly put by a local designer, whose commercial success is built on sensual body-conscious clothes for young Singaporean women: "In Singapore, the only protest you can make is how you look, short of taking off your clothes. So people make a statement with what they wear" (Peter Teo, *The Sunday Times*, 8 June 1997).

Excesses of Consumerism

In addition to being criticised for being 'Westernised', youth are also criticised for their 'excesses'. However, in this instance, youth is but part of a larger critique which indicts the entire society: that the society has turned 'materialist'. The society is thus economically and morally/ideologically couched within a language of 'thrift' of the past and of 'older' generations against the spending ways of the present and the 'younger' generations. The 'past' is constructed and recalled fondly as inhabited by individuals and families who were 'frugal' by attitude and/or character. Yet, the fact is that the older generations lived in underdeveloped conditions, in which 'poverty' and 'frugality' were indistinguishable phenomena; by force of circumstances, frugality was the only available response to poverty. The critique of the excessive materialism of the present is thus a classic case of ideology formation: the historical response of being frugal is being 'naturalised' or 'essentialised', making a moral virtue out of necessity. The question remains: would those of the 'older' generations have been frugal if they had the relative wealth of today's younger generations?

Just how spendthrift are the young? It remains an empirical question that requires serious research. For example, in a newspaper-financed national survey, Singaporeans as a whole and youth in particular were found to be responsible about money, rather than being 'excessive' consumers, the popular perception promoted by the media themselves in their role as moral crusaders. It was found that if Singaporeans desired a consumer item but had no money at hand: 67 per cent would save up money before making the purchase; 53 per cent would forget about buying; no more than 20 per cent would borrow from family members, friends or banks to make the purchase or pay by instalments (*The New Paper*, 15 May 1994).[11]

At an abstract level, the question concerns the actual rate of change in people's attitude towards money: how quickly do people move from being frugal, borne of circumstances, to being spendthrift in newly-industrialising nations? It would appear from the Singapore example that attitudes before rapid economic development have longer staying power than it is ideologically assumed by moral gate-keepers, from government to media.

Shifting up age-groups, from youth to new entrants to the workforce and newly-formed families, the ability to consume is severely hampered by the very high costs of housing and cars, two of the 'normal' items within the expected horizon of consumption by the middle class elsewhere. In a 1996 survey (*The Straits Times*, 27–29 June and 26 August) of young professionals aged 21–30 years, 36 per cent were not expecting to be able to afford a flat for 6 or more years from 1996 and more than 60 per cent could only afford government-subsidised public housing flats. In terms of cars, although up to 67 per cent planned to purchase a car, 51 per cent estimated that they were only able to buy the smallest, second-hand car in the market at a cost of around S$40,000.

Indeed, beyond individuals, young families often live tightly on the margin of their income or slightly beyond (Foo, 1995). In 1996 the Prime Minister commented publicly that "For the top 10 per cent, maybe there is enough money, but for the middle-income Singaporeans, there is not enough money" (*The Straits Times*, 28 April 1996). What they have is tied up in property. "The rising level of household indebtedness on account of leveraged property purchases, and the increased exposure of financial institutions to the property market, pose systematic risks in the event of an economic slow-down and collapse in prices" (Monetary Authority of Singapore, quoted in Koh and Ooi, 1996: 7). These official statements should raise scepticism about the perception of Singaporeans as 'excessive' consumers. Meanwhile, most people still have discretionary expenditure; consumption continues to expand, albeit at a slower rate and at the expense of lower household savings.

Local Reception of Global Consumption Goods: Some Instances

This section will first substantiate the argument that cultural consumption of imported American products does not necessarily require the consumption of a symbolic 'America' as represented in advertisements and television programmes (although the cultural underpinnings of consumption are a much more complicated phenomenon that cannot be examined here). Producers of globalised commodities are not primarily interested in the cultural mission of 'Americanising' the rest of the world — in this instance, Singapore — but are more focused on profits and capital accumulation. Finally, the section will also illustrate rising Asian confidence, both in its economy and its culture, as seen in the marketing of Asian-produced jeans. All these instances are but illustrative vignettes, thus fragments, of how the consumption sphere in Singapore is constituted; indeed, in any attempt to subject the entire sphere to analysis, it would quickly be realised that the task is endless because 'big-ticket' items and the number of small consumer items keep proliferating, each generating its own consumers, and its own symbolic significance.

Some Ads Don't Travel Well

With global distribution, advertisements of particular products often have to travel across cultural spaces and differences. Since the differences define the ways the ads are received and interpreted, some ads travel well while others do not; most fall in between. Two ads that might be said to be 'difficult' to consume culturally by Singaporeans were those for Calvin Klein's 'unisex' *eau de toilette* products, cK1 and cKbe.

Perfume is a difficult product to advertise. The ads must hide perfume's real purpose, which is to overpower the odours produced by the natural body. In contrast to many physical qualities which are desired, the lack of body odour of any kind is a lack to be celebrated; transforming the suppression of body odours to the 'scent-in-industry'. An additional difficulty in advertising perfume is that the product is intrinsically intractable. It is a liquid, substantial and heavy when sold in 'designed' bottles. What is consumed is the vapour, insubstantial and ephemeral; consumption of the imaginary.

That perfume consumption is consumption of the insubstantial explains largely the bifurcation of conventional ads of female and male perfumes. In ads for male 'scent', the odour of sweat is still kept in the foreground; sweat and 'manliness' are inseparable. Masculinity is to be preserved at all costs; even the word 'perfume' is taboo lest one feminise the hunk. In women's perfume ads, the imaginary is given full expression: memory, mystery, romance, sensuality, seduction and sexuality (deodorised) and decadence (in lifestyle). Even the names of the perfumes are exercises in the imaginary: Opium, Diamonds, Romeo (Gigli) all conjure up allure and fantasy.

Klein's cK1 and cKbe subverted all that by erasing the masculine-feminine division, marketing themselves as 'unisex' fragrances — 'perfume' has been downgraded; the vapour has been taken out of the scent. First, the bottle, conventionally the focus of design attention in perfume marketing, has been radically neutralised. In cK1, it resembles an old-fashioned medicinal bottle of frosted glass, with an aluminium screw-on bottle cap. While in cKbe it is simple and black: no cut glass, no rich amber liquid — just dense, pitch darkness. It is unimaginatively there.

The ads feature, in black-and-white photography, a serial arrangement of twenty-something males and females, apparently at a party, engage in conversation, even in heated arguments. The imaginary of femininity, which resides in the private, even solitary — the better to relive the memory of romance — is eliminated; replace by the public-ness of a party. The 'hunk' also has been replaced. The male and female models are all 'grungily' attired in black jeans and nondescript tops. They look anaemic — both the clothes and the bodies suggest the need for a wash. The group is homogenised and androgynised; as befits a 'fragrance' for both genders. They are unmistakably American ads, unable to traverse the cultural distance and be meaningful to twenty-something Singaporeans.[12]

This may be surmised from the fact that the full multi-page ads, each featuring an individual model, with everyone equally grimy and anaemic, were never used in Singapore in the selling of cKbe, which was marketed after cK1. Instead only the picture of a very plain young woman in a crumpled black day-wear tube-top, not deserving of any further visual attention, was featured. Her face is naked with no trace of make-up and she has matted hair. The fact that she is supermodel Kate Moss is incidental. It is her ordinariness that is emphasised. Just like her plain self, a reader is invited just to 'be' himself or herself.

Twenty-something Singaporeans are on the make, impatient for success. Deprivation from car-ownership, contextually the ultimate success symbol, has made their bodies the locus of consumption. Clothes and other body accessories have elevated status as expressions of 'success'. Their fashion statements do not include anaemia and dirt. That does not mean that targeted Singaporeans will not buy the perfume. Far from it: these two fragrances were instantly quite successful in Singapore. This attests to the fact that consumer behaviour is governed by many factors, never by advertisements alone.

The Cultural Difficulties of Consuming American Television

Although local television programmes are immensely popular with Singaporeans, Singaporeans are simultaneously avid consumers of imported American programmes — hence, the concern for their possible 'Americanisation'. Yet, when one looks into the details of a particular piece of popular music, movie or television programming, obstacles to consuming the embedded cultural values become apparent.

One of the currently running, late-night TV sitcoms popular among younger Singaporean viewers is *Friends*, which revolves around a group of six middle-class friends, cardboard versions of American 'generation Xers', who seem to have an immense amount of free time. The three men and three women are always hanging out at the café in which one used to work as a waitress or in the sitting rooms of their apartments. Every episode is built around the personal disappointments of different group members.

Of the men, one is a palaeontologist who works in a museum, is divorced and has a monkey as a live-in companion; another 'knows' that he is destined for 'something' in life — he does not know what. He works in a low-end, managerial job in data-processing. The third man is an aspiring actor who always 'almost' gets a meaningful acting part. Of the women, one is an aspiring cook who came closest to a calling when she worked in a 1950s-style theme restaurant; her apartment mate is a poor little rich girl who has left the comfort of wealth to find herself, only to work as an incompetent waitress in the café where they hang out (she later achieves her ambitions as a department store purchaser of fashion); and the third is a sometimes taxi-driver, sometimes massage-lady, who is so 'blur'[13] and off-the-wall that everyone of her on-screen statements requires a double-take from the viewers. Each is an exemplar of 'generation Xers' with a McJob and a dream.

An episode generally opens with them coming together at the café, before each goes off pursuing their own hopeful events: a romantic evening with a new friend, a job prospect or a collective endeavour to 'do something' together. Anticipations of happiness will be dashed subsequently. The episode then ends with them returning to either of the two hang-outs to lick their wounds. One may say that it is these personal wounds that bind them together; a bunch of 'beautiful losers' against the rest of the cold, real world out there.

Each role in the programme constitutes a 'subject position' which a viewer may be able to occupy in his/her imagination. However, that they are all occupational losers makes them unlikely role models for Singaporean viewers in a similar age-group. This is reflected in a young Singaporean's comment: "How could they have so much free time?" The question reflects the Singaporeans' all-too anxious pursuit of their careers: they can hardly understand, let alone realise, the desire to chase one's dream — acting, cooking or the search for 'self' — at the expense of a future defined in terms of material comfort. A survey of Singaporeans aged between 21 and 30 years old found that their greatest concern was their career (*The Straits Times*, 29 June 1997), especially since they felt that the future was going to be more difficult in the face of escalating prices. Indeed, the 'Singapore Dream' — a trope which engages local politicians and policy-oriented academics from time to time — is cast entirely in terms of property and cars. Their unaffordability has cast a pall of pessimism among young professionals (Koh and Ooi, 1996).

To young Singaporeans faced with an absence of affordable accommodation, *Friends* may have cultural resonance at one level. To live independently from family in one's own pad and meet freely with close friends is something attractive to young professionals here, as anywhere. But, then, these young professionals do not need American television to tell them of this desire. At this level, *Friends* is probably consumed as a sublimation of this desire. In the end, however, without the ability to occupy the subject positions provided by the characters in the show, the series is consumed as mere entertainment, as comedy for a laugh, providing some relief from the day, and immediately to be forgotten: little, if any, Americanisation potential there.

New Asian Confidence and the Marketing of Jeans

Giordano, an Italian name, is actually a very successful Hong Kong company which manufactures and markets casual wear for youth, largely jeans and t-shirts.[14] In 1996, the company produced a series of advertisements with the theme: 'World without Strangers'. The ads ran in Singapore movie houses, and presumably in the rest of East and Southeast Asia.

In one of the ads, a young East Asian woman, donning Giordano jeans and a casual shirt, is planted in a dusty Latin American landscape, signifying the Third World. She meets some idling locals and strikes up a musical exchange with them, in a seamless weaving of the sounds of her *erhu*, a two-string Chinese musical instrument, with the strumming of the guitar of one of the locals — the two instruments standing as icons of their respective cultures.

A second ad features a similarly-attired young East Asian male in a village setting. A group of poorly-clad, barefoot children playing soccer on an unpaved road run away as he approaches. He then picks up an empty tin can and, using it as a 'ball', shows off his own soccer skills. A man with leathery skin and deeply-etched face flashes a smile and throws him a ball from behind a pillar. The children merrily reappear and chase the young man and his ball down the dirt path. Again, the scene represented is Third World, Latin America.

The conceptualisation of these ads is not accidental. They depict clearly the new Asian confidence, fuelled by capitalist economic success. The new confidence and the new wealth have carried, and are carried by, well-dressed and adventurous Asian youth into the Third World. No longer satisfied with the well-trodden tourist routes of Europe and North

America — once the beacons of modernity that attracted aspiring Asians — the new Asian youth are seeking new territories. They are the new Asian cultural tourists, exploring poor countries, promoting South-South cultural exchange.

Inscribed on the confident new Asian youth is new Asian capital itself. Behind or, perhaps, ahead of the adventurous youth is the adventurous entrepreneurial penetration of Asian capital into the Third World. The new Asian youth not only signify their new spending power, but are also an extension of the new Asian investment power.

The above analysis of selective examples of media-cultural commodities is ideologically motivated by the desire to raise doubts about all simplistic reductions of cultural consumption in non-Western locations as one of homogenisation of culture globally, with a unitary Western culture as the centre.[15] First, what the analysis has disclosed are some of the material and cultural conditions in Singapore which stand in the way of simple identification with representations of the American way of life in American fashion and media products. Secondly, this has also demonstrated that local political and economic conditions are equally ideologically important considerations in the marketing of globalised products. It should be apparent that, with respect to both points, questions of how the selected instances are actually consumed remain unexplored.

Conclusion

Singapore is a node of global finance and a site of global marketing for both locals and international tourists. This is plain from its architectural landscape of corporate buildings and miles and miles of shopping complexes. This landscape represents two sides of the economic transformation of Singapore; the relentless drive for national economic growth, and its translation into improved material life for citizens through the expansion of consumption. Both processes are constitutive of the legitimacy of the PAP government and serve to underwrite certain undemocratic practices in the nation (Chua, 1995a); they provide the discursive space for the government to define ideologically 'good government' against 'democracy' (Chan, 1992).

However, while the drive for continuing economic growth remains unabated through the promotion of the idea of a 'learning' society — that is, constant skills upgrading among workers — consumption expansion appears to be an emergent social and political issue. First, the effects of income and consumption inequalities are increasingly apparent and are becoming politicised. A Cost Review Committee, convened first in 1991 and again in 1996, concluded that household spending had risen by 76 per cent between 1988 and 1993, with inflation accounted for less than 15 per cent of the increase; the increase was largely due to Singaporeans consuming 'more and better quality goods and services' (*The Straits Times*, 7 August 1996). Nevertheless, the Committee recommended measures to ensure that future cost increases are moderated; for example, government was urged to maintain its very substantial subsidy of tertiary education.

Secondly, more significantly, severe controls on consumer credit were introduced. For example, since 1992, the minimum qualifying annual income for obtaining a credit card was raised to S$30,000. Credit is not to exceed twice the card-holder's monthly salary; card-issuers must suspend the use of the card by card-holders whose outstanding balances exceeds this credit level. Card-issuers are prohibited from aggressive advertising, from issuing unsolicited pre-approved cards, from including gifts, discounts and incentive schemes to promote consumer spending in their advertisements, and from being financially involved in incentive schemes sponsored by merchants. Violations of any of these controls could lead to a moratorium on the issuance of credit cards in the future (*The Straits Times*, 24 March 1996). Loans on expensive cars and mortgages were also subjected to stringent controls. These measures were aimed at reducing household indebtedness which had been edging up in recent years causing a steady decline in private consumption in other, particularly retail, goods. This decline led to a severe downturn in the retail sector in Singapore; in 1995, combined losses at large department stores exceeded S$130 million, leading to serious downsizing and outright closures.

In so far as the legitimacy of the PAP government is tied to improving the material life of Singaporeans, measures to constrain consumption are likely to have their political effects; however, given the already very high standard of living in Singapore, disaffection may be readily contained. What is altogether surprising is that, compelled by economic factors, the government itself had to introduce changes to these constraints. In early 2003, with the economy facing the most severe downturn in the brief history of Singapore as an independent nation, the government lifted constraints on housing and car loans to stimulate consumption. The massive overhang of surplus flats in the public housing sector and private condominiums forced the government to reduce the 20 per cent cash down-payment for home purchases by half, easing cash outlay requirements and facilitating home purchases. The same was done for car loans; the previously stipulated 30 per cent down-payment and a loan period maximum of seven years were removed completely, leaving the banks and credit companies to negotiate with their respective clients on the terms and conditions of loans. This radical change of policy shows that the Singapore government, with its hegemonic political position, must nevertheless abide by the logic of capitalism in stimulating domestic consumption to generate some level of economic growth in the face of economic downturn. Such is the inherent logic of capitalism: high savings and asceticism are necessary in the period of economic 'take-off', while hedonism is the necessary ethos of a mature economy.

Notes

1. Similar discomfort with the rise of consumerism, especially of the young, can be found in most of the newly-industrialising economies in East and Southeast Asia, see Chua (2000).
2. Hall (1991: 20) further points out that 'we suffer increasingly from a process of historical amnesia in which we think that just because we are thinking about an idea it has only just started'.
3. While details of how the people work out some aspects of the two sets of attitudes and practices, including use of different objects of consumption, are anthropological research topics in their own right, I would merely suggest here that the workings out are not as traumatic as some might assume. For examples of anthropological research on incorporation of 'modern' products in Third World locations, see Howes (1996a).
4. In the case of the overwhelmingly Chinese population, even the Chinese-language educated were modernist in their political orientation, as they were divided between republicans and communists rather than loyal to the decaying Ching dynasty. Their modernity is reflected in the fact that the Chinese vernacular schools in Singapore have used Mandarin as the language of instruction since 1910, influenced by the May Fourth intellectuals in China.
5. For example, for the first time, between 9 June to 9 July 1997, the National Computer Board and the Singapore Tourist Promotion Board combined their efforts in promoting shopping by Internet during the annual month-long 'Great Singapore Sale', which involved the entire retail sector and attracted shoppers not only from the region, but from as far as South Asia and South Africa.

6. As Appadurai suggests (1991: 5), the relative 'homogenisation' of culture as a result of the global reach of capitalist production and consumption 'often subspeciates into either an argument about Americanisation, or an argument about commoditisation, and very often the two arguments are closely linked'. For a discussion of this simplification under the concept of 'Coca-colonisation', see Howes (1996a: 34).

7. Perhaps because of its past status as a colony of Japan, Taiwan is the only location in Asia where there are concerns with Japanisation, see Ching (1994).

8. This classification of Japanese goods as 'technological hardware' and Western products as 'cultural' is one of the plausible answers to the question: 'When Japanese exports to the United States exceed American exports to Japan, is not the spectre of Western consumer imperialism an outdated myth' (Classen and Howes, 1996: 187–88).

9. For a discussion of the similarities between conservative traditions in Western political thought and 'Asian' values, see Rodan and Hewison (1996).

10. As with all ideologies, official anti-Westernism has its supporters and critics. Space limitations do not permit extensive discussion of the positions of local critics. A good sampling of these latter positions can be obtained from the themed issue of *Commentary*, 'On Democracy' (1993), a journal published by the National University of Singapore Society.

11. Similar concerns with excessive consumption may be found in Taiwan and South Korea. In one survey of South Koreans, more than 90 per cent of respondents thought that excessive consumption was a serious social problem in Korea, but more than 80 per cent of the same respondents say that they were not excessive consumers themselves (Kim, 1996).

12. It has been exposed that the models used were either actual heroin-users or made out to look like them. This would make it even more unacceptable in Singapore, where possession of a very small quantity, 15 grams, of heroine could lead to a sentence of death by hanging.

13. 'Blur' is a Singaporean idiom for someone who is always missing the point. Such individuals are sometimes referred to as *sotong* — the Malay word for squid, assumed to swim in its own dark ink.

14. The founder of the company is Jimmy Lai. Notably, he had angered the PRC by his crude critical remarks regarding the late Deng Xiaoping, which led to the shutting down of his shops in Beijing and the PRC's divestment of shares in his company. After resigning from the chairmanship of Giordano, he subsequently founded his own newspaper, the popular *Apple Daily*.

15. In fact, these are summaries of articles which first appeared in Singapore's English national newspaper, *The Straits Times*. The motivation behind the series of analysis of popular cultural instances is precisely to contest claims of 'Americanisation' of Singaporeans, either by state agencies or by private individuals.

AN ETHNOGRAPHY OF CONSUMPTION CULTURE

3

Bodies in Shopping Centres: Displays, Shapes and Intimacies[1]

Orchard Road, Singapore's hotel and shopping strip, was developed between the mid-1960s and the mid-1990s to position Singapore as Asia's premiere shopping destination, in competition with Hong Kong, and later, Bangkok. Each year, the entire month of June is dedicated to the 'Great Singapore Sale', designed to attract consumers from neighbouring Malaysia and Indonesia, from other Asian countries — Taiwan, Japan and India — and from even further afield, Australia and South Africa. However, it is undeniable that the clients of these shopping establishments are as often local Singaporeans as they are tourists. In the case of upmarket women's boutiques, clients are more often local. The ubiquitous shopping complex embodies the now conventional view that mass production has made goods that were once consumed only by the socially privileged available to all.

By the mid-1990s, the sprouting of shopping centres appeared to have gone beyond the saturation point to overbuilding; according to sociologist Mike Featherstone, walking through the heart of Singapore is like walking through a series of large shopping centres (Featherstone, 1998). The overbuilding contributed to serious economic difficulties in the entire retail sector, and some large department stores closed, including the French chain Galleries Lafayette and the American chain K-Mart, in a time of robust economic growth. However, by then, 'shopping' had become a national leisure activity for Singaporeans (*The Straits Times*, 18 August 1996). Furthermore, and ironically, during the 1997 Asian financial crisis, 'shopping' might have become a more frequent activity for those made unemployed by the crisis.[2] In the analysis of consumer culture of

41

Singapore, the shopping complex must be included among the prime sites for research.

Within academic social science writings, department stores and shopping centres have been elevated to the status of 'dream palaces' or 'cathedrals' of contemporary consumer culture (Williams, 1982; Ferguson, 1992). This echoes the self-serving claim of Selfridge, pioneering UK department store entrepreneur that customers 'came to the store and realised their dreams' (Shields, 1992:3). The image that emerges from the extensive postmodern literature on shopping is one of consumers freely whizzing through shops, gazing on and purchasing, or even shop-lifting, whatever they desire, in order to (re)invent their own identities. This image of the 'unrestrained' consumer in 'dreamland' is often theorised into existence by updating the trope of the 'Flaneur' (Falk and Campbell, 1997; Featherstone, 1998; Tester, 1997), rather than undertaking ethnographic observation of visitors to the shopping centres. Given its unsubstantiated and overly 'romantic' claims, this body of literature has been aptly described by Meagan Morris as "'Edenic' allegories of consumerism in general" (1988:193). Such writings contrast to those which continue to condemn consumerism as morally evil or just another ploy to trap the exploited masses (Crawford, 1992). The behaviour of visitors to the department store and shopping mall, the very location of both visual and actual consumption, remains unexamined ethnographically. This chapter is therefore concerned to fill this lacunae by documenting some of the activities of shopping centre visitors in Singapore.

The term 'visitor' designates those for whom 'shopping' is a mundane metaphor for idling away time at a shopping centre, as a leisure activity. It is common knowledge that for many urbanites the actual buying of objects of desire or necessity is not the primary purpose of 'shopping'. Browsing is. Browsing, however, is itself also often a euphemism for what one may term 'wasting' time, in contrast to spending time 'productively'. Idling, while moving or stationary, is thus the primary purpose and activity for many who visit shopping centres. Visitors, particularly the young, constitute a very significant component of the population that is present within a mall at any one time.

For these visitors, the shopping centre is a public space filled with desire-stirring commodities but also cluttered with strangers. The strangers are phenomenologically perceived as impersonal 'bodies'. The late Erving Goffman suggested that a pedestrian "can be considered a pilot encased in a soft and exposing shell, namely his clothes and skin" (1971:7). When a visitor navigates as a pedestrian-vehicular body/unit through the circulation spaces in the centre, he/she is not only aware of the commodities but also of the presence of other moving bodies, and of the shifting gazes of the latter. This awareness of other bodies is captured by the proverbial 'to see and be seen'.[3] The behaviours that issue from this doubled awareness of goods and strangers should be directly observable from the way visitors carry their vehicular body-units through the spaces in shopping centres. This essay is concerned with some of these behaviours drawn from ethnographic fieldwork in Ngee Ann City Shopping Complex, along Orchard Road.

Takashimaya Square, Singapore: Where Nothing is Happening

The Japanese department store, Takashimaya is the anchor tenant of Ngee Ann City. At the basement of the store is a double height open space labelled Takashimaya Square. The Square is architecturally planned as a space for occasional and changing exhibitions, festivals, and promotions of themed-commodities. Like other shopping areas, the Square is highly policed by security guards and not so-hidden-video cameras. Such surveillance has received much analytic attention and negative commentary by scholars, some of whom label shopping centres as the 'new panopticon'. Such comments issue from the assumption that visitors desire to conduct themselves so as to subvert the organised orderliness of shopping centres (Goss, 1993:40–43). Empirically, as we shall see, this is far from the case, and the presumed subversive desire, if it exists, is distinctly a minority feeling. Furthermore, the injunction against behaviours that are subversive of the social order of public spaces is not exclusively the desire of the shopping centre owners but is also to be found in the policing of such spaces by users themselves. This is evident in the behaviours and activities of visitors to the Square.

When not occupied by goods, the Square is filled with visitors: free-loading on the comfort of shopping centre air-conditioning is a common phenomenon in tropical Singapore.[4] In most shopping centres, free-loaders tend to clutter up the interior circulation paths, causing inconvenience for the actual purchasers of goods. By gathering and accommodating such visitors, the Square acts to free up circulation paths, giving purchasers the relative comfort of not having to compete for space with the freeloaders. In this sense an empty Square is functional as an unintended consequence of the architectural design and planning, as 'an aberration of local performance' (Morris, 1988:206).

Thus, when empty of goods, the Square is transformed into a space for young visitors, the most prevalent users of shopping centres as places to just hang-out (Lewis, 1990). On any Saturday, beginning at about eleven o'clock in the morning, it starts to fill up. First come students in school uniforms, flush-faced and observably sweaty, wearing 'fashionable' brand-name sports shoes in spite of their ungainly chunkiness. They have just come in after their extra-curricular activities at school, delaying their return home. They are followed by young office workers in jeans with all sorts of 'tops'; Saturday being only half a work day, the office dress codes for both male and female employees are relaxed to allow informal wear. White-collar workers with family responsibilities are a distinct minority.

At the Square, everyone is accorded a place on the steps, each keeping a respectable distance from and for the others, co-present but not intrusive. In spite of being a space that is privately owned by the landlord of the building, it is a public space in the best sense of the term. It is a space open to all who wish to use it, where the norm of civility of citizenship rules (Scruton, 1984). In the simultaneity of the temporary denizens, the Square does not discriminate. There is one exception. A single woman idling on her own is still a relatively infrequent event and when it does occur, she is usually noticeably aware of herself as being a 'spectacle' of the male gaze. In Singapore, gazing remains unequally gendered.

From our observations, as a rule, courting couples do not idle at the Square beyond the necessary time to consume their fast-food, bought from the food-court next to the Square. They then hurry off to where they can be alone-in-the-crowd, as shall be discussed later in this chapter. Individuals over thirty tend to be focused shoppers. They skirt around the Square, go straight to the stores they have in mind, make their purchases and head for the exit; for them, shopping is for buying. The Square is thus the space for youth, and there are few better places in Singapore to idle.

Activities at the Square are always the 'same' every Saturday; however, the individuals involved in enacting the 'same scene' are constantly changing, not only on different Saturdays but during a given afternoon. As in the case of all shopping centres, the same scene is repetitively enacted by different individuals (Morris, 1988:204), as the public that use the Square is not a stable or homogenous entity. The 'same-ness' comes from the Square being a 'hang-out'. 'Hanging-out' is an activity without specificity but derived from a phenomenological, generalised sense of 'nothing is happening'. So, for example, when a new arrival at the Square spots and approaches a group of friends who appear to have been there forever and inquires, as a mode of greeting, 'What's happening?' the answer is invariably 'Nothing', or versions thereof. This 'nothing' is, of course, metaphorical. For indeed, there are always lots of happenings on the Square, otherwise it would be pointless to hang-out there. It is just that whatever is taking place is so much within expectations as to be unremarkable, the events are not 'happenings'. All these activities constitute the 'normal' for one who is a 'regular' at the Square, thus 'nothing is happening'.[5]

This 'nothing' is but a shorthand version of "the enduring scene of all the changes, fluctuations, and repetitions of the passing of everyday life" for those who hang-out at the Square (Morris, 1988:205). The fluctuating yet repetitive activities include eating ravenously with school mates after vigorous workouts during sports practices in schools, with food conveniently bought from adjacent food-courts; splitting apart a daily newspaper, each with one page or section to read; staring at the multi-screen MTV, with what's on the screen being often of secondary importance; studying in solitude, where one is anonymous in the crowd (there is no study space in public housing flats, and no escape from noise due to the density of residents); sitting around and being bored, preferably collectively rather than alone, perhaps painting each other's toe-nails (why not?); and, of course, parading self-consciously, wanting to be seen. All these 'normal' activities take place on the steps that skirt the Square, significantly not at its centre, as we shall see.

Managing to Self-Display

That urbanites must call attention to themselves if they wanted to break through the 'blazé' and inattentive attitude of the throngs of strangers around them was noted long ago by Georg Simmel (1950). Indeed, making oneself a spectacle is an intentional feature of hanging-out anywhere. Yet self-display can be risky business and must be managed judiciously, as some observed instances at the Square serve to illustrate.

The Square is the size of a small recreational ice-skating rink. In fact this was its original design intention, to provide an exotic leisure activity in tropical Singapore. However, it is perceptually 'vast' and intimidating to idlers. This may be read from the fact that almost everyone skirts around the Square rather than cross the centre to get from one side to the other. Crossing it appears to be an intimidating experience because it 'exposes' one to the gaze of all who are present. To cross the Square is a conscious display of the self, and there is a tacit assumption that others will stare at anyone who does so. This assumption/ awareness places limits on the desire of the visitors to 'be seen', suggesting that self-display is far more intimidating than commonly assumed.

In one observed instance a group of teenage Caucasian girls danced across the centre and upon reaching the other side, they turned to the crowd and took a bow, to applause from the sedate audience.[6] The bowing signalled the girls' awareness of having put themselves on public display, while the applause affirmed the assumption that there was an audience of strangers. The episode demonstrates that such calling attention to oneself must be conducted without excessive disruption of the norm of civility, without the 'bad taste' associated with 'showing off'. The act of taking a bow transformed the grabbing-of-attention into a 'spontaneous' act of 'fun', a ludic act, thus minimising (but not erasing) the show-off component of the act itself. This phenomenon of managed self-display is further refined in the next observed event.

Pagers and Parody

An obvious way in which a person calls attention to oneself is of course bodily adornment. No matter how functional, all objects that are carried on the body can become objects of fashion. In Singapore, the newest entrants to the pantheon of functional yet fashionable ornaments of adornment are modular-mobile-phones, which have largely replaced the once ubiquitous, inexpensive 'pager'. Their elevation to status-imbued, ornamental goods can be discerned in their designs. Each successive generation of the two items strives to be more 'sleek' and 'attractive' than their predecessors; industrial goods fused with design concerns of fashion. In this 'ornamentalising' process, the once rather self-consciously 'cool' matt-black or dark-grey of mobile phones, which imparted a sense of seriousness and formality, presumably of commerce, has followed ixn the footsteps of pagers, breaking out into carnivalesque colours. Pagers metamorphosised from small square black boxes, whose prominence when clipped on to the belt was accentuated, perhaps undermined, by their ugliness, to colourful, crystal-like objects that glowed in the dark.

As items of adornment, mobile-phones and pagers are conspicuously displayed in use and also when dormant. This is why the ringing and the 'beeping' sounds, respectively, are so noticeable, intended to announce to the world that their owners have been summoned. The sounds signify the importance of the owners and are thus self-identity-enhancing. However, the self-deprecating, even self-incriminating 'embarrassment' of being so indiscreetly summoned publicly must be displayed; hence, the frenetic scrambling into the pocket or the handbag in search of the 'offending' objects. The tension between identity-enhancement and 'embarrassment' suggests the always present possibility of the 'excess' of the former sliding into the latter and transforming the owner into a 'show-off'. Precisely because of this possibility of excess and identity transformation, all items of adornment contain the potential for their own subversion, the potential of self-parody, as the following observed instance at the Square illustrates.

A mixed-gender group of late-teens had been hanging out on the steps of the Square for quite awhile. They formed the core of a group whose composition expanded and shrank according to the coming and going of friends and acquaintances, without any apparent prior arrangement. Every so often, the entire core group would get up and walk away from the Square, only to return to approximately the same spot after a brief time. During one of these short departures from their perch, one of the guys collected all the pagers from group members and hung them randomly but prominently all over his clothes. Pagers of different colours were hanging on his shirt-sleeves, the outside of his breast pockets, on the belt-loops of his trousers. He walked rather gingerly along with his friends, taking care that the pagers would not fall off. His excessive adornment and his careful gait were calculated for the loud amusement of his friends and the potential audience of strangers. Those who saw him could not help but laugh or suppress a smile.

He had turned himself into a public spectacle. He had made a 'fool' of himself. He had accomplished this by showing how ridiculous the wearing of pagers as ornaments among teenagers has become. The excess number of pagers on him exposed the underlying pretension of many pager-wearers — a pretension of immediacy and self-worth, such that others cannot wait to get hold of one. In his self-ridicule he was redeemed. He showed that he knew that the pager is just a kind of 'show'. In truth, days may go by without anyone paging one, and when pages do come they usually concern an insignificant matter. Significantly, this self-parody would only be executed in public by teenagers, whose social honesty about the self often surpasses those of adults. Indeed, it is impossible to imagine a thirty-something doing the same anywhere in public.

This scene of self-parody through excessive ornamentation of the body shares the same ludic elements as the instance of teenage girls crossing the Square mentioned above. The self-mocking does not erase the simultaneous effect of calling attention to oneself, of being 'seen and noted' by others in the crowd, rather than absorbed into the 'seen but unnoticed' quality that pervades when 'nothing is happening'.

Intimate in the Light

If groups of teenagers are relatively immobile within a shopping centre, courting couples tend to keep on the move. At Takashimaya, for example, couples do not hang-out at the Square in the basement. They are moving bodies, browsing through displays; each partner may break away from the other led by different interests and attentions, but always in close proximity. Or, in many cases, the man trails along after the woman, tapping his toes in impatience and having difficulties placing or focusing his eyes on all the bodies around him, especially in women's merchandise sections. Often the woman, in addition to 'shopping' for herself, has to interest her male companion in items for himself. In all these instances, the behaviours of courting couples are generally not remarkable — until they reach the escalator.

On the escalators, a seen-but-unnoticed sight in shopping centres in Singapore is repeatedly enacted by different couples.[7] The woman changes from one who leads, as mentioned above, to one who is 'dependent' on her partner. As if overcome by the exhaustion of shopping, she appears no longer able to hold up her own body and stand on her own. She leans back on to him and he supports her body with his, props her up, eliminating all physical distance between them; bodies pasted together until the landing at the top or the bottom of the escalators. Again as if in gratitude, she may even give him a pecking-kiss. All these little gesture are what Goffman (1971) calls 'tie-signs'. In Singapore, where physical distance between genders is still relatively rigidly maintained and public expression of emotions are still culturally frowned upon by many, courting couples do not come to shopping centres to be intimate in public. Such displays of intimacy on escalators therefore deserve analytic attention.

Parenthetically, one should not overlook this need for simple reassurances like the 'we are still together' gestures. Elaborate everyday cultural practices are built around and through these little assurances. Anyone who has been to an American home would have noticed that the names of the married couple seem to have disappeared, replaced by 'dear', 'honey' and 'darling' and other more private terms of endearment. This replacement discloses the routine practices of reassurance of 'love and concern' through constant explicit expressions and little gestures.[8]

In the context of shopping, the brief intimacy, snatched in full public exposure, has its own logic: having been enticed and hailed by the glittering merchandise while browsing through the displays, thus neglecting each other for the duration, it is necessary to re-establish their connectedness. One can imagine each member of the couple, perhaps more so the man, feeling less-than-the-merchandise while on the shop floor. The little reassuring intimacy can constitute both an admission of having been mesmerised by the objects in the 'palace of desires' leading to temporarily mutual negligence, and thus also a gesture of apology for the temporary dizziness. This brief moment re-seals their relationship as a couple, before they are separated again by yet another whole new set of desired objects at the next floor of the department store or shopping centre.

Nevertheless, there remains the question of why the escalator is the privileged space for such an act of contrition.

Pedestrian traffic in successful shopping centres, especially one as crowded on a Saturday afternoon as Takashimaya, is too dense for a body to stop comfortably in mid-stream along any circulation paths between displays or shops. If two bodies were to stop to catch a little 'reassurance' in the middle of a path, it would immediately create collisions. These pile ups of bodies, with their eyes on everything but other moving bodies, would resemble accidents on expressways when a driver is forced to stop suddenly, and fast moving traffic slows suddenly during rush hour. In a shopping centre, browsers of windows have to trust others not to walk into them, and avoid walking into others who have stopped in their paths. Hence, throughout the shopping centre, there are no convenient stopping points without entering a food outlet, or in the case of Takashimaya, going to the Square. Indeed, there is often hardly any room to hold hands and a couple has to resort to different body gestures, different tie-signs, to signal to others that they are an 'item' not to be separated unnecessarily.

For this reason of traffic flow there is, therefore, no better place than the escalator to catch a little reassuring intimacy in a shopping centre. The escalator is a physical oxymoron. It allows a body to move while staying stationary, in stationary movement. The need to move along is taken care of by the mechanical movement of the escalator itself, with no risk of a traffic jam. At the same time, the need to stay stationary for physical contact is provided. So, where else but the escalator for a little intimacy in the light?

Changing Shapes of Bodies in Shopping Centres

A body changes shape over time naturally. It can also be altered by regimes of diet and exercise, increasingly common 'beauty' practices. It manifests different shapes when it is wrapped differently by different costumes, a fundamental principle of fashion. As a vehicular unit moving through a shopping centre the body changes shape in yet another manner. As a body navigates through the circulation paths created by display counters, racks of clothing and lines of shops, it 'expands' and 'shrinks' in response to the objects which entice the eyes and the hands.

Upon entering the ground floor of Takashimaya, the department store, one is confronted by an apparently random arrangement of counters of small objects, such as inexpensive women's accessories. The informal character of such displays invites anyone who passes by, hailing one to reach out, touch, pick up and try on the items, and if dissatisfied, just throw them back on the counter. A browser has the maximum degree of freedom here in relation to displayed commodities. With hands extending to maximum reach, the body is stretched to gain the greatest amount of space that it can potentially occupy (Miller, 1998:36).

Freedom of the body is increased among the clothes that hang on free-standing racks stationed along the circulation paths. Fingers, grease and all, feel the fabric, hands pick up the clothes, hold them against the body so as to imagine oneself in them, and if desired, take them to the changing room to try them on. Clothes are thus donned and doffed at will. As the intention to purchase is not a prerequisite, fantasies of image-change are free. As shall be shown later, it is among these free-standing displays that one comes closest to the realisation of the idea of the shopping centre as a palace of desires and house of dreams.

As one ascends the escalator to the upper floors of the departmental store, where up-scale 'branded' goods are displayed within clearly bounded stalls, the body begins to 'shrink'. An invisible line seems to have been etched on the ground keeping the body to the side, away from the merchandise. If there are stalls on both sides of the body, it stays within the corridor space defined by the two boundaries, one on each side. The invisible lines constitute 'thresholds' beyond which a visiting or browsing individual does not cross, kept in check by the awareness of the high prices of merchandise that attracts the eyes but not the hands. A visitor will no longer touch the goods on display, afraid of being accosted and embarrassed by a designer-uniform-clad sales person, whose refrain of 'Can I help you?' sounds more like a put-down than an offer of assistance (Peretz, 1995).

Avoidance of crossing thresholds of shops reaches its limit when visitors are confronted by very high-price boutiques that are 'empty', as they are devoid of customers for most part of the day.[9] Significantly, the emptiness of these shops, their sparseness of both display and customers, does not signal to visitors an invitation to walk in, freely interact with the merchandise and let their imaginations run their course. On the contrary, the emptiness signifies exclusivity. The transparency of the plate-glass walls, with their imperceptible glass door, invites the eyes but keeps the object out of reach of the hands and the body outside the store.

When it violates this keep-out rule, the body shrinks further. When a visitor unwittingly steps into one of these glassed-in boutiques, casually flipping one of the price tags on a very 'ordinary' item, like a plain white shirt, the fingers are quickly retrieved, reflexively, as if burnt by a source of heat, that is the price. The body now holds itself in, hands 'glued' to the side, afraid of coming into contact with the merchandise again, for fear of contaminating the latter. Eyes are focused on the exit and the legs beat a quick retreat out of the shop. The relationship between browser and merchandise has been reversed: instead of the browser abusing the goods, the goods intimidate the browser. The intimidation is only intensified by the presence of the above-mentioned designer-uniform clad sales people, who often outnumber customers at any one time in the shop, and their 'attentiveness'.

These instances of the shrinking body disclose the consciousness of purchasing power, or more generically of social class, between the browser and the merchandise. It is a consciousness that severely constrains the freedom to browse and handle objects of desire, in contrast to the imagined expansive if not unlimited freedom generally implied in social science theorising of shopping.

Intimidation by merchandise reaches its limit when the body shrinks to its smallest; this is when one arrives at the crystal section of the department store. Here, the merchandise positively threatens the customer with a promise to break if mishandled. Imagined the fear in the eyes of the boyfriend when his girlfriend swings around with her sling bag to check on his whereabouts; hence, he makes sure that they stay out of this section. Families with children are absent for similar reasons. Consequently, crystal sections are seldom visited by the throngs that pass daily through the department store. Defined by absence of visitors, the crystal section is a place of quiet respite, a sanctuary, for visitors before they return to confront the world of goods and strange bodies again.

Conclusion

The above observations and interpretations of bodily behaviour of visitors to shopping centres permit us to reconsider the idea of unbounded consumer freedom in such centres. First, visitors are highly conscious of their 'presence' in a world of strangers, which they can either choose to 'thematise' by consciously bringing the attention of strangers onto themselves, or ignore, by staying anonymous, as in the 'self-absorption' of couples on escalators. Second, visitors do not have unrestrained freedom *vis-à-vis* the commodities on display. The degree of freedom permitted is signalled by, among other cues, (i) the manner in which the commodities are displayed and (ii) shoppers' own awareness of their financial ability to consume. The latter helps up-market vendors to maintain the status of their merchandise and shops, signalled, significantly, by 'emptiness', a space devoid of customers, as visitors have placed the merchandise beyond their means and thus keep themselves out of the shops. Third, visitors tend to employ self-discipline, independent of, or in addition to, the surveillance devices that are installed by shopping centre owners. This self-discipline is as important as the 'panoptic' gaze of hidden video cameras, security guards and undercover, plain-clothes shop-floor 'police' looking out for shop-lifters.

However, it should be noted that self-expressive and self-disciplining behaviour observed in any shopping site are highly culture specific. In this case, it is apparent that Singapore remains culturally a space in which public expression of emotion is not encouraged, if not exactly frowned upon; where gender distance in public is seriously observed and where sartorial conformity rather than individual expressiveness is the norm. All of which combined to 'explain' some of the behaviour observed. Bodily behaviour observed in Singapore will not necessarily be reproduced in other sites, where different modes of expression and discipline will be observed, although locally-conventional restraints on visitors' freedom will undoubtedly still prevail.

Finally, to end on a methodological note: In making observations, descriptions and interpretations of bodily behaviour, no confirmation of the interpretations is sought through actual contact, such as interviews, with those who were the object of the research gaze. Readers who are familiar with the writing on the figure of the 'flaneur' will recognise that in this particular instance, the sociologist/anthropologist of the urban space is operating as a 'flaneur'. He is an intentional observer in and of the crowd. As a 'sovereign' observer he orders the world by his definition and attributes meanings to the spaces and activities that fall into his gaze.[10] Confirmation of meaningfulness of these observations and interpretations, however, is achieved when Singaporean readers smile in self-recognition upon reading of the antics of the visitors described.

Notes

1. Earlier versions of this paper were presented at the Seminar on 'Cultural and Social Dimension of Market Expansion III', Goethe Institute, Jakarta, 26–27 August 1996 and at the Conference on 'Body and Culture', Kalam Foundation, Jakarta, 14–15 August 1998.
2. It is beyond the scope of this chapter to take on board a discussion of the economic crisis in the retail sector, which took place even before the 1997 Asian regional economic crisis. It should be noted that to the extent that the larger regional crisis had caused greater unemployment in Singapore, the number of visitors idling away time in shopping centres might have increased during the crisis period. However, the fieldwork for this chapter was carried out before the crisis, thus the observations are made under so-called 'normal' economic conditions.
3. The analytic focus on pedestrians in shopping malls is also suggested by Morris, who suggests that an alternative title to her own on-going project on 'Things to do with shopping centres' is 'Pedestrian notes on modernity'.
4. Many shopping centres are crowded with large number of domestic workers from the Philippines, Indonesia and Sri Lanka during the weekends. This has led the management of some shopping centres to place security guards in the corridor spaces to move the foreign workers along and prevent them from idling in air-conditioned comfort.
5. Ironically, some adults fail to read this as the metaphor that it is. For example, Lewis (1990:130) suggests that 'mallies' are always 'waiting for something, anything, to happen' and then proceeds to quote from the youth he interviewed at the mall a whole list of activities which the latter engage *in situ*.
6. In this instance I am refraining from commenting on the fact that the group of teenagers are Caucasians, i.e. foreigners, in this Asian city. In the eyes of many of their ready-made audience is a perception and belief that only 'Western' youth with their 'liberal' up-bringing will engage in such self-display and frivolity. This essentialised division between 'conservative/Asian' and 'liberal/Western' is part of a public discourse inscribed on the Singaporean body-politic by the state and the long-governing dominant single-party, the People's Action Party.
7. We say 'seen-but-unnoticed' because such acts are so 'familiar' to Singaporeans that they are no longer 'noticed' as an 'event'. My students upon hearing the description provided by me during lectures generally laugh in recognition.
8. To buttress the earlier claim that public display of sentiment remains relatively 'tabooed' culturally, such replacement of names by terms of endearment is not found in Chinese households in Singapore. I remember distinctly my own discomfort when confronted with such practices when I first went as a student to Canada.

9. In Singapore, clients of these shops make purchases within a very narrow band of three to four hours during the afternoon, after a leisurely lunch and before it is time to arrange dinner. See the next chapter.
10. See the essays in Tester (1997).

4

Steps to Becoming a Fashion Consumer

Introduction

"Ours is a consumer society." This statement calls attention to the idea that consumers are 'socially produced'; i.e. individuals are socially transformed into consumers. This distinguishes the social historical components from the biological needs behind an individual's consumption activities. An intentional merging of the historical and natural processes has enabled purveyors of commodities to place the goods they market in the language of needs and necessities. On the part of the willing or unwitting individual-turned-consumer, the presence of the natural need to consume serves as an alibi for the purchase of said goods, if such an alibi is even necessary. To emphasise that consumers are socially produced and socially sustained is to argue that the 'needs' are themselves embedded in a social-cultural 'matrix' of consumption (Featherstone, 1987:57).

The network of social processes that effects the transformation of an individual into a consumer include, of course, marketing strategies used at every level of the social organisation of sales, with advertising as the most prominent and widespread (Ewen and Ewen, 1992; Baudrillard, 1981; Haug, 1986; Wernick, 1991). Advertising stands at the apex of abstraction in the social organisation of sales, and the shop floor of a retail outlet is at its bottom rung. An advertisement may successfully compel an individual to seek out a particular consumer item; however, it is the sales staff at the retail outlet that is responsible for transforming the individual into a client who makes repeated purchases. This chapter aims to provide an account of the stages in the behavioural transformation of an individual into an avid consumer, based on direct observations of the behaviours employed when sales transactions are achieved and retail establishments acquire loyal clients in high-end fashion boutiques in Singapore's premier shopping district. The interest is, therefore, not in the sartorial behaviours of Singaporeans but in the processes of their being transformed into fashion consumers.

Background to the Research

Fieldwork was conducted for a month in four high-priced designer clothes boutiques that cater mainly to women clients, located in the same up-market shopping complex; three of the boutiques have minor sections for men's clothes. These boutiques functioned as the interactional sites within which the transformation of individuals into consumers was accomplished: the entire process from the moment a 'seeking' individual steps through the door to the moment the same individual becomes an established client.[1] The boutiques' proprietors imposed some conditions: the researcher was not to engage the clients either in conversation or interviews; conversations with the sales people were to focus on their job activities and not on labour relations, and no attempt should be made to discover the profitability of the trade. With these constraints, my role as researcher was essentially a passive one; I remained entirely an observer and never became a participant. The focus of observation was mainly on the actual behavioural interactions between sales staff and customers.

Absence of verbal exchanges with the clients served to reduce my presence in the small spaces of the boutiques. My too-intrusive male presence in the small boutique was unavoidable, given the high rent for these premises, all the floor area in the stores is utilised and there was no space for me to place myself without being seen. The oddity of a male sitting in full view of everyone in the store, scribbling away into a notebook was readily noted by many of the clients. Furthermore, the process of shopping for clothes is often a rather private affair, especially given the need to keep changing outfits. It might have given rise to more discomfiting conjectures if I had attempted to hide my presence! Nevertheless, my presence caused many enough discomfort that they would not step out of the fitting rooms when trying on clothes! Fortunately, all the fitting rooms in these premises had mirrors on all four walls and were large enough to comfortably accommodate both the client and a sales person.

The collection of observed data and the interpretation of their significance proceeded concurrently as meaningful conceptual clusters emerged and became identifiable. The soundness of these interpretations was clarified by submitting the final report to the proprietors, as a kind of 'member's check'. These proprietors were themselves working proprietors in that they would double up as sales persons when they were in their stores and were, therefore, thoroughly familiar with the activities on the premises.

Before presenting the substantive findings, it is necessary to provide a general description of up-market fashion retailing strategies.

Fashion Retail Strategies

With mass production, the lure of fashion has been democratised. However, as Ewen and Ewen suggest, "The hidden secret of fashion democracy was the class dimension, demarcating differences between the hand-sewn originals and the cavalry of often shoddy copies that followed with varying degrees of loyalty" (1982:181). With the emergence of a middle class worldwide, the fashion industry has introduced a new line of clothes between the hand-sewn original and the poor imitation; namely, designer label ready-to-wear clothes. These are machine-sewn limited editions of original designs, produced often in low production cost areas in Asia (Morawetz, 1981). In terms of price, these designer clothes are not exorbitant one-of-a-kinds but they are definitely up-market merchandise given their relative exclusivity. The development of ready-to-wear, along with international advertising efforts, have made French, Italian, Japanese and American designer labels — often unpronounceable to the locals of the consuming nations — household names in the entire spectrum of the middle class everywhere.[2] Exclusivity of the clothes is maintained by franchise arrangements and marketing through small independent boutiques, as is the case in Singapore.

Designer Boutiques as Client Recruitment Centres

To maintain exclusivity, the boutiques are 'hermetically' sealed with plate-glass windows and doors. The setting is intimidating in its emptiness, with the emptiness being itself a measure of exclusivity. As soon as a shopper passes through the glass doors, she immediately becomes the centre of attention among the staff, for there are generally more sales people than clients in the shop, and someone who is not used to such attention can only respond with nervousness. Occasionally, an inadvertent browser may cross the barrier and wander into the store, only to be shocked by the price on the goods and beat a hasty retreat out of the shop without uttering a word. The doors are therefore barriers of intimidation to browsers who cannot afford the high-priced designer items. Inside, they are furnished so as to make shopping comfortable and leisurely and are small enough for a client to view the entire store and its range of clothes without much effort. The latest issues of fashion magazines are readily available and in their pages, the represented designers' clothes are featured and tagged to draw the clients' attention.

Designer boutiques never rush their customers into making purchases; clients have ample time to deliberate on each and every item. Individualised service to every customer is the norm. Customers' inquiries, needs and desires are immediately attended to, from the moment the customer enters the store till she leaves it. Usually, two sales persons serve one customer. One helps the customer directly with the fitting, while the other puts aside selected items, puts away unsuitable items and returns with new outfits. Even when packaging the purchased items, the former makes out the bill while continuing to interact with the customer and the latter does the actual packaging. The two sales persons work in tandem and share the sales commissions. The extended interaction is not just for making a sale on a particular day, but more to encourage sustained and repeated purchases from the customer in future — to 'cultivate' a prospective customer into a client. Such highly-personalised service is more for the benefit of client recruitment than mere retail practices.

Routine Activities at Boutiques

The stores open from ten in the morning to seven in the evening. Staff arrive and depart at staggered times, with full staff strength between noon to six in the evening. Mornings are generally very quiet. The bulk of the business is conducted between half past two and half past five in the afternoon; the three-hour period between lunch and dinner. Even during these peak business hours, the number of customers coming into the stores is small. Hours can easily go by without any browsers or customers. Significantly, more customers than browsers come to the store because the high-price tags keep browsers at bay. I observed that the maximum number of customers at any one time was five and the sales staff was barely able to cope due to the preferred tandem serving arrangement. Sales people usually lament that customers do not space themselves throughout the day. They prefer to visit the stores during the three-hour period in the afternoon and shop in the company of one another.

The overwhelming majority of customers were regular, established clients. This is certainly a case where the proverbial 80 per cent of the goods are sold to 20 per cent of the clients (Prus, 1987:336). According to one proprietor, the clients are "either self-employed professionals or unemployed", that is, they are either born or married into money, or have some other source of wealth. The majority of the clients are housewives, with professionals in the minority. This accounts largely for the activity pattern in the stores — the three-hour period in the afternoons is when the need to engage in housekeeping activities is at its lowest. The regularity with which some of the clients frequent the stores is astonishing to anyone unfamiliar with the trade. Sales people claim that some clients come every day. Even if this were an exaggeration it, nevertheless, highlights the frequency of the visits. Some clients who travel in the same social circles are at the stores so often that they readily become meeting places for them. The stores may be considered 'the third place' for these clients, that is, a setting that is neither home nor workplace but one which is accessible and well integrated into the daily life of the clients (Oldenberg and Bissett, 1982).

Two features of designer clothes shopping contribute to this high frequency of visits. First is the set of activities that altogether constitute a completed purchase; this set of activities will be discussed later in the chapter. Second is the very nature of fashion itself as a social phenomenon. Fashion is characterised by constant and rapid change. Its cultural value is perishable and, therefore, requires repetitive consumption (McCracken, 1986). To be 'in fashion', one needs to keep pace with these changes ceaselessly; one must be vigilant, watching the latest trend, make the purchases and wear the clothes before others do. This explains the frequency of store visits.

During lull periods, sales staff are engaged in miscellaneous activities such as keeping minor inventories of immediate sales; major inventories are carried out in the evenings or on Sundays as overtime work. The most important and frequent of these miscellaneous activities is keeping in touch with clients through the telephone. This serves two purposes: to keep clients informed about new arrivals, and to find out the reasons why a particular client has not been in the store for a period of time. A common reason for the absence is that the client is abroad — itself a measure of wealth. This is confirmed when clients appear in the store togged out in their purchases from abroad.

The stores are generally quiet from five till closing time at seven in the evening. Saturdays and public holidays are no different, though business is often slower, perhaps because clients are away on weekend trips.

Steps to Becoming a Fashion Consumer

The Inadvertent Browser

The career path to becoming a client logically begins when an individual becomes a browser in a boutique. Shopping is becoming more a leisurely than a functional activity in developing countries (with the possible exception of food-buying). As a form of leisure, one walks the streets, peers into windows and goes in and out of stores on a whim. Such activities are normally uneventful happenings, especially in self-serve, mass market stores. However, drifting into an up-market designer clothes store transforms this uneventful phenomenon into a notable one for the shoppers themselves.

Instead of being the usual 'seen-but-unnoticed-just-another-browser', there is an immediate awareness that one becomes the focus of attention among the entire sales staff the instant one steps into the store. The store is small and normally empty of customers. As a consequence, anyone who passes through its door draws immediate attention. This immediate sense of presence transforms the uneventful 'just browsing' trip into 'an event' that often transforms the individual into an 'inadvertent browser'. This refers to someone who has stepped into the store by mistake. A flip of a price tag will confirm this mistake, subsequently the inadvertent browser does not touch anything else. In one example, a middle-aged woman who accompanied a friend to the store read the price tag on a shirt and could not contain herself, exclaiming, "Are you out of your mind, $300 for a plain white shirt!"

Having made a 'mistake', corrective action is required. The inadvertent browser will try to retreat from the store as quickly and as unobtrusively as possible. The speed is obvious. Some inadvertent browsers stepped into the store, made a quick visual survey without taking another step, then turned around and took their leave. Others are more self-composed: they might do a circuit of the store without touching any item of clothing, and then walk right out of the store before the sales people have a chance to offer assistance. If approached, they simply answer with a quick 'just browsing, thank you'. The unobtrusiveness is extended not only to the sales staff but to the clothes themselves. The inadvertent browser's movements are drawn in and kept along the circulation path of the store in order to avoid the displayed items themselves.

The Intimidated Browser

As opposed to one who inadvertently walks into a designer clothing store, some browsers go in with the intent to buy. The sales people, who are unaware of their intentions, will treat these browsers as they do all strangers who walk into the store. Consequently, the sales person, after an initial greeting, will tend to hang back and wait for the browser's next move.

Any gesture on the browser's part — such as pulling out a specific item, checking its price or feeling the texture of the material — will immediately draw the attention of a sales person. These gestures, therefore, are a summon for service, much like a ringing telephone is a summon to be picked up. At the slightest indication of deliberation, the browser is urged to try on the item in question. If she succumbs and tries on the clothes, she is urged to step out of the fitting room to look at herself under better lighting. The sales person then steps up close to adjust the dress for a better fit. Further commentary is offered as sales talk.

However, the very attentiveness of the sales persons poses a serious interactional problem for the browser. Once the sales person has been engaged, the browser would not want to be looked down upon as being unable to afford the clothes and merely out to waste the sales people's time. There is, therefore, a question of 'face'. In this sense, a prospective buyer may be threatened by any attempt at personal contact by a sales person. The browser's interactional concern at hand is the best way to extricate herself without embarrassment, after declining to make a purchase.

The social psychological pressure of 'face' is intense enough to prevent some browsers from trying on the clothes at all. To try them on is to intensify the interaction with the sales person and increase the obligation to buy, thereby, intensifying the difficulty of making an acceptable retreat. Consequently, browsers tend to respond minimally to sales talk from the sales people. The intimidation reflected in the minimal gesture is in sharp contrast with the nonchalant, careless gestures of browsers in self-serve, mass market department stores. In these stores, browsers freely go through the merchandise, and pick up and try on several items at a time. If any of the items are found unsuitable, they are simply put back on the racks or handed to the sales person at the fitting room, without so much as a nominal word of thanks.

A browser's avoidance of interactional engagement creates a dilemma for the sales people. If the browser does not try on the clothes, there will be no sale. Yet, if the sales person hangs back and leaves the browser alone, this may be misinterpreted as snobbery. The browser might presume that sales person does not think she can afford the merchandise. Nevertheless, sales people tend to stay close at hand, commenting on any item that a browser happens to be focusing her attention on and also pulling clothes off the racks for better inspection. In short, the sales person performs all the activities that a customer in a self-serve store would do on her own.

Ironically, the most effective strategy for a browser to avoid 'losing face' is not through minimal interaction but to accept the services of the sales person. Since it is always possible to find any number of slight faults with the colour, texture, form, detailing and fit of any item of clothing, it is not such a difficult task to decline to make a purchase without shedding unfavourable light on one's ability to purchase. This strategy of extrication may be further backed up by investing some time in reading fashion magazines, so as to acquire the necessary fashion vocabulary. When appropriately used, this vocabulary shows evidence of a familiarity with fashion trends, thereby affirming one's status as a fashion consumer. At no time during my fieldwork, however, did I see this strategy being used.

Furthermore, during my fieldwork, there was little evidence of sophisticated fashion talk between the sales people and customers. Such sophisticated language seems to lie exclusively in the domain of fashion writers and readers, for whom fashion may be merely a matter of visual consumption. For regular fashion consumers, talk seems limited to 'Does it fit? Does it make me look fat? Is it the latest?'

From Browsing to Trying-On

If the sales person manages to persuade the browser to try on an outfit, her role changes from being intimidating to that of being a significant other to the browser. This change in interactional status is, in part, a result of the expertise attributable to the sales person: "Their job is to interpret the couturier's idea, as demonstrated in the Collection and to supervise the fittings of the customer" (Amies, 1973). It is also a significant result of the sales person's position as the immediate audience to the browser trying on the new clothes. As an audience, the sales person's comments can be influential in the final decision to purchase. For example, there was an instance during my fieldwork, when a customer was contemplating buying a full white skirt and white top with tight long sleeves. However, at my own casual — and from a business point of view, careless — remark that it resembled a bridal outfit, the customer could no longer visualise herself in it, and no sale was made. This instance discloses how a social psychology of clothes is at work at the point of a customer's decision to make a purchase. We shall, therefore, suspend for now the progress of the transformation of an individual into a fashion consumer and switch the analytic focus to the social psychology of making a purchase, as part of the social psychology of fashion.

Programming Appearance

In terms of fashion, the store is a place where one gets in and out of clothes assessing them in terms of how they fit one's self-image, and their appropriateness in the possible scenarios in which they might be worn. Just like a dressing room in the privacy of one's home, the store is an experimental stage on which clothing configurations are tried out. The shopping situation provides us with some opportunity to observe part of the process of 'programming' our appearance.

Appearance is a composite concept that includes all the physical attributes and movements of a person, namely, (i) the body and its gestures, and (ii) the transformation of this given physical body by adornments such as clothes, accessories, and cosmetics. Of the two, the latter is subject to a greater degree and ease of manipulation at will; the ways in which a given body is wrapped by different bodily adornments, including clothes, could significantly change how others assess a person's physical attributes. Indeed, conceptually, one may argue that once the adornments are identified, the physical body itself may recede into the background and lose much of its relevance in the ensuing interaction. For example, a person in a police uniform is immediately responded to as the embodiment of public authority as symbolised by the uniform, rather than by his/her bodily attributes. Appearances thus enable individuals to recognise each other's 'identities', or more accurately, 'identity claims' (Stone, 1962), claims that are affirmed or otherwise in subsequent conversational exchanges. In the meeting between individuals, particularly for the first time, appearance has therefore very significant effect on subsequent social interactions. 'Appearance' is therefore a major component of the social self.

The process of putting together the components of appearance can be conceptualised as 'programming'; one "programmes one's appearance according to the identity one desires to project" (Stone, 1962). Clothing is undoubtedly both a vehicle and a means of encoding and communicating features of the intended self projection; although, of course, the others as audience may not necessarily read accurately the intended meanings of the self. Significantly, this programming of appearance is, necessarily, a backstage activity (Goffman, 1959). In everyday life, this backstage activity is the privacy of the dressing space in one's own house. However, interestingly, the shopping space where one tries on outfits is a functional equivalent to the private dressing space. It serves as an experimental stage in which clothing configurations are tried and changes made; that is, it is a space in which programming experiments take place. This explains the earlier-mentioned observation that some customers to the boutique were reluctant to step out of the fitting rooms when trying on clothes, with my presence in the shops. In this space, therefore, the social psychology of fashion consumption is manifest and made observable, involving the interaction between the consumer, who programmes herself, and the potential audiences that the programmed self is supposed to impress.

The Sales Person as Audience

The very first audience for a customer is the sales person. As the sales person's long-term financial interest benefits from turning a customer into a long-term client who will make regular purchases, she needs the customer to rely on her professional judgment. Any inappropriate purchase may be blamed on the sales person, threatening future transactions and casting doubts on the latter's professionalism. If the outfit that is being tried on were obviously 'right' to a browser, the sales person tends to be more encouraging and persuasive in pointing out the details and the fit to the browser. Sales persons will unavoidably have reservations about some of the choices made by the customer. In such instances, the sales person's comments are generally guarded and will tend to respond to the browser's own comments and defer to the latter for the final decision; her own negative evaluations are communicated without offence to the customer who selected the outfit to try in the first place. No hard-sell strategies are used.

Shopping Companion as Audience

The next audience for a fashion consumer is made up of shopping companions. Three categories of shopping companions may be identified. First, it sometimes happens that the persons with whom a customer arrives at the store are not her shopping companions. Rather, they happen to be together when the customer decides to drop into the boutique. Such incidental companions are immediately identifiable as they are dressed very differently from the client. Understandably, such a companion's comments are completely irrelevant, because to the customer the companion is not 'in the know' about fashion. Evidence of this often comes from the companion herself, who might be stunned at the prices in the shop. One illustrative example involved a regular customer in her mid-20s who was accompanied by a middle-aged lady. The latter was so stunned by the US$250 price tag on a white shirt that she could not suppress her remarks, "You've got to be out of your tree. Who would know where you buy your clothes from!"

Second, a 'proper' shopping companion of a customer is readily identifiable by compatible attire. In such instances, the latter's comments are treated as informed opinions. Knowledge is displayed by the companion's comments not only as to the fit of the clothes on the customer but also other relevant aspects such as form, texture and detailing and further, comparative references to other pieces of clothes by the same designer, or to other designer clothes that the client has. Critical comments issued from such knowledge are highly valued by the consumer.

The above two types of shopping companions tend to be women. The third type of shopping companion is the male friend or husband of the customer, who either abstains from or engages actively in the selection of clothes. In either case, his comments are always sought, whether or not he is knowledgeable about fashion. He tends to provide minimal comments of either agreement or disagreement with the general look of the clothes tried. These comments almost always amount to the decision to make or decline a purchase. One may say he has a veto power over the customer's decisions. This apparent veto power issues not only from the fact that he is possibly the one that will pay for the purchase, but more significantly, from the fact that he is most likely the one who will be seen with the customer when the latter wears her purchases at social events. During such events, the male presentation of himself is as important as that of his companion, so his involvement in shopping may be seen as collaborative rather than judgemental. However, it cannot be denied that there is an element of power in the purse strings, and this is apparent when we consider the absent audience.

Audiences in Absentia

Arbiter as Audience

One common practice in boutiques is for customers, especially established clients, to make what is known in the trade as 'on approval' purchases, contingent on the approval of someone not present at the shop. Although no specific person may be named in such instances, there is no doubt that this someone is the one who holds the purse strings. Since the overwhelming majority of the clients are housewives, it is generally assumed that this someone is the husband. Evidence to support this assumption may be gleaned in the store, where it is common to hear clients hankering after certain outfits but lamenting that, unfortunately, their husbands did not like them.

Since the process of seeking approval is done in the privacy of the customer's home, the actual interactional exchanges that lead to a decision cannot be observed. We may assume that the husband's approval is used as the final decision to ratify a customer's own choice in deference either to his position as the holder of the purse strings, or as the one who will most likely be seen with her in social settings. On his part, his decision would be partly based on whether he likes the way his wife looks in the outfit. He is, therefore, the *arbiter elegant* — a judge of elegance and matters of taste with reference to his wife's appearance. The absent audience may or may not be fashion savvy but, as the saying goes, 'he knows what he likes'.

Social Propriety as Audience

Finally, another audience for prospective fashion buyers that is invisible but nevertheless present at the shop is social propriety. As social propriety is bound by culture, it is shaped by the general norms of a society. Every culture not only defines what is socially appropriate attire for different occasions but also maintains sanctions against overt exposure of different parts of the body. Rules not only vary across cultures but also change with time within the same culture. For example, Malay women will swim in the sea fully clothed, while the two-piece swimsuit that was once uncommon on Singapore's beaches is increasingly used among those below 30 years of age, even away from swimming pools, in parties or clubs. Indian sari-wearers have always bared their midriff, way ahead of the pop music idol-inspired young girls of today. Yet, on the whole, the different ethnic groups in Singapore are still generally inclined to rhetorically maintain sanctions against overt exposure of the body, even as individuals keep breaking these sanctions, ostensibly without penalty. Undoubtedly, clothing norms have changed. Plunging necklines are now common, as are spaghetti-strap tank tops, so too are body-conscious clothes that show the curves of the body. Yet, bralessness, although ubiquitous in contemporary designs, is still seldom seen in Singapore. Teenagers and women in their mid-20s will more often than not wear tubes and halter-tops with bras in this island in the tropics, in contrast to their counterparts in Europe and America, during summers. At the time of fieldwork, a woman in her mid-40s, when shown a braless evening dress in a store, exclaimed, "I am a mother of four children, not me!" Apparently, the established wisdom of "one wants to keep in step with the fashion without being ahead of it" (Konig, 1973) continues to operate as a check on purchases, arising from a concern that the boundaries of good manners in adornment are not transgressed. The *avant garde* of fashion pay the price of being considered strange or weird in the eyes of the majority.

As such norms of social propriety affect customers' choices, they also play a significant part in determining the clothes that are available in stores, which in turn reinforce the norms themselves. The norms of propriety complete the list of audiences to which a female fashion shopper will orient herself when deliberating on a purchase.

The Browser-Turned-Customer-Turned-Client

Assume that after having given all due consideration to the different levels of audience, present and absent in the boutique, the browser who has tried on a selected item decides to make a purchase. This will take her on to the next step towards a career in fashion consumption. Once a purchase is made, the browser is immediately transformed into a customer. All the repressed concerns about 'face' can be shed instantly. Having demonstrated the ability to buy, the browser-turned-customer is now interactionally in the dominant position with reference to the sales people. As a customer, she has the privilege to try out all the clothes in the store if she so chooses. A sense of adventure may prompt her to spend more time trying on different outfits, without actually making a second purchase.

Interactionally, the pressure is now on the sales person to serve and sell to the customer. Convinced of the browser-turned-customer's ability to buy, the sales person seeks to increase sales with suggestions that may be of interest to the new customer. Selling is conceptually differentiated from serving. To serve is to simply give the customer what she requests, while to sell is not only to fulfill the requests but to make additional suggestions to the customer (Sofer, 1965). It should be noted here that sales people place strong emphasis on an ability to judge the 'style' of a customer and make appropriate suggestions. According to sales people, if these judgments are accurate, then selling is easy. This judging of the 'style' of the customer is a sense of helping the customer to visualise herself in a particular configuration of clothes on offer.

Once a person becomes a customer, particulars such as name and mailing address are requested by the sales people, and entered into a client book. The customer is now on the mailing list for information on new goods and sales. Becoming a customer is the first step to becoming a 'client'. With further purchases over time, a customer literally enters the memory bank of the sales people in the store, especially if the store encourages each sales person to build up her own client list. When a customer's name enters the short list of memorised names, she has arrived at the status of the established client; and the interactional pressure on the sales person intensifies substantially.

An established client's behaviour at the store is readily recognisable. She is greeted by name by the sales people. She does not look through the displays, and this not from a lack of temerity. Rather, she does not need to look through the displays. She has not only seen but possibly tried on and rejected many items when they first arrived at the store. So she walks in, usually in the company of one or two other shopping companions who are just as likely to be established clients, and will simply be shown the latest items. It is her privilege to be kept informed of new arrivals by the sales people. New arrivals that are within the range of her style and taste will be reserved for her till the day she is free to shop, usually within a few days of being informed. If the sales person fails in her responsibility to keep the client informed, she is deemed to have failed in her job. For example, if a client were to see somebody wearing an outfit that is to her taste, she would want to know why she was not informed of its availability. She would consider herself poorly served and be within her rights to be angry. This reflects the social inequality that exists between sales person and client — one's responsibility is the other's privilege.

The sales person must also have knowledge of a client's social circle. It is her responsibility to inform a client when a member of her same social circle has already bought a particular outfit. This is to prevent both clients from turning up at the same occasion in similar clothes — wholly unacceptable in the social phenomenon of fashion, in which uniqueness is the norm even if the clothes are mass-produced. If a client insists on purchasing similar clothes even after being informed, the sales person is relinquished of any future blame. Presumably, the clients will co-ordinate their dressing so as to avoid the embarrassment of turning up in similar outfits.

Beyond these specific clothes-related activities, sales people must also possess some personal knowledge of clients' families, occupations and friends. This information is gleaned either directly from the clients themselves or overheard from their conversations with one another. Changes in personal status are noted by sales people to avoid possible *faux pas*. For example, a sales person may unwittingly ask a client who has just separated from her husband to look at items for her husband. Or she may ask a client if she liked the dress her husband had picked up earlier when, in fact, she had received no such dress! Generally, a sales person will not make general inquiries about a client's family members unless the client mentions them first. While conversations between clients and sales persons in such highly-personalised settings are inevitable, a sales person's conversational position must be guided by responding only to a client's initiatives, and picking up conversational threads and topics offered by the client. No matter how friendly the conversations, the social distance between client and sales person is maintained. The sales person's awareness of this distance is a significant social and sociological phenomenon.

As for all working class individuals, the daily work of the sales people is itself a constant reminder of their class position and their material deprivation in relation to the clients they serve. Different sales people, however, react differently to this consciousness. Generally, sales people who have to deal with family finances have a greater tendency to react resentfully. They are more inclined to make disparaging remarks behind their clients' backs on how freely the clients spend time and money — "it must be crazy to pay such prices for just clothes" — that their "husbands work hard to earn". On the other hand, the single, younger sales people who do not have financial cares tend to enjoy their work more because they readily get excited and involved with the fashionable clothes they are selling, including defending the high prices of the clothes. To them, their jobs bring them as close to the glamour of the fashion trade as they can get, and the fact that they wear the designer clothes while in the store reinforces this commitment to the designer labels they sell. It may not have occurred to them that they are live mannequins in this function!

Completing a Purchase

As mentioned earlier, in addition to keeping up with fashion trends, a set of activities that collectively adds up to making a completed purchase contributes directly to how often clients visit a store. If a client decides to buy an item, she either takes it immediately or leaves it at the store for alterations, which may range from simply replacing buttons to substantial changes to the outfit. Changes are exceptional because the lure behind wearing designer clothes is the design itself, however peculiar it may be. With alterations, another trip to the store is necessary. As a rule, no home deliveries are made unless the client is rushing to leave the country. Clients also prefer to do their fittings at the store where further alterations may be attended to immediately.

If a client makes a purchase 'as is' but changes her mind within a couple of days, it would mean another trip to the store to return and exchange the item for another. No refunds are made. If no suitable items for exchange are found, a credit account is established for future purchases. Subsequent purchasing trips are thus required, until the credit is spent. If a client is hesitant about a certain item, she can request for it to be held while she decides. If she decides to make the purchase, another trip is required, and a subsequent third trip for any alterations. Finally, an established client has the privilege of taking the items home to consult her significant other(s) for approval, as mentioned above. If approved, the item is purchased, otherwise, it is returned.

All the above possible trips are made in rapid succession because clients cannot wait to wear their new purchases, and unsuitable items must be returned to the store immediately before they become dead inventory. Fashion changes too quickly for either party to dally. With all these purchasing trips and the 'just browsing' trips, the same set of women can be seen in the boutiques with stunning frequency. One could say that sales persons have an ambivalent attitude towards these frequent visits and visitors. As their wages are entirely dependent on the volume of sales, frequent visits potentially mean higher incomes. These same sales persons also, however, express frustration at clients who drop in and create work for the sales staff by trying on rather than buying.

Throughout the above description of the purchasing processes, I have alluded to privileges enjoyed by established clients at designer clothes stores. This client status is attained only after a substantial period of association with the boutiques. Furthermore, these privileges cannot be taken for granted because a client is bound to lose them if she does not spend regularly at the store. The client's status has to be maintained through regular consumption. The stages that an individual progresses through — from taking the tentative first step into a designer boutique to becoming a client — may be conceptualized as a career, with explicit benchmarks and processes (Prus, 1987). Each stage has its own interactional routine that is enacted by the sales persons and the customers. The stages and interactional patterns that constitute them are the processes through which an individual is transformed into an avid consumer, and they form a part of the total network of processes that socially produce and sustain a consumer.

Conclusion

The social status of an up-market consumer is realised and reinforced by the level of personalised service she can command from the sales people, especially against the backdrop of functional and impersonal mass marketing strategies. Satisfaction with the service received is essential to sustaining the client's consumption activities. Hence, the pattern of social interaction between sales people and clients is fundamental to the ongoing social reproduction of up-market consumers. This chapter attempts to bring out interactional activities in the career of a consumer, from initial involvement with a product and/or vendor to becoming an established client within the setting of highly-personalised service stores. The following conceptual and substantive generalisations may be induced from the present investigation.

Settings that contain highly-personalised services should be conceptualised as client-recruiting settings rather than as mere retail outlets. In these settings, sales people invest their time and energy to cultivate long-term client-sales person relationships, rather than just immediate sales transactions. The path towards a stable client-sales person relationship is a progressive series of interactional patterns enacted by the two parties involved. At the core of these interactional patterns is the reversal of the 'domination/subordination' relationship between clients and sales people. The presence of this reversal is itself a consequence of the up-market prices in these highly-personalised service settings. It discloses an aspect of the social psychological disposition of the customers in such settings; namely the fear of being held in low esteem by the presumably fashion-savvy sales people.

The up-market prices and highly-personalised services drastically reduce the number of casual browsers, thus enabling the few sales staff to be highly attentive to those who do come into the store. The attention, in turn, has an intimidating effect on browsers. The glaring visibility of a browser to the sales staff exerts a strong social psychological pressure on the former to buy, or risk feeling snubbed or looked down upon by the sales staff. The presence of this sentiment undermines the customer's self confidence and subverts the conventional belief that in retail business that 'customers are always right'.

Relief comes only from making a purchase. Once a purchase is made, the interactional pressure is then on the sales person to serve and sell to the browser-turned-customer. This starts the interactional subordination of the sales person to the client. This subordination intensifies when a customer becomes an established client, as a client can command personalised service without even being in the store. The sales person must constantly look out for and inform the client of new arrivals of goods. In this way, she helps directly to keep the client in fashionable consumption. This subordination extends beyond the service at hand to include paying attention to aspects of the client's personal life that may jeopardise her public image as a fashionable consumer.

Finally, the sales person serves as the immediate audience to a customer's appearance in a new outfit and is, therefore, very influential in the customer's decision to purchase. Conceptually, this position as the *in situ* significant other to the consumer makes the sales person an important link in the diffusion chain of the transfer of cultural values to consumer goods.

Notes

1. The research approach adopted is known as naturalistic inquiry; see Lincoln and Fuba (1985). The range of research processes and strategies are summarised in Belk, Sherry and Wallendorf (1988).
2. Indeed, the names have even penetrated the consumption horizon of lower income individuals, as there are plenty of fakes that bring the labels within their reach, even if they cannot afford 'the real thing'.

5

On the Power *Cheongsam* and Other Ethnic Clothes

As suggested in Chapter 1, the global character of Singapore has been reinforced by constant governmental investment in communication infrastructure, keeping pace with the latest modes, means and mechanisms of communication. These investments are both a cause and an effect of the integration of Singapore, both as a location and as an economy, ever deeper into global capitalism. Indeed, in the early 1970s, long before the term 'globalisation' gained its current popular and analytic status, Singapore had already declared itself a 'global' city.[1] On the other hand, the cultures of everyday life of Singaporeans, as in many other colonised locations, are the enduring results of the mixing, or hybridisation, of the cultures of groups of people who came to Singapore in search of a living; from commercial transactions to chance encounters among strangers, interactions among Singaporeans involved extensive ethnic and linguistic code mixing. Responding to this situation, Singapore, declared itself, constitutionally, a multi-racial society at the very beginning of independent statehood in 1965.

Constitutional multiracialism had serious consequences for the subsequent cultural and political development of Singapore, the mapping of which far exceeds the task set for this chapter.[2] Suffice it to say that multiracialism as an official ideology has provided the government with a two-prong ideological imaginary to push Singapore into the contemporary world; namely, continuing globalisation of the economy and racialisation of the cultural sphere. The first offers a national economy that unites the population behind national competitiveness in global capitalism, the second divides the population by races in a way that justifies constant political intervention for the sake of national 'unity'. The PAP government never strays far from this ideological configuration. While it placed overwhelming emphasis on economic development in the early years of statehood, there was no attempt to erase race and race-cultures in an integrative, even utopian, imagination of a 'national' culture. The resurrection of the race-cultures always remains a possibility, even a necessity in giving substance to constitutional multiracialism.

Ideologically, cultural hybridity is not an irreversible process. Beneath the hybridisation, every group that contributes to it has the ideological possibility of resurrecting an imagined 'pure' culture of its own; even if this (re)discovered 'indigenous' is a cultural invention. Witness the different types of cultural 'indigenisation' programmes found in many, if not most, postcolonial societies. Official multiracialism in Singapore, indeed, keeps in the foreground this possibility, which haunts cultural hybridity in practice. However, the desire for race-cultures is not evenly distributed throughout the society. Consequently, the processes of cultural globalisation, hybridisation and (re)racialisation operate concurrently within Singapore with varying degrees of interactive mixing, at both abstract levels of intellectual and political thought and in the cultures of everyday life. This chapter provides an illustrative instance of the concurrent operation of these tendencies in the fashion practices of multi-ethnic and multi-religious Singaporeans.

Re-racialisation after Economic Success

Significantly, and ironically, at precisely the time when economic success had been achieved, race-cultures were given new emphasis. In the late 1970s, as economic 'take-off' got under way, the government began to experience ideological despair. In its view, the Singapore population, enticed by the individualistic competition for advantages in consumption, had become callous about familial and other social responsibilities. To inject cultural 'ballast' against individualising tendencies and the supposed consumerist hedonism that come with economic growth, moral education based on the population's racial and religious cultural values was to be taught to the young. However, neither economic growth nor expansion of material consumption could be allowed to slow down, as both were essential to the legitimacy of the single-party dominant state. All three goals, therefore, had to be promoted concurrently. Herein lies the root of the 'Asian values' discourse, popular among and popularised by the PAP leadership in the early 1990s and maintained until the 1997 Asian regional financial crisis swept through the hyper-growth Asian countries.

In brief, rapid economic growth in East and Southeast Asia from the 1960s was to be explained in terms of the cultural values — Asian values — found in these societies. The explanatory value of the 'Asian values' discourse for economic growth was dubious at best. Indeed, the first Minister of Finance of Singapore, who had been most responsible for the economic take-off, declared Confucianism to be insignificant to the economics of global capitalism, shortly after having been responsible for setting up a research institute of East Asian philosophy (read Confucianism).[3] On the other hand, the Senior Minister, Lee Kuan Yew remains a vocal champion of the Asian values discourse. At the peak of the 1997 economic crisis, exasperated by constant badgering by journalists, Lee argued that the crisis was the result of corruption of individuals in governments rather than the failure of Confucian values.[4]

While the 'Asian values' discourse undoubtedly lost much of its triumphalism after 1997 it nevertheless continues to have more than passing cultural effects on life in Singapore. After close to a decade of popular usage and circulation, the ideological and cultural effects of the 'Asian values' discourse continue to be felt. The discourse has reinforced the possibility of an ideological resurrection of multiracial 'traditions' as counters to a constant 'cultural' invasion, or cultural 'imperialism', originating in the developed capitalist West. The 'suppressed' values and cultural practices of decolonised Asians/Singaporeans can be resurrected as icons of cultural pride and continuity with a culturally-distinguished past. By the mid-1990s, many Singaporeans across class lines, generational divides and educational levels were apparently willing to adopt an 'Asian' identity and be subject to the constraints that such an identity would impose. Phrases like, 'We Asians...' and 'We are Asians...' were commonly heard, as a trope to distance oneself from supposedly less desirable features of imported cultures of/from the 'West'. Everything, from the economy to the single-party-dominant state and its illiberal attitudes to forms of daily cultural practice, were embraced by the discourse, and a general 'Asianisation' process took place.[5] Among the cultural practices elevated to icons of cultural pride in this Asianisation process, clothes surpass abstract entities, such as history and social values, because of their material capacity for public display as explicit cultural claims. Clothing thus constitutes a significant site upon which the crosscutting effects of globalisation and re-ethnicisation are inscribed, and as is usually the case, particularly on women's clothes, the focus of this analysis.

Emergence of the Power *Cheongsam*

The Asian values discourse and re-ethnicisation have their greatest effect on the clothes of Chinese and Malay women, in different ways and for different reasons.[6] From the early 1990s, the *cheongsam*, began to be a palpable presence on public formal occasions. It is true that for some Chinese women, for example Mrs Lee Kuan Yew and novelist Catherine Lim, the *cheongsam* is the exclusive dress for all formal occasions big or small, including business meetings. What is significant is that women educated in English, locally and abroad, had hitherto seldom, or never, been seen in a *cheongsam*, but now began to attend public, formal occasions adorned in this clearly Chinese identity marker. Among the most obvious were wives of politicians and other significant power players in and out of government, and women who were significant in their own right, such as directors or heads of government or non-government institutions, senior lawyers in private practice, entrepreneurs and senior academics. The *cheongsam* emerged, under the Asianisation process, as power clothing for women with power or in close association with power. Meanwhile, it remained absent from everyday life and celebratory occasions, such as wedding banquets, among middle and working-class Chinese women.

In its original form as a formal garment of Manchurian women in the Ching Dynasty, the *cheongsam* was a straight-cut dress that reached the ankles, with a high collar, and sleeves cut wide just above the wrist but narrowed towards the shoulder. A slit was cut on each side of the dress and undergarments were worn to avoid displaying the lower limbs. After the collapse of the dynasty, the garment was popularly adopted in different guises in China. Influenced by the 'modernity' of the republican era, the *cheongsam* was reshaped and mixed and matched with various garments. For example, a version that was shortened as a top and worn with a 'western' skirt became common as a school uniform in urban areas. By the 1930s, it had stabilised in its present stylised form. Today, the *cheongsam* is a single piece, tight-fitting sheath dress, of varying length, "with a high cylindrical collar, with an opening at the front, from the middle of the collar, following the upper contour of the right breast to the armpit and down the side" (Lam, 1991:4). The opening is fastened with either cloth buttons or press-studs. Sleeves are of varying length, or may be omitted altogether. The slit on either side of the dress remains. The length of the slits depends on the tightness of fit, "the tighter it is the higher the cut", to facilitate movement "as well as a decorative means of showing shapely legs" (Lam, 1991:4).

The semiotics of the *cheongsam* are complex. It is the garment of choice for self-marking as a Chinese; like "the kimono for Japan and the sari for India, the cheongsam has served to designate the Chinese women to the West" (Fairservis, 1971:118). Other modulations of self-representation are embedded in this generalised ethnic marker. Depending on the context in which it is donned, the degree of 'body consciousness' of the fit, the length or depth of the slits and the age, social class and status of the wearer, the meaning of the garment ranges from sleazy to elegant and respectable. At the sleazy extreme is that most Orientalist image of the Chinese prostitute, *a la* 'The World of Suzie Wong', or of a low-status Chinese restaurant waitress; such images continue to be used in Singapore in advertising posters for beer, brandy or stout found pasted in local coffee shops. At its most respectable it is associated with Chinese school teachers etched in every Singaporean's memories of student days. Thus, stylised representations of women in *cheongsam* are not entirely fictive.

The *cheongsam*'s presence had greatly diminished during the 1970s and 1980s, the period of rapid economic growth in Singapore. Labour force demand drew increasing numbers of women into the job market, while the ideological dimensions of economic modernisation spilled into the cultural practices of the population. In such circumstances, the *cheongsam* all but disappeared from the everyday life of Chinese women, replaced by company uniforms or 'office' attire. The noticeable few exceptions stood out, precisely for their difference. Moreover, clothes were increasingly bought off-the-rack in the mushrooming shopping centres and department stores, replacing the earlier practice of home dress-making. By the mid-1980s, few young Chinese Singaporean women could imagine themselves in a *cheongsam* (Lam, 1991).

The visible re-emergence of the *cheongsam* as 'power clothing' for Chinese women is thus a 1990s phenomenon, coinciding with the

impressive economic development of the past four decades that lifted
Singapore from the despondency of underdevelopment to a per capita
income higher than almost every nation in Europe. This rise of local
affluence was jump-started by globalised capital in search of inexpensive
production platforms, under what is now known as the new international
division of labour. However, Singapore has since the 1980s moved beyond
being a production site for low-end consumer commodities to become
a capital-intensive centre for high technology industrialisation, with a
greatly expanded financial and capital market.

Nevertheless, according to official discourse, this rise in affluence has
been achieved by 'bootstrapping' the 'traditional' values of the people. For
the Chinese, this meant a Confucian emphasis on hard work, education,
pragmatism and family cohesion, values that have been ideologically
distilled into a set of 'Asian values'. (This is, of course, a very narrow
reading of the cultural underpinning of capitalism for it has screened out
the routinised cultural demands and practices of a proletarianised
population reduced to the status of wage labour, albeit on different scales
and incomes.[7]) The *cheongsam* for Chinese women of power in Singapore,
in the 1990s became a symbolic expression of Chinese-ness, of Chinese
values as constitutive parts of 'Asian values'. On occasions graced or tinted
with cabinet ministerial presence, hence the presence of power and
official ideology, it represents acquiescence to, if not affirmation of, the
national ideology.

Parenthetically, the re-emergence of the *cheongsam* as a sign of Chinese
cultural pride, due to the rise of capital, was taken to a higher level in
Hong Kong by the "flamboyant, cigar-chomping entrepreneur-cum-
socialite", David Tang, in his attempt to market jazzed-up, 'traditional'
Chinese fashion in New York — from *cheongsam* to velvet Mao jackets
— after such clothes enjoyed success in Hong Kong. The US$12 million
venture on Madison Avenue failed after 20 months. In the opinions of
an American retail consultant, "that store was too exotic".[8]

Cover-Up with *Baju Kurung*

In contrast to the increased visibility of the Chinese *cheongsam*, one of
the traditional costumes for Malay women has disappeared. The *kebaya*
is a tight-fitting, long-sleeve top that drapes over the hip, and is usually

made of thin and transparent cotton, with elaborate embroidery work along all the edges of the garment. The open front is held together by ornate silver or gold pins. It is worn with a tight-fitting, colourful batik *sarong*. The *sarong-kebaya* combination is a garment of the Malay world and until recently was commonly worn by Malay women in Indonesia, Malaysia and Singapore. While it is still commonly seen in Indonesia, it has disappeared in the latter locations, under the globalising force of the resurgence of Islam.

With rare exceptions, all Malays are Muslim, and Islam is a central identity marker of Malay ethnicity. In the 1970s, the global resurgence of Islam caught up with Malaysia and Singapore, most keenly among Malay youths, especially those with early religious education and a university education. The Muslim Society at the National University of Singapore was a central organisation in Malay students' re-affirmation of faith and moral and theological injunctions. Others in the community gained interest and knowledge through religious lessons offered by several Muslim educational institutions.[9]

Arguably, the most visual part of this Islamic resurgence is inscribed on the women's body through the donning of the veil, the aggregate effect of which, in Malaysia, is captured by an anthropologist:

> The sarong-clad girls and women of the 1960s and early 1970s have been transformed by renewed ideals of Islamic feminine modesty into virtual facsimiles of their Arab sisters of the Middle East. Now they are shrouded in many layered and loose garments (*baju kurung*), which obscure all hint of body form. Women have also adopted a modified short veil somewhat resembling the nun's wimple, although they still reveal their face. A small minority does veil the entire face and even covers their hands and feet with gloves and socks.
>
> (Nagata, 1984: xviii)

Veiling is a religious injunction to cover up the entire body. It is believed that exposure of parts of the body which are not to be seen by another person (*aurat*) who is not a family member is an act of 'provocation' that could potentially induce unnecessary trouble from men, including being the cause of their temptation to rape. In its strict definition, even the voice of the women is *aurat*, thus a woman is to refrain from speaking in public and, when that is absolutely unavoidable, to avoid eye contact with men. The ideological and disciplining effects of covering up the body are often expressed in the subjective narratives of young Malay women. For example, one who wears the head-veil said:

> If we wear the veil, there is no attraction. Men look at us and they say, "Ah! She is *kolot*" (old fashioned). If we dress sexily, it will only attract men. It can destroy a marriage. If we go to work and wear a tight *kebaya*, with our hair all beautifully styled, the men at work would not care if you're married or not.
>
> (Yohanna Abdullah, 1990: 29)

The subject position and subjective narrative of a Malay woman who does not abide by the cover-up injunction can be pictured as follows:

> Sally's dress sense is rather provocative. According to her when she meets friends in the *baju kurung* with a veil upon their head, she would almost always cover part of her body, which she thinks is most offensive due to the show of skin, with her bag or file. If wearing a low-cut top, she will cover her chest with a file, and if her skirt is too short, she walks with her bag in front of her to cover her thighs. Her reactions are conscious but sometimes are almost reflexive.
>
> (Suziela Yassin, 1999: 39)

For Malay/Muslim women in Singapore, braced with religious beliefs, clothes have thus become a constitutive part of the 'technologies of the self'. Such technologies "permit individuals to effect their own means or with the help of others a certain number of operations on their own bodies and souls, thoughts, conduct and way of being so as to transform themselves in order to attain a certain state of happiness, purity, wisdom, perfection or immortality" (Foucault, 1988:18). This is apparent in the self-narrative of a young Muslim at the time she started to don the head-veil:

> I was experiencing a turmoil or crisis in life. I turned to God. I was helped by my religious background. Since I have found help from God, it's only logical that I follow what he asked me to do. I thought it was an obligation.

People thought it's a selfish reason. But *alhamdulillah* (all praises to Allah), its God's way of bringing us back to Him. Its really natural. If I didn't have a religion, I don't know how I would have cope with it.

(Yohanna Abdullah, 1990: 53)

One should not assume, however, that there has been no resistance to the covering up. There is the above-mentioned case of Sally, who continues to wear 'figure-hugging' clothes, among other behaviours that the Muslim community deems as deviant. There are women who continue to think that the *'purdah'* — veiling of the face usually accompanied by very large black Arabian coat — is extreme and point out that it is not required by the religion, a position supported by the Muslim religious authorities in Singapore. Nevertheless, taking the Malay/Muslim women community as a whole, the injunction against exposure of the body, including its outline or form, has obviously taken hold, as evidenced by the demise of the *kebaya*.

The tight-fitting *kebaya*, which displays the contour of the torso, and by ending at the hip brings visual attention to it, is no longer a normatively acceptable garment. It has been replaced by the *baju kurung*. The latter consists of a long tunic that reaches the knee as a top, worn with a loose sarong that reaches the ankle. The two pieces are either the same colour or colour coordinated, often with bold prints on the tunic and sarong skirting. The usually very bright and vibrant colours of the *baju kurung* appear to be a drawn line that emphatically stops the total 'Arabisation' of Malay women's clothing practices. Instead of the solid, matt-black robe worn by Arab women in public, the Malay women are defiantly bright and colourful, with orange, red, lime green, purple, retaining and reasserting the colours of Southeast Asian batiks, only brighter because the fabric is often shining polyester rather than matt cotton. In their insistence on using strong colours, the Malay women in their *baju kurung* share a common trait with the powerful Chinese women in their *cheongsam*, recalling that both Malay and Chinese cultures favour strong colours in women's clothes.

Youth in Black

The 'contest' between 'Oriental' colours and mass produced, internationally distributed designer-labelled, or 'branded', casual clothes is interestingly, summarised in a journalist's account of the demise of David Tang's store in New York: "Maybe it was the fashions in lime green, electric orange and eye-popping fuchsia in a city that prefers basic black" (*Far Eastern Economic Review*, 29 July 1999: 25). The same may be said of the difference between the English-language educated middle-class young Singaporeans and their mothers. (As we shall see in the next section, young lower-educated Singaporeans have quite different dress codes.) The colour of choice of these youth, including young Malays who do not abide by the code to cover-up, is basic black, and the limited colour palette used in the diffusion lines of internationalised American and European designers, such as Calvin Klein, Donna Karan, the late Gianni Versace and Gorgio Armani. Their presence is ubiquitous in exclusive franchised shops, in separate stands in department stores and in fakes with their namesake in night markets. In contrast, black *cheongsam* and black *baju kurung* are rarely seen, except in connection with funerals and mourning rituals.

The colour black in clothes is polysemic in the 'West'. Its elevation from associations with death and the satanic to being "the quintessential colour of modern fashion" has been schematically charted by fashion historian Valerie Steele. Since the Middle Ages, black has been associated with evil, and "satanic black that is perversely erotic" (1996:191) is found in fetish fashion associated with sadomasochistic sexuality. This counter-cultural perversity slides into and expresses itself in a larger and also more diffused sense of 'rebelliousness' linked with black. According to Wilson, black as anti-bourgeois adornment, already worn by the dandies in the nineteenth century, was intensified after the Second World War, in Paris where the bohemians adopted "black sweaters, black shirts and black trousers", which were "originally inspired by the Fascist tradition" (1985:187). This rebellious use of black, however, exists side-by-side with black as the colour of bourgeois sobriety, as in formal dark suits and the cliché 'little black dress' of the bourgeois woman, popularised by Coco Chanel. The most important moment of black's escape into popular, mainstream fashion was in the 1980s, when Japanese designers working in Paris, such as Rei Kawakubo and Yohji Yamamoto, paraded all black clothes on contemporary fashion runways. By early 1990s, black had become the quintessential colour of contemporary fashion. Throughout this trajectory and, according to Steele, accounting for its mainstream popularity, is black's association with "night, death, danger, nothingness, evil, perversion, rebellion, and sin" (Steele, 1996:192).

It is difficult to assess with any degree of accuracy how much and with what intensity elements in this string of symbolic associations with black get transported to Singapore and appropriated by young Singaporean fashion consumers through internationalised fashion. However, black's popularity is without doubt, as is its symbolism of rebellion. Evidence of its popularity is readily observable wherever English-medium educated youth are found in significant numbers, such as the central shopping area of Orchard Road and the local university campuses. For example, in 1991, an entire class of about 30 students turned up for the final examination of a course in the sociology of popular culture attired in black. As recently as 1999, one student in the same course said that she had just totally abandoned her totally black wardrobe because her friends were beginning to ask why she was always wearing the same clothes, as details in her black garments were too subtle to be noticed. These students have become so enamoured with black that, when questioned, they admit to being unable to imagine themselves in the vibrant colours that are 'traditional' in Malay, Chinese and Indian ethnic clothes.

As for expression of 'rebelliousness', this is evident in the disagreements between black-adorned youth and their more 'traditional' parents, during celebratory occasions, such as birthdays, weddings and especially, Chinese New Year. Among older Chinese in Singapore, black is still associated with death, funerals and the generally inauspicious, as in 'black brings bad luck'. Where parents are able to exercise control, even grown-up children will be denied the wearing of black on such occasions, lest it constitute an affront to the celebrants. This is especially so on Chinese New Year's day, when red clothes and gold jewelry are traditionally the only acceptable colours for daughters to greet their parents on the New Year morning. Yet, such ritual occasions are precisely the times when Chinese youth want to appear cool and sexy in the most fashionable black. The insistence of preferences across the generational divide is thus a site of disagreement, between upholding and rebelling against 'tradition'.

As consumers of internationalised fashion, the English-language-educated middle-class youth draw their fashion lessons from the image bank constituted by international media, from television programmes, movies, popular music and MTV. Unlike Malay/Muslim women who suffer from moral disquiet when their own dressing defies the religious injunction to cover-up, these young fashionables do not have any deep commitment to appearances at any moment. They change as the international fashion changes. As colours (rather muted compared to the brightness of *baju kurung* and *cheongsam*) have returned to international casual wear, young people seem to have suffered from a surfeit of black and have come to find black 'boring', as in the case of the above-mentioned university student who threw out all her black clothing. The colours and cut of the English-educated young will therefore always be tied to the international fashion scene, scanned and adopted through Singaporean editions of the international fashion magazines, Hollywood movies, MTV programmes and other sundry mass media.

Bright Colours from Japan via Hong Kong and Taiwan

In contrast to the English-educated middle-class young, with their skimpy tank tops, spaghetti straps and basic blacks, the lesser-educated Chinese youth are influenced by different cultural flows. The latter are unlikely to have successfully completed the four years of secondary school. They have been pejoratively termed locally as 'Ah Beng' (for males) and 'Ah Lian' (for females). The terms are abbreviated derivatives of common Chinese dialect names. For example, this author's name Beng-Huat might be shortened to Beng or Ah Beng; similarly, a Chinese girl named Lian-Huay might be addressed by family members or friends as 'Ah Lian'. However, the English-educated have discursively transformed such abbreviated addresses into generic categories of their own 'other'. Initially appearing in the argot of English-speaking youth, the terms have acquired popular usage in Singapore.

Given their lowly-formal education, this lesser-educated population has a very mixed linguistic code, not always by choice. They speak a mixture of Hokkien, the main dialect among Singaporean Chinese (similar to the Minnan dialect of Taiwanese), Mandarin and/or Singlish, a local *patois*, which uses English words with a Hokkien grammatical structure. Furthermore, there is a tendency to mispronounce multi-syllabic English words. This linguistic characteristic provides the basic template for the discursive construction of this group as 'other', by English-educated youth. As the 'other' to the English-educated, the figures of Ah Beng and

Ah Lian are not simply lowly educated, they also have supposedly 'pre-modern' or *sua-ku* (hill tortoise, metaphor for 'backward') modes of behaviour.[10] Until recently, the English-educated used Singlish as a means of belittling this group.

However, in the late 1990s, there was an apparent change in this attitude. Being 'Beng' or 'Lian' became 'cool' among the English-educated. Many local television personalities began to declare themselves to be Beng or Lian at least 'on the inside' or in their past. This is because most of them were from working-class backgrounds, before success in English-language education propelled them into the media industry. In such instances, the individual may choose to speak Singlish by choice as a different 'English'. The popularity of Singlish as an identity-proffering practice has caused alarm in the government, leading the Prime Minister, among others, to criticise its proliferation in a National Day Rally Speech, the annual state-of-the-nation speech (*The Straits Times*, 23 August 1999).

What separates the two youth groups is a class divide, with all its differences in education, occupation, income and adornment. In contrast to the black and muted pastel shades of the middle-class youth, the clothes of Ah Beng and Ah Lian are filled with bright, or to the English-educated, 'gaudy', colours. For example, frilly lime green tops of polyester material may be matched with 'day-glo' yellow jeans or short skirts and white patent leather platform shoes. Generically, against the understatement of the middle-class youth, Ah Beng and Ah Lian go 'over the top' in every item of bodily adornment, including dyed bronze hair. All the colours on the body from hair to nails are big and bright, with every intention of drawing attention to themselves.

On the surface, the lesser-educated youth appear to be continuing the use of the colours of their elders. However, like youth everywhere, few if any self-respecting Singaporean youth would imitate the dress-sense of their parents; the fashion of each generation almost always defines itself against that of the generation immediately before it. So, to see the use of colours among the Chinese youth as continuity or recuperation of their mothers' colourful *cheongsam* is to miss a significant part of the cultural traffic within Asia. Instead, for the trained eye, the garments of Ah Beng and Ah Lian may be recognisable as pared down derivatives of the highly-eclectic styles of urban Japanese youth; the 'bronzed' hair being the most obvious point of emulation. However, lacking the radical individualistic eclecticism of Japanese youth, Singaporean youth's appropriations of Japanese fashion elements follow an indirect circuit, by way of circuits of cultural commodity flowing from Japan through and mediated by Hong Kong and/or Taiwan fashion practices to Singapore. The latter two locations are sources of popular cultural products for non-English-speaking Chinese Singaporeans. Hong Kong movies and television serials, whether in Cantonese or dubbed in Mandarin, and Cantonese popular music, '*Cantopop*', are consumed in huge volumes by these Singaporeans. In recent years, Taiwanese cultural products have also gained popularity among them. For example, there is a fledgling tea-house culture imported from Taiwan, and Minnan or Hokkien songs are popular in karaoke singing among working-class Chinese. The most popular musicians from both locations have reached pop icon status among their fans in Singapore, with an entire industry trafficking in the paraphernalia of fandom (Soh, 1995).

Both Hong Kong and Taiwan have greater popular cultural connections with Japan than Singapore. Taiwan was a colony of Japan from 1897 until 1945; among those who lived under the Japanese colonial regime, there is often a perverse nostalgia for the colonial days. Elements of Japanese culture have become incorporated into current Taiwan popular culture; Japanese words often slip into Taiwanese conversation, Japanese sounds and rhythms are very noticeable in Taiwanese popular music, Japanese television programmes, music videos and fashion are popular in Taiwanese youth culture. For example, in the relatively small city of Tsingchu, about 40 minutes drive south from Taipei, there is an entire narrow street of small shops that sell exclusively fashion items from Japan. The entire streetscape, with its narrowness and small shops, is reminiscent of urban Japan.

On the other hand, Japanese influence on Hong Kong popular culture, including youth fashion, is much less straightforward, and the explanation for it is more elusive. Although a British colony until 1997, Hong Kong has always been very much a Chinese city, with Cantonese rather than English the lingua franca, unlike Singapore. Nevertheless, the Hong Kong Chinese population has always read the people and culture of the People's Republic of China as backward relative to themselves. They seldom, if ever, look towards the People's Republic of China for any popular cultural inspirations, let alone trends (Ma, 1999). Thus, instead of being oriented towards either Britain or the PRC, Hong Kong's popular culture tends to look elsewhere for inspiration. Its television stations are filled with Japanese cartoons, its young consume a large number of Japanese 'manga' comics translated into Cantonese, and its fashion designers embrace Japan as part of the international fashion scene and as a source for ideas.

In contrast, there is a general lack of familiarity with the Japanese language and culture among Singaporeans. Furthermore, the victimisation of Singaporeans under the brutalities of the Japanese Occupation during the Second World War is a constantly invoked item in the ideological landscape and social memory of Singapore. This historical memory is particularly acute among Chinese Singaporeans. All these elements obstruct direct and positive popular Japanese cultural influence in Singapore. Finally, the Japanese emphasis on child-like 'cuteness' has, in general, a rather negative image among Singaporean youth.[11] For Ah Beng and Ah Lian, this child-like cuteness is in sharp contrast to their self-representation as 'tough' and 'street smart', expressed through their public (mis)demeanours of cursing, smoking and other behaviours that draw attention to themselves.

Under the official policy of multiracialism, Chinese children in Singapore have been schooled in Mandarin but many continue to speak their respective dialects as home languages, giving them access to popular cultural commodities from Taiwan and Hong Kong, and even the PRC. It is from the vibrant popular cultures of Hong Kong and Taiwan, often ideologically identified as fellow Chinese, that Ah Beng and Ah Lian draw much of their popular culture commodities, including sartorial inspiration. This is reinforced by the fact that the fashion importers catering to this group source their clothes predominantly from Hong Kong and to a lesser extent from Taiwan. Imported through the popular cultural commodities circuits, items of Ah Beng and Ah Lian's clothes are thus the result of local appropriation of Japanese-Taiwanese-Hong Kong creations. It is entirely plausible that the Ah Beng and the Ah Lian are unaware of the Japanese elements in their sartorial statements. Perhaps, as far as they are concerned, their fashion is a 'sharing' with their Chinese counterparts in Taiwan and Hong Kong.

Conclusion

This empirical analysis of clothing practices of different groups, along racial, religious, class and generational divisions, discloses a complex set of cultural flows and their respective and relative absorption in Singapore. It underscores the by now commonplace realisation that the term 'globalisation' is but a short-hand manner for talking about complex sets of cultural exchanges between spaces and times in late capitalism. More significantly, it substantiates the conceptual point that in any given multi-racial or multi-ethnic location there is co-present a multiplicity of cultural references, each serving its respective racial or ethnic constituency, instead of a single cultural flow from any metropolitan center, particularly one in the West, dominating a local hybrid culture. Indeed, the case of the *cheongsam* suggests that the metropolitan flow from the West was the one met with greatest cultural resistance. On the other hand, veiling and the *baju kurung* suggest that the particular cultural flows of an internationalised Islam, which resonate with the 'past' of local Muslims, has been re-appropriated and renewed as an identity marker. The ideological reversibility of cultural hybridity is obviously open to cultural flows not only from metropolitan locations but also from the locations from which the different components of the hybrid community were hewn. Registering and substantiating these multiple references and multiple flows disrupts the simple mindedness of any ideological construction or suggestion that Singapore, or any other place in Asia, is subject exclusively, or even largely to the cultural imperialism of the West. It also disrupts attempts by any regime to use the 'West' or other preferred locations as an ideological decoy to hide their own ideological preferences.

Finally, perhaps, it may be only in Singapore that clothing practice is a privileged site for the disclosure of the above conceptual points. In other locations, other cultural objects may be more efficacious for similar tasks. Nevertheless, every instance of substantiation of multiple flows is an instance of clarification of the complexity and contestations within the ongoing configuration of the cultural sphere within globalisation.

Notes

1. See Rajaratnam (1987).
2. For detail discussion of the effect of multiculturalism on national language policy in education, see Purushotam (1998), on public housing see Chua (1977) and Lai (1995), on community welfare assistance see Rahim Ishak (1994) and on political representation see Chua (1995a).

3. See Chua (1995a), Chapter 7, 'Confucianism Abandoned'.

4. For a sampling of the statements on Asian values from official Singapore see, Tommy Koh, 'The ten values that undergird East Asia strengths and success', *International Herald Tribune*, December 1994; Kishor Mahbubani (1998) and Fareed Zakaria (1994). Lee's statement is quoted in *The Straits Times*, 23 May 1998.

5. For a sympathetic view of how the PAP leaders tried to 'Asianise' its single-party dominant rule, see Vasil (1995).

6. I have left out of this essay the analysis of clothing practices of Indian women for lack of empirical information. Impressionistically, the *sari* has never been discarded or even marginalised by the Indian women even in everyday life, particularly among those more mature in age, its presence has always been visible. This maintenance of the *sari* may have to do in part with the absolute numerical minority of the Indian community.

7. For an in-depth discussion of the changes in the everyday life of Singaporeans see Chua (1989; 1997, Chapter 8).

8. The information for the failure of the enterprise is drawn from *Far Eastern Economic Review*, 29 July 1999, p. 59.

9. For a detailed discussion of the politics of the Malay community in Singapore during the 1970s and 1980s, see Mariam Mohamed Ali (1989).

10. The characterisations of the Ah Beng and Ah Lian have become highly stylised in a very popular local sit-com built around the life of a small-time building contractor, Phua Chu Kang, and his wife. This show has been at the centre of the government's expressed concern over the proliferation of Singlish, accordingly, the main character was sent, in mid-season, to upgrade his English in night classes ran by the National Trades Union Congress for workers.

11. For details on the 'cute' or '*kawaii*' culture among Japanese youth, particularly females, see Kinsella (1995).

6

Food, Ethnicity and Nation
(with Ananda Rajah)*

Food is promoted by the Singapore Tourist Promotion Board as one of several compelling reasons for visiting Singapore. A large variety of cuisines are presented as icons of the different ethnic communities which make up the 'multiracial' nation; in both official and popular conceptions and representations, food is a register for ethnicity in Singapore. This large variety of food is much too extensive to be considered in its entirety in this chapter, making it necessary to delimit the boundaries of empirical concern. We will not be concerned with calendrical and festival food; neither will we be dealing with the daily, weekly or annual structures of food consumption and their attendant complexities in domestic contexts. We will limit ourselves, instead, exclusively to cooked food that is publicly and commonly available, in restaurants or other establishments including hawker stalls, and is consumed at any time throughout the day, either on its own or in combination with other items. As they are publicly available, the items of food which we propose to consider are relatively well codified in their ostensible ethnic manifestations; that is, consumers are able to identify the ethnic 'origins' of the items in question without much difficulty.

The very public-ness and inscribed 'ethnicity' of a particular item of food is, of course, itself the result of a social process in which a style of cooking and its results come to be a representation of an 'ethnic' cuisine. A first step towards the inscription and codification of 'ethnic' food is when it is (re)presented to a consuming public by vendors through a 'menu'. The menu is part of the process of giving an 'ethnic' identity to an item of food that was previously not necessarily identified as 'ethnic', the codification that renders the food recognisably 'ethnic', and generally an extension of the 'ethnicity' of the cook who produced it. The next stage of codification takes place with the (re)presentation of the food in recipes in cookbooks (see also Appadurai, 1988). It may then be said to be fully inscribed with 'ethnicity', as anyone can prepare an 'ethnic' dish by following the recipe. The food is detached from the ethnicity of the producer and circulates freely among those who are prepared to take the trouble to (re)produce it. It is this process of inscription that we have chosen to examine in connection with food that is publicly available and recognisably ethnic to ordinary Singaporeans in everyday life.

In the official representation of Singapore as a multiracial nation, the component peoples who constitute it are 'Chinese', 'Malay', 'Indian' and 'Others'. Accordingly, Chinese, Malay and Indian food co-exist in an ostensibly harmonious, national smorgasbord, while retaining distinct, separated culinary and thus 'racial' or ethnic identities. Where the homology between the supposedly 'racial' cuisines and the 'races' of the nation in these depictions collapses is in the failure to indicate what the cuisine of the 'Others' might be. 'Others', in official censuses and Singaporean popular conception is generally taken to refer to 'Eurasians', eminently an ethnically hybrid community whose cuisine is no less hybrid. However, it is erased from the cuisine of Singaporeans in tourist promotion brochures. Interestingly, hotels and other organisations in the tourist industry may proffer, as part of the multiracial smorgasbord, Peranakan food as a 'unique' blend of Chinese and Malay cuisines, although it is distinct and separate from Chinese, Malay and Indian food. By the logic of official racial classification, Peranakan food ought to place it in the category 'Others' in culinary and racial terms alongside the Eurasians, and it is noteworthy that this is not the case. Indeed, the blending of food is not restricted to Peranakan and Eurasian foods alone, but also takes place within the so-called ethnic foods. Chinese, Malay and Indian cuisines appropriate in a promiscuous and voracious manner from each other, creating a far greater culinary variety through hybridisation than each possesses in its exclusive representation. We are concerned in this essay to deal with such 'borrowing' across officially and popularly conceived ethnic boundaries, which conventional and popularly-held depictions of food in Singapore apparently fail to recognise.

Substantively, food, cooking and cuisine in general constitute in long-term human history a cultural field in which cross-fertilisation, appropriation, re-appropriation, infusion, diffusion, absorption, invention and bricolage practices proliferate. The central issue is not what permits appropriation or borrowing but, rather, what prohibits it. And what prohibits must be placed in the realm of cultural constructs, such as food taboos, which are often religiously derived, or notions and regimes of health and aesthetics. The field of food, cooking and cuisine involves freedom and creativity, and the imposition of limits to hybridisation.

Hybridisation is the tendency to critically appropriate elements from the master-codes of the dominant cultures and in the process subvert dominant cultural forms through creolisation. As Young observes,

> Hybridization as creolization involves fusion, the creation of a new form, which can then be set against the old form, of which it is partly made up. Hybridization as 'raceless chaos' by contrast, produces no stable new form but ... a radical heterogeneity, discontinuity, the permanent revolution of forms (1995:25).

In referring to certain categories of food as hybrid we wish to draw attention to the fact that it is the social actors, the producers and consumers of food in Singapore, who assume the existence of 'pure' cuisines, despite the hybridisation that has occurred in 'their' cuisines. This tendency to 'racialise' even hybrid food is, in the final analysis, a form of 'misrecognition' in Bourdieu's (1977) sense of the word. The racial imprinting of the population is partly a product of colonialism, but it has been inscribed in far more rigorous, thorough-going cultural-ideological ways by local nationalist politicians and the government of post-colonial Singapore than it was by the British colonisers. These acts of misrecognition and the related regimes of classification produced by the state — as well as historically-embedded typifications of food and ethnicity — are pivotal to the way in which styles of cooking and their products finally reach their own essentialised, ethnic representations in Singapore. In analysing this process, any of the cuisines associated with the ethnic groups found in Singapore could, of course, serve as a point of departure. However, we will take 'Chinese' food as a locus of analysis, so that any reference to change, borrowing and appropriation is concerned in the first instance with changes in Chinese food through contact with other cuisines, and secondarily with transformations brought about in other cuisines in contact with Chinese cuisine.

Fujian and Guangdong Food as Base

Within the predominantly Chinese population in Singapore, the largest dialect group is the Hokkien (Fujian), followed by Cantonese, then Teochiu (Chaozhou), and Hakka, with smaller groups of Hainanese among others. We shall therefore use Hokkien and Cantonese food as the baseline of our discussion, supplemented when appropriate by items from the minor dialect groups. In the regional-geographical classification of Chinese food, Hokkien is considered eastern cuisine and Cantonese as southern (Anderson, 1988; Lai, 1984), and each has its distinctive ingredients and cooking strategies. According to Lai, the three most characteristic qualities of southern food, typified by Cantonese food, are 'clearness, blandness and freshness'. Clearness may be represented by double-boiled chicken soup which should be completely transparent; blandness connotes a certain neutrality in taste, along with moderation in the application of salt, vinegar and spices; freshness refers to the state of being newly slaughtered, harvested or prepared (1984:23). The best example in which all three features are present is steamed fish:

> Properly cleaned, topped with a slice or two of ginger and steamed until just right, the fish has a firm, yet tender, texture. To enhance its flavour, it is necessary to pour over it spoonfuls of boiling chicken stock followed by very hot lard or peanut oil, and finally to scatter over it pieces of spring onions (1984:23).

In Singapore, steamed fish is produced by Hokkien, Cantonese and Teochiu cooks in variations of the theme set out by Lai, but the 'lightness of touch' is in popular imagination associated more with Teochiu cuisine. The Teochiu dialect is closer to Hokkien than to Cantonese but the Teochiu are to be found in Guangdong province and so, in popular view, this feature of Teochiu cuisine (the 'lightness of touch') is to be explained by the fact that the cuisine straddles the cuisines of the Cantonese and Hokkiens.[1] This is, if anything, hybridisation at work, yet it is associated with the Teochiu in an essentialised sense. What is also interesting, both in Lai's view and popular conceptions in Singapore, is how counter-factual evidence is ignored. If, for example, 'clearness, blandness and freshness' are the distinctive characteristics of southern, especially

Cantonese, food, what are we to make of that other 'distinctive' Cantonese dish, braised whole duck? This is rich and heavy. It consists of a whole duck rubbed with five-spice powder (C. *ng hiong fun*) and dark soya sauce, and then stuffed with stewed chestnuts, dried oysters and diced pork liver.[2] The whole duck, head, neck, feet, webs and all, is then braised in a wok in a liquid containing soya sauce and Chinese wine, to which leftover stuffing is added, yielding, after a minimum of two hours of cooking with constant turning, a tender bird with a dark, rich stew and stuffing. It is eaten with rice and a chilli dip usually consisting of pounded chillies, vinegar and grated ginger.[3] It seems evident that depictions of dialect-based or Chinese regional cuisines and hybrid foodways (resulting from a 'straddling' of such cuisines) are inevitably essentialised representations.

In contrast to the lightness of the Cantonese, Hokkien cuisine is said to be heavier. This is partly because of the widespread use of pork lard as a cooking medium. It "is virtually the only area in all East Asia where this occurs. It developed because the area is mountainous, with much fodder for pigs but little land to raise oilseeds; now it is simply a preference" (Anderson, 1988:163). In contrast to Cantonese cuisine, according to Anderson, the Hokkien focus on soups and stews has influenced the cooking method. Hokkien food "is apt to be cooked more slowly than other Chinese foods: the influence of slowly-simmering soups and stews". For example, "mixed vegetables that would be flash-fried in seconds in a Cantonese home are apt to be slowly simmered in lard in a (Hokkien) one" (Anderson, 1988:163). Perhaps the best exemplar of Hokkien cuisine, as depicted by Anderson, to be found in Singapore is braised belly pork which is stewed in dark soya sauce together with ginger, whole cloves of garlic, and five-spice powder or other variations. In restaurants, this is consumed with steamed buns, but a somewhat more robust version of the dish can also be found in hawker centres where it is eaten with rice.[4] Another distinctive feature of Hokkien cuisine is the common use of dips: "Many dishes have their particular accompaniments: garlic crushed in vinegar for poultry, sweet malt syrup for fried fish balls, and so on" (Anderson, 1988:163).

As with idealised depictions of Cantonese cuisine, it is possible to identify Hokkien dishes that subvert the representation of Hokkien food in the terms described above. In Singapore, a once common dish sold by itinerant hawkers consisted of a clear soup made by simmering pork bones, meat, offal (heart, lungs, kidneys, large and small intestines) and salted vegetables (H. *kiam chye*). Pork liver is also used, but this is cooked twice. The first cooking is nothing but a quick blanching to seal the chunks of liver after which the liver is taken out of the soup; the second takes place after slicing, and is quick blanching immediately before serving. This is to prevent the liver from turning hard. The clarity of the soup is ensured by skimming off the fat and scum which rise to the surface. The meat and offal are then taken out and set aside, to be sliced and then placed in a bowl of the soup to be eaten with rice on demand. The dish is eaten with a dip consisting of pounded chillies, grated ginger, pounded garlic and vinegar.[5]

In referring to these representations of Cantonese, Teochiu and Hokkien food, and the variety which contradicts these representations, we wish to indicate that regional Chinese cooking suffers from essentialisation. The representations are attempts to depict these cuisines as pure types, when in fact there is considerable criss-crossing of culinary influences over regions and dialect groups. The tendency to associate cuisines, dialect groups and regions or provinces as organic wholes is part of this attempt.

There are, of course, certain continuities in the food prepared and consumed between the Chinese in Singapore and that in their historical places of origin in China, but the continuities similarly reflect the crossing of influences. Indeed, the fact of migration to Southeast Asia (or the *Nanyang*, the 'South Seas') and the resulting daily contact with the cuisines of the Malays and the Indians, have changed palates significantly, so that in some instances, the food consumed by Chinese in Singapore would be unrecognisable to Chinese in China.

Peranakan Food

According to the aunt of a young Baba, "The test of a true Baba was to eat chilli without flinching."

A young Nyonya's perception of Chinese, when she was a teenager, was that 'these people were really *cina* (Malay word for Chinese) because they don't eat chilli, they don't have *sambal belacan* and their food is different.[6]

The terms 'Baba' and 'Nyonya' refer to Peranakan Chinese, male and female respectively. There is now an extensive academic and popular literature on Peranakans (Tan, 1988; Clammer, 1980; Chia, 1980, among others) and, as in all such instances, the definition of who is a 'true' Peranakan constitutes a field of disagreement, which we will not explore here. Taking descent as the criterion: a Peranakan is a child of (i) a Chinese man and a Malay woman, a Sino-Malay couple or, (ii) a child of a Chinese man and a Sino-Malay woman or, (iii) a child of two Sino-Malays. This is only a minimalist definition. What is significant, from a historical perspective, is the absence in these definitions of a Malay man married to a Chinese woman as an original genitor, or indeed anywhere down the line of descent. There is, in other words, an asymmetry. What this asymmetry reveals is that, historically, Malay men could not marry a non-Muslim without compromising their Muslim-ness whereas Malay women could. However, this no longer applies to contemporary Singapore. Today a Chinese man who marries a Malay woman is almost invariably required to convert to Islam; in Malay, this is to *masuk Melayu*, to 'enter into Malay-dom'. So too with a Chinese woman who marries a Malay man. Being a Peranakan is thus more than just a matter of descent; it is to be part of a particular cultural milieu and its practices. The contrast between contemporary Chinese-Malay marriages and the kinds of inter-ethnic marriages which gave rise to Peranakan culture in the past reflects important social and political changes over time.[7]

Peranakan culture is the result of cultural hybridisation, of creolisation, between Chinese and Malay and this is to be found in language and cuisine. The language is a creole of Hokkien and Malay called 'Baba-Malay' while the cuisine combines elements from Chinese (predominantly Hokkien) and Malay foodways. If a Chinese from anywhere outside Southeast Asia were to be confronted by a full-scale Peranakan meal, there is little he or she would find recognisable. Neither would he understand the language spoken by the hosts or cooks. The little that was recognisable, however, would nevertheless be very familiar. Peranakan cuisine has since the mid-1970s emerged from household kitchens and entered into cookbooks (Lee, 1974; Oon, 1978; Tan, 1981) and restaurants. The inscribing of Peranakan domestic cooking as recipes in cookbooks and as features in restaurant and coffee-house menus, as well as hawker fare, has resulted in the formalisation of a cuisine. It codifies the cuisine into a public and recognisable form to consumers and renders it reproducible by all, Peranakans or otherwise.[8]

In contrast to the 'blandness' and 'freshness' emphasised by Cantonese cuisine, Peranakan food, as the quotations above make apparent, is highly spiced by a very heavy use of chilli, an essential ingredient of Malay food, as well as other ingredients of Southeast Asian origin. The quotation above is interesting because it reveal how some Peranakans, at least, distinguish themselves from non-Baba Chinese through the consumption of chillies. Yet, as we shall see, the Singaporean Chinese are no mean consumers of chillies. Chilli can be used on its own, whole or pounded into paste; furthermore, chillies are often pounded together with a pungent (or to unaccustomed noses, 'smelly') shrimp paste, called *belacan* in Malay, to make a chilli-based preparation associated with the Malays and known as *sambal belacan*. The association of *belacan* with Malays is so close for some Chinese, or at least Cantonese, that it is often referred to in Cantonese as *Malai-chan*. Alternatively, the pounded chillies may be fried with pounded dried shrimp (H. *he bi*), garlic, onions and sometimes ginger. The resulting paste is known as *he bi hiam*, a Hokkien term.

Among Chinese consumers of Peranakan food, it is sometimes thought that with the use of chillies and other spices, the 'freshness' of meat, fish, and even vegetables, becomes unimportant. This is a mistaken impression. Whether cooking for domestic or public consumption, Peranakan cooks value freshness in meat and fish no less than Chinese. Indeed, in general, Southeast Asian cuisine, including Peranakan cooking, is highly sensitive to freshness because of an awareness of spoilage by climate. Meat and fish are generally cooked without undue delay. The reason for the attribution of a higher tolerance for lack of freshness in Peranakan cuisine is because of the 'masking' effect of the spices used, which leads to the view that what is masked is a lack of freshness. Popularly available Peranakan food does not help to disabuse Chinese consumers of such views because restaurants and hawker stalls selling Peranakan food do not usually offer 'fresh' vegetables. But this is for the simple reason that 'fresh' vegetables do not feature in Peranakan cuisine, except when they are thoroughly cooked until they are soft or 'overcooked', as with Malay vegetable preparations such as *sayur lodeh*, vegetables cooked with spices in coconut milk. In the domestic sphere, however, a common feature of Peranakan meals, as with domestic Malay meals, is raw vegetables which can only be fresh, served together with fried salted fish in dishes known by the Malay term *ulam*, which are eaten with *belacan* and other dips and as an accompaniment to rice and other dishes.

This, of course, raises an interesting problem: why do purveyors of Peranakan food, at least in Singapore, not include *ulam* in their menus? In general, Chinese cuisine does not include raw vegetables. The vegetables have to be cooked in one way or another, ranging from minimal cooking by the high-heat, stir-fried method attributed to the Cantonese or by the long stewing attributed to the Hokkiens.[9] The absence of *ulam* in the menus of Peranakan food establishments is thus to be seen as a concession to Chinese tastes, because the Chinese are after all the predominant customers in such establishments. Malays/Muslims are absent because the restaurants use pork. It is ironic that such a concession results in the odd typification of Peranakan cuisine as being more tolerant of a lack of freshness. Such a concession suggests an understanding of Chinese gustatory preferences which is not always reciprocated; but then such typifications are essentialised identifications writ small.

A common, highly-spiced Peranakan dish is a small local fish (*ikan-selar, ikan-kembong*) which is fried or grilled whole, very similar to a Malay dish. The fish is stuffed with chilli paste and other spices and often marinated in tamarind juice. Perhaps the most representative Peranakan dish, however, is *ayam buah keluak* (chicken cooked with *keluak* nuts).[10] This dish is so named because it is based on large black nuts from Indonesia which are scrubbed clean, prised open at one end and soaked for three days to leach the nuts because otherwise they are slightly toxic. The nuts are then cooked in a stew with chicken, lemon grass, candlenut (M. *buah keras*), pounded chillies, *belacan* and tamarind juice among other things. A richer variant of this dish entails the removal of the flesh of the nut which is then mixed with freshly-minced prawns and pork and stuffed back into the nuts. All the spices used are of Southeast Asian origin. Indeed, there is little that is 'Chinese' in this dish, except for the long simmering process reminiscent of Hokkien cooking and the presence of pork, which places it outside of Malay/Muslim cuisine!

However, reflecting their part-Chinese origins and continuing gastronomic attachments, many Peranakan dishes do not contain chilli and remain basically Chinese. An example is *chap-chye*, a term that is readily familiar to the Hokkien or Cantonese ear. This is either a stir-fried or braised dish of cabbage, mixed with dried bean-curd skin, mung-bean vermicelli, black fungus and dried lily buds cooked with mashed preserved bean curd.[11] There is nothing in this dish that is Malay, neither the ingredients nor the mode of cooking.

While more-or-less exclusively Malay and Chinese dishes are present within the menu of Peranakan cuisine, hybridisation is apparent in many of the dishes. To begin with, the names of the dishes are generally given in Malay, except in instances where a Malay term does not exist, in which case a Hokkien term may be used (but this hardly constitutes a rule). So, one gets a dish such as *bakwan kepithin*, a clear soup of meatballs made of minced pork (H. *bakwan*), crab (M. *kepiting*) meat and bamboo shoots. The Chinese element in this dish is, of course, pork; a taboo for Muslim Malays. Yet reflecting a relaxation of ethnic boundaries, the Malay name for crab is used. The same is true for another common dish, duck and salted vegetable soup, which is known as *itek tim*, where *itek* is the Malay term for duck.

As we have mentioned, Peranakan food is popularly thought of and represented as a unique blend of Chinese and Malay food with the vague, implicit connotation that each dish is such a blend. As we have sought to show, however, this is not the case. Cultural hybridity especially where it concerns food is not a simple matter of blending. It is a matter of reconstituting, in part and in whole. Thus, while we may find dishes such as *ayam buah keluak*, which will not be found in a Chinese or Malay meal, there is also *sambal belacan*, *ulam* and *chap chye*. Culinary hybridity is to be found as much in individual dishes as in the totality of the meal in which some dishes are recognisably Chinese and Malay. As far as Peranakans are concerned, however, this very hybridity, in part and in whole (together with their creole language) is uniquely emblematic of their Peranakan identity.

What is significant about Peranakan food in Singapore and Malaysia, where non-Peranakans are concerned, is how it resonates on the register of Chinese cuisine as a marker of Chinese ethnicity, in spite of the hybridisation. The cuisine remains a 'Chinese' cuisine because of the presence of pork, which is, as pointed out above, taboo for Malays/ Muslims. The tenacity with which Chinese-ness is attributed to Peranakan ethnicity in this instance of ethnic contact is significant. At the point in time when the emergence of Peranakan culture was historically possible, the Chinese were a largely male minority, and they married local Malay women. However, they were not absorbed into the majority indigenous culture, and a creole culture emerged. It is not the minority Chinese food practices that have been appropriated by the Malays and nativised (but see below), which is the usual pattern for the absorption of new foods into an ethnic community (Douglas, 1984); instead, the majority Malay culinary practices were appropriated by the Chinese.

Chilli as Gastronomic Index

In Peranakan cuisine, there is a crisscrossing of the cuisines of different ethnicities and even sub-ethnicities, which allows us to label it a creole cuisine. Beyond this point, however, the crossing of ethnic boundaries by Chinese cuisine is limited; Chinese cuisine stays largely Chinese but takes on local ingredients selectively, largely because the Chinese constitute the overwhelming majority ethnic group. Even so, the selective incorporation has to be seen as a process of hybridisation.

The most prevalent expression of the absorption of local ingredients into Hokkien and Cantonese cuisines is the ubiquitous and complex uses of chilli in street or hawker food.[12] This is most readily observable in the case of noodles, a staple Hokkien food. According to Anderson, "[Hokkiens] often get half as many calories from wheat as from rice". Most of these are in the form of soup noodles, but all sorts of stir-fried noodles are popular, from wide, thick rice-flour noodles to hair-thin wheat ones. The variety of forms and names is comparable to the variation in pasta in a comparably-sized region of Italy; nowhere else in China do noodles reach such apotheosis (1988:164). However, noodles are to be found everywhere in Singapore and not just among Chinese dialect groups. They also figure prominently in Malay and Indian cooking.

The gastronomic index to the array of noodles is chilli-based dips or sauces. Noodles are consumed in two ways, with a sauce ('dry') or in a soup. In the dry version, the sauce invariably has chilli as an essential component, accompanied by other ingredients, such as vinegar, light soya-sauce, tomato ketchup, garlic, chopped small red onions, *belacan*, and/or pounded dried shrimp (H. *he bi*).[13] The same is true of fried noodles, where chilli paste of one kind or another is added to the dish during frying or, occasionally, placed by the side for the consumer to stir into the noodles at his discretion. Even when noodles are eaten in soup, a side dish of fresh-cut chilli in light soya-sauce is served as a dip.

The ubiquitous chilli is processed and served in a great variety of ways. Each type of noodle dish has its own chilli accompaniment. To list a few, Hokkien prawn noodles (H. *he mee*) are either served dry or in soup with three different chilli dips. In both modes, a light powder of fried chilli may be sprinkled on the noodles, but the noodles are invariably accompanied by a chilli paste made with *belacan* as well as freshly-cut red chilli in a light soya sauce as a dip. The chilli paste is virtually identical to the Malay and Peranakan preparation. The dry noodles may also be tossed with a chilli sauce. The same fresh-cut chilli in light soya sauce is used for Teochiu noodles with fishballs in a soup. The freshly-cut red chilli is replaced by pickled green chilli when it comes to Cantonese wonton noodles. No Singaporean would accept substitutes for the types of chilli accompanying their order of noodles from hawkers.[14]

The same insistence on the 'correct' chilli exists with other food items. For example, pork rib soup (H. *bah kut teh*, literally 'pork bone tea') which is consumed by Chinese Singaporeans for breakfast, lunch, dinner, and as a late-night snack, is accompanied by freshly-cut red chilli slices in dark, thick sweet soya-sauce. Hainanese chicken rice, "probably at its best in Singapore rather than Hainan" (Anderson, 1988:164), is accompanied by a dip of chillies, garlic and sometimes grated ginger in which pieces of chilli are still pounded, but identifiably intact. Chilli paste, on the other hand, is reserved for other food, especially fried noodles and local tropical vegetables.

In all these instances, there is no mistaking that one is consuming Chinese food, in spite of the appropriation of chilli as an important ingredient to complete the preparations and satisfy the palate of Singaporeans. The range of chilli preparations and their consumption embodies a store of local knowledge which a Singaporean acquires through time and gustatory practice. In fact, Singaporeans often judge the food they consume by the quality of the chilli. This complex taste for chilli may be said to be a marker which distinguishes Singaporean Chinese from others in the Chinese diaspora. If the different kinds of chilli sauces, dips and accompaniments are indexical of the different kinds of noodle and other dishes consumed by Chinese Singaporeans and Malaysians, the general all-consuming need and desire for the gastronomic pleasures of chillies is an index of their differentiation from other ethnic Chinese and, indeed, Chinese in China, including Hunnanese and Sichuanese.

Although the origin of dips may be traced to the gastronomic practices of the Hokkien, as mentioned earlier, and for that matter the Cantonese and Teochiu, such condiments have become hybridised through elaboration by the incorporation of Southeast Asian ingredients or the outright appropriation of equivalent dips, e.g. *sambal belacan*, found in the region.

Hybridity in Malay Cuisine and the Islamisation of Chinese Food

Strange as it may seem, elements of Chinese food have found their way into Malay cuisine, most notably in hawker or street vendor dishes in Singapore. The appropriation has been so thorough that Singaporeans, regardless of race, typically think of these dishes as being Malay. Noodles are not indigenous to Malays. One such hybrid noodle dish is *mee rebus* (Malay: quick-boiled noodles). The dish consists of thick, yellow wheat noodles served in a thick gravy or sauce made from a base of fermented soya bean paste (H. *tau cheo*), garnished with diced, fried bean curd (H. *tau kwa*), bean sprouts (H. *tau ge*), half a boiled egg, chopped Chinese celery or coriander, and sliced green chillies. Another dish is *tahu goreng* which, as the name implies, is made from deep fried soya bean cake (*tau kwa*). The bean curd is fried, cut into squares and served in a peanut-and-chilli sauce with a garnish of scalded bean sprouts. Indeed, nothing in these dishes is of Malay origin!

Mention must also be made of two other dishes which represent even greater hybridisation. The first is *mee siam* (literally, 'Siamese rice noodles') which uses thin rice vermicelli served in a thin spicy soup made from *belacan*, dried shrimp, tamarind juice, pounded chillies and fermented soya bean paste among other things. The dish is garnished with chopped spring onions, chopped Chinese celery or coriander leaves, diced fried bean curd, half a boiled egg and deep-fried sliced small red onions. Despite being called Siamese noodles, the dish is identified equally with the Malays and Peranakans!

The other dish is *mee soto*. Although thought of as a Malay food, its original provenance is in fact Javanese as the term *soto* suggests. It consists of a soup with strips of chicken, yellow noodles, and bean sprouts topped off with a lashing of extremely hot pounded chillies. The soup is made by boiling a whole chicken (which provides the strips of meat) with a formidable array of spices, such as grated ginger, curry leaves, *belacan*, ground turmeric, ground coriander seed, ground cummin, ground fennel, black pepper and ground nutmeg. These four examples are clear instances of how Chinese food may be hybridised through its appropriation into the foodways of others.

In recent years, however, an interesting variation of Chinese food has emerged in Singapore, namely, through what may be called the 'Islamisation' of Chinese food. As we have already noted in the case of Peranakan cuisine, the culinary crossing of ethnic boundaries between Chinese and Malay is an asymmetrical process: the Chinese can readily cross over to Malay food but Malays, as Muslims, had been prevented from doing the same by the prevalent use of pork and often lard in Hokkien and Cantonese cooking. Until the late 1960s, it was common for Malay/Muslims and Chinese to dine together in hawker centres or even Chinese restaurants where Malay/ Muslims might sometimes partake of food which they were assured did not contain pork or lard. This mode of commensalism has all but disappeared. Increasingly, as the practice of Islam has become more strict in recent years, a gathering of Malays and Chinese to celebrate an occasion, such as the annual dinner of a firm or company, is unequivocally marked by a separation of the two ethnic groups.

Owing to a greater consciousness of Muslim sensitivities and in deference to the Islamic prohibition on the consumption of pork, many Chinese restaurants, especially those in hotels which cater to a cosmopolitan clientele, will provide halal (i.e., religiously approved) Muslim food, served at separate tables from Chinese food. Parallel to this is the emergence of restaurants, run either by Chinese Muslims, Malays or Chinese entrepreneurs and/or cooks, which serve halal Chinese food — Chinese cuisine prepared without the use of pork or lard, and where all other meats, such as chicken and beef, have been slaughtered in the manner prescribed by Islam. These restaurants now invariably display an endorsement by the *Majlis Ugama Islam Singapura* (Muslim Religious Council of Singapore) indicating that the food and the establishment are halal.

Significantly, the structure of Malay meals, which consists of rice and several side dishes (M. *lauk piring*) all served at the same time, might have contributed to the development of halal Chinese food restaurants. The domestic consumption of food among the Chinese and the Malays is in fact similar.[15] However, apart from Malay royalty and other elite groups, there is no Malay tradition of 'formal dining' or 'banquets' even on communal-ceremonial occasions. There is no sense of a multi-course meal where the dishes are served individually and in succession. What makes Chinese food amenable to restructuring in the form of banquets is in fact firstly, the food itself, and secondly, historical imperial and upper-class demands for social diversion, culinarily or otherwise.[16] Because Chinese food is not generally spicy, it can be eaten on its own in small amounts successively. Malay food, on the other hand, is spicy and each dish is savoured with rice as a foil. It is difficult, indeed impossible, to conceive of a Malay banquet consisting of, say, *ulam* (raw vegetables, fried dried salted fish and *belacan*) or *sop-buntut* (ox-tail soup) for a starter, followed in succession by *sambal udang* (prawns in *sambal* sauce), *ikan asam pedas* (fish in hot tamarind gravy), *kari ayam* (chicken curry), *rendang* (dry beef or mutton curry) ending with *nasi goreng* (fried rice)!

Halal Chinese restaurants, common in Malaysia, are not found in large numbers in Singapore. Such restaurants offer a convenient compromise solution for companies seeking to accommodate both Muslim and non-Muslim staff in their annual dinners. In many respects, it is a solution preferable to the above-mentioned segregation of tables for Malay and Chinese food. It preserves the symbolic, socially constitutive elements of commensalism (Rajah, 1989) through the consumption of common food. In short, the asymmetry noted above has provided the impetus for restaurateurs to develop a variation of Chinese food that is acceptable to the Muslim community.

Islamisation, however, is not confined to the kinds of Chinese food generally served in restaurants. It is also to be found in hawker fare where Chinese noodle dishes, Hainanese chicken rice, and Cantonese and Hakka *yong tau foo* (stuffed bean curd) have been Islamised.[17] Of these dishes, possibly the most notable, in terms of the first appearance of Islamised Chinese hawker food, is the adaptation of *yong tau foo*. The 'original' Hakka version (for there are many versions now) consisted of soya bean cake, dried bean curd, egg-plant, chillies and bitter gourd filled with a stuffing of fish paste (see also Anderson, 1988:170), cooked in a soup made by boiling dried anchovies with whole soya beans. The absence of pork, in general, made the dish amenable to appropriation, though in the process of appropriation the soup or stock has been replaced by one usually made from chicken. The Malay/Muslim version may be eaten dry or in a soup accompanied by chilli sauce whereas the Hakka version has two sauces or dips, a chilli sauce and another sauce made from mashed fermented bean curd (red or brown). The Malay/Muslim version of chicken rice closely resembles the Chinese, the crucial difference being the use of halal chicken. This applies to other noodle dishes which include meat. Where Chinese noodle dishes entail the use of pork or pork bones for the making of stock, this has been supplanted by chicken. These days, at hawker centres, halal Chinese food may be served by either Malay or Chinese Muslim hawkers.

It is difficult to place with authority the actual origin of the Islamisation process, in time or space. In Singapore, Islamised Chinese hawker food made its appearance, to the best of our knowledge, in the early to mid-1970s, most notably at a hawker centre opposite the Botanic Gardens, popularly known as 'the halal hawker centre', not far from the then-University of Singapore at Bukit Timah. But it is possible that there may have been other places where the trend set in, for example in Geylang Serai, which formerly had a large Malay population. Food here was prepared and sold by ethnic Malays and not Chinese. Some informants also claim that halal chicken rice first made its appearance at a stall in a coffee shop near the Rex Cinema near Serangoon Road, Singapore's 'Little India'. Halal Chinese restaurants, on the other hand, emerged in the early 1980s in the East Coast area and in Geylang Serai.

There are several reasons which might account for the emergence of Islamised Chinese food. Chinese food vendors may have sought to expand their market by catering to Malay consumers.[18] It is perhaps more likely that Malay food vendors Islamised Chinese food through culinary innovation. At the same time, Chinese converts to Islam, who must abide by the religious injunctions against pork, yet desire to continue to consume Chinese cuisine, may have helped to Islamise Chinese food. Growing affluence among the Malays has resulted in consumer demand expressed in, among other things, culinary diversion and an emulation of the foodways of the Malay upper classes, part of which has taken the form of halal Chinese food in different modes of consumption, for example, in the style of banquets. The emergence of halal Chinese restaurants thus reflects growing affluence and a differentiation of gastronomic desires, and at the same time fills an increasingly frequent social need in a multi-ethnic society for formal dining acceptable to both Malays and Chinese.

The Islamisation of Chinese food is in effect a very simple process, for all it requires is the slaughter of animals in accordance with Islamic rules and the elimination of pork and lard. It is surprising that it has occurred only relatively recently. Perhaps, the innovativeness of Malay hawkers revealed a hitherto hidden ambivalence towards Chinese food: gastronomic revulsion and desire. While the revulsion derives from the Islamic prohibition on pork, it would be hard to explain the success of Islamised Chinese food establishments if there were no desire. In the context of Singapore, Chinese food with pork is exclusivist, for it excludes Malays and other Muslims; Malay or Muslim food, on the other hand, is inclusivist because non-Muslims can consume it. Through Islamisation, Chinese food is made inclusivist which means to say that the consumer base is expanded for it now includes Muslims. Of course, Chinese gastronomic purists often scoff at the food provided in Islamised Chinese restaurants and criticise it as not 'authentic' because it does not contain pork or because lard is not used to cook the food. What is interesting about this view is that not all Chinese dishes, even in proper Chinese restaurants, contain pork. Lard is rarely used. The common cooking medium is in fact peanut oil.

In terms of our theoretical orientation, it would be a mistake to view halal Chinese food as a deracinated version of 'pure' Chinese cuisine. The omission of pork and lard is yet another aspect of cultural hybridisation, for such hybridisation is not necessarily the product of the presence of alien or foreign elements: hybridisation, where it involves the crossing of culturally-constructed boundaries, can also be the product of absences. This process of 'deletion' is significant but much neglected in the discussion of hybridisation.

The Hybridisation of Indian Food

In a process similar to the hybridisation of Chinese food in Malay cuisine, elements of Chinese food have been appropriated by South Indian migrants in Singapore. The resulting culinary creations are thought of as being intrinsically Indian and distinctive to the ethnic group. In some respects, this identification and attribution cannot be faulted, if only because these hybrid creations are not to be found together with food associated with other ethnic groups.[19] There are several such dishes of which we shall consider three: *mee goreng, mee kuah* and 'Indian' *rojak*, as it is known, to distinguish it from 'Chinese' *rojak*.

Mee goreng (Malay: fried noodles) refers to a dish of yellow wheat noodles stir fried in a wok, to which is added chilli powder, a generous teaspoonful of monosodium glutamate, a large dose of tomato sauce, a sprinkling of chopped green vegetables (H. *chye sim* or C. *kailan*) or canned peas and sometimes bean sprouts and some finely chopped, boiled mutton or lamb. The result is oily noodles, classified as dry because of the absence of gravy or soup, accompanied by a small side-dish of tomato sauce into which sliced cucumber is mixed. *Mee kuah* is the 'wet' version of this dish; *kuah* being the Malay term for gravy or sauce — the 'wetness' is the result of the addition of copious amounts of chilli powder and tomato sauce-based soup.

Indian *rojak*, on the other hand, appears at first sight to be unrelated to any dish of Chinese origin, though fried bean curd and Chinese lettuce are ingredients. The dish consists of a wide variety of fried or deep fried foods: bean curd, prawn in batter, potatoes, hard-boiled eggs in batter, among others. One selects what one wishes to eat and the items are then cut, sliced or chopped and placed on a dish garnished with chopped Chinese lettuce and sliced cucumber. The items are served with a dip made from tomato sauce and chillies. It is impossible to trace the ancestry of this dish but we would note that the employment of deep frying, the mode of presentation, display and serving as well as the sauce are remarkably reminiscent of a Hokkien hawker preparation which includes a wide variety of deep fried foods, e.g. pork or pork liver rolls (H. *ngo hiang*), prawns in batter (H. *he piah*), bean curd, Chinese sausages and century eggs. This is accompanied by two dips, a bland, starchy red dip and a chilli sauce. The dish is simply referred to by the term *ngo hiang* which acts as a synecdoche for the entire fare. Indian *rojak* is nothing like Chinese *rojak*, which is a mixture of tropical fruits such as pineapple and mango, raw vegetables such as cucumber and turnip, cooked ingredients such as vegetables like *kangkong* and bean sprouts and sliced dried deep-fried bean curd, all stirred together with a sharp smelling black shrimp paste, tamarind juice, ground peanuts and sugar. The fact that raw

vegetables are used is indicative of the non-Chinese origin of *rojak*;
indeed, *rojak* is Javanese in origin (*rujak*) and was most likely brought to
Malaya by Javanese settlers in the late nineteenth century (Brissenden,
1996:160). The fact that both the Chinese *rojak* and Indian *rojak* are
described by the same term means, puzzlingly, that the two are cognitively
grouped within the same larger culinary category.

Where South Indian restaurant food is concerned, there is one dish,
fish head curry, which is commonly believed to be Indian. In all respects
but one, it is Indian in the sense that the spices and method of cooking
are similar to those used in South Indian fish curry. The exception lies
in the use of fish head, usually that of a large garoupa or snapper. South
Asian fish curries invariably use fish steaks or fillets, and fish heads are
never consumed. The dish was invented, in the early 1960s, by a Malayalee
whose ancestry is said to go back to Kerala State in South India. This
Mr. Gomez opened the first fish head curry restaurant in Singapore at
Selegie Road. The fish head is cooked in coconut milk in the style of
South Indian fish *ntoolee*. The dish itself is said to have been created to
cater to Chinese tastes for the exotic, but this may be apocryphal. It has,
however, since spread to other South Indian restaurants where it is now
consumed by Indians and non-Indians alike.

Ethnic Identities, National Identity and Food

Singapore's close to 40-year history as an independent nation is a short
one. Since independence in 1965, the political leaders of Singapore have
been trying, quite consciously, to create a national identity, both as a
nation and as a state. The attempts range from the serious to the frivolous.
Among the serious are compulsory national service in the armed forces
for all men, the daily recitation of a national pledge by students in
schools, and grandiose National Day Parades which display, amongst
other items, the military hardware and capability of the Singapore Armed
Forces, and specially choreographed ethnic dances that are supposed to
represent the multiracial character of the nation-state (see, e.g. Leong,
1995; Rajah and Sinha, 1994; Benjamin, 1976). The frivolous include the
now-abandoned search for a national dress, which tended to be a pastiche
of different elements of clothing from the three major ethnic groups, and
the invention of icons for the tourist trade, such as the 'Merlion' — a

grotesque hybrid creature with a lion's head, (symbolising the 'lion city') and a piscean body and tail signifying the city-state's livelihood as a seaport.[20]

As the case of the search for a national dress suggests, an abiding preoccupation has been and continues to be the construction and representation of a Singapore national identity as a multiracial society living in harmony, in contrast to other multiracial nations that are plagued by racial tension and violence. This has given rise to many derivative representations produced by government agencies, statutory boards such as the Singapore Tourist Promotion Board and private establishments such as hotels. Among the derivative representations is that which may be found in the menus of the 24-hour coffee houses in international hotels in Singapore where there is inevitably a page for 'local fare'. On the list of food, a multiethnic presence is de rigueur. This smorgasbord may be intended to represent the ethnic cuisines of Singapore to tourists, but the array is just as likely to represent Singapore to Singaporeans. They also frequent such coffee houses where they can be waited upon and enjoy the tastes of Singapore in air-conditioned comfort. Though the food is often little or no better than that available in hawker centres and is much more expensive, Singaporeans have no qualms about paying for these luxuries. Finally, it is worth noting that similar versions of this array of food are also often offered at less formal official functions hosted by government leaders and by Singapore's overseas missions when celebrating Singapore's National Day or other occasions of national significance.

The array of multiracial foods, generally, includes as Chinese food, Hainanese white-cut chicken, Teochiu stir-fried *kway tiao* or carrot cake, Cantonese wonton noodles, Hokkien prawn mee soup; Peranakan *laksa* (rice noodles in a spicy, thick coconut-milk based soup, with slices of prawns, dried bean curd and hard-boiled eggs); Indian curries and Malay satays or *mee rebus*. While the Chinese dishes outnumber the Indian, Malay and Peranakan dishes, there is no question that the array symbolises the multiracial composition of the nation-state, comprising Chinese, Malay, Indian and Others. This representation, however, does not quite reflect the official categories in censuses and on identity cards. While Peranakan food is represented on such menus as a category unto itself instead of under Others, Peranakans are certainly not represented in censuses and identity cards. Anyone claiming Peranakan descent is automatically classified as Chinese by virtue of his or her Chinese family name. And, as noted at the beginning of this chapter, Eurasian cuisine is generally not in evidence. At the same time, while the relative diversity of Chinese dishes is suggestive of the dialectal diversity in the Chinese population, the relatively limited number of Indian and Malay dishes suggests limited cuisines and virtually eradicates the considerable ethnic, linguistic and dialectal diversities in the communities represented by these latter two labels. The official category Malay, for instance, obscures the fact that those who are so classified are in fact made up of Riau Malays, Orang Laut ('sea people'), Orang Selat ('straits people'), Bugis, Boyanese, Minangkabau, Kelantanese and Javanese to name a few. Likewise, the Indian category embraces South Indian Tamils, Jaffna Tamils (from Sri Lanka), Sinhalese, Telugus, Malayalis, Gujeratis, Bengalis, Hindis, Sikhs, Parsis and so on.

It would perhaps be more true to say that the ethnic communities which make up the nation-state have in fact been misrecognised and misrepresented in the construction of the menus of coffee houses and tourist-oriented literature. These documents seek to present the foodways of the people of Singapore through a concordance with the doctrinaire, official representation of Singapore's national identity based on an essentialising conception of the multiracial composition of the people-as-nation.

Conclusion: Imagined Cuisines and Communities

In sociology and anthropology it is generally recognised that ethnic identities and boundaries are associated with markers such as language, religion, dress and food. The analytic interest is to reveal the tenacity of such markers in ethnic identification, whether of the Self or Other. In Singapore, Benjamin (1976) has argued that the logic of Singapore's multiracialism leads Singaporeans to see themselves in 'racial' terms and this is indeed true in many aspects of social life. The ideology of multiracialism and its consequence — the tendency for Singaporeans to racialise themselves — also expresses itself in the realm of food. While this is apparent, what we have tried to demonstrate in this chapter is that beneath this there are, nevertheless, historically-embedded typifications of food-and-ethnicity.

Chinese, Malay, and Indian are unambiguously identified through a fantasmatic fixing of definitive and defining foods and cuisines to these ethnicities. This is not to deny that at some level certain foods are representative of ethnic and sub-ethnic groups; yet doing so ignores the culinary hybridisation which vitiates even this level of representativeness in the domain of ethnicity and the popular culture of food in Singapore. It only serves to show that ethnically pure cuisines are imagined, just as pure ethnic groups are, *pace* Benedict Anderson's (1993) imagined communities. There are, to state the obvious, clearly no boundaries to the imagined and the fantasmatic, for how else can we explain the essentialisation of hybrid foods such as 'Hokkien' *he-mee-with-sambal-belacan*, 'Malay' *tahu goreng* and 'Indian' *rojak* as markers of pure Chinese, Malay and Indian ethnic identities, let alone *ayam buah keluak* and *chap chye* for Peranakan identity, the latter an identity the state does not recognise?

Notes

*   We would like to thank Geoffrey Benjamin, James Gomez, Ho Kong Chong, Kwok Kian Woon, Steven Lim, Sidney Mintz, Alexius Pereira, James Poon, Nirmala Purushotam, Mavis M. Thurairajah, Tong Chee Kiong and James Watson for comments on an earlier version of this chapter or otherwise sharing their culinary expertise and highly-informed views on food in Singapore with us. In this chapter, we have not adopted a standard orthography for representing terms in the non-English languages and dialects to be found in Singapore but we provide an indication of what these languages and dialects are according to the following convention: C. = Cantonese; H. = Hokkien; T. = Teochiu; M. = Malay; Mn. = Mandarin (*Putonghua*).

1.   This straddling of the two regional cuisines is also noted by Anderson (1988:163), but, clearly, straddling connotes hybridity.

2.   Chinese five-spice powder is now considered to be quintessentially Chinese or at least Southern Chinese and perhaps, quite arguably, it is unique in terms of the combination of spices and use. However, it is often forgotten that the spices include cinnamon, star-anise, fennel, cloves and Szechuan pepper, all of which except for Szechuan pepper and star-anise were historically obtained from Southeast Asia as early as Ming times (Wheatley, 1961).

3.   In Singapore, as in China, a braised goose dish is often associated with Teochiu cuisine and the dish is therefore iconic of Teochiu-ness. Unlike the Cantonese braised duck, however, the dish does not include stuffing though the chilli dip is similar. The Hokkiens also have their version of braised duck, but again it lacks the stuffing associated with the Cantonese dish.

4. Ironically, it is increasingly difficult to find Hokkien restaurants in Singapore, as a result of the invasion of the restaurant business by Hong Kong entrepreneurs and cooks, who tend to serve seafood and Cantonese food.

5. It is interesting to note that this soup, as sold by hawkers, is what might be called a 'living' soup not unlike the stews of the South American natives encountered by Claude Levi-Strauss as recounted in his Tristes Tropiques. At the end of the day, soup left in the pot is replenished by the addition of water and more bones, meat and offal.

6. These quotes are taken from interviews with Peranakan informants conducted by Rudolph (n.d.).

7. There is, of course, much to be written about the changes that have taken place in the outcome of Chinese-Malay marriages. It is, at least, one of the indications that Peranakan culture is threatened with extinction, because one of its sources of continuity has been radically severed. Another reason for the disappearance of Peranakan culture, at least in Singapore, is the official policy (related to the official ideology of 'multiracialism') that the 'mother tongue' of Chinese citizens is Mandarin (*Putonghua*). All Chinese students in primary and secondary schools are, therefore, required to learn Mandarin. Peranakans are officially classified as Chinese by virtue of their Chinese family names and Peranakan children thus have to learn Mandarin leading to an erosion of any competence they might have in Peranakan creole.

8. This is not a unique phenomenon. Indeed, most if not all cookbooks historically are codifications of domestic culinary practices. In premodern times, this served the courts (which also contributed new creations and methods to 'national' cuisines partly because of their monopoly over trade) and in modern times, this has served the consumer in capitalist economies. Where both have come together in an unusual fashion is cordon bleu cooking which, at its core, is based on French provincial cooking (compare, for example, the recipes in Carroll & Brown Limited [1994] and Reekie [1975]). See also Appadurai (1988).

9. It should be borne in mind, however, that where Hokkien cuisine involves the stewing of vegetables, this generally entails the use of preserved vegetables such as mustard greens.

10. Pork, especially pork ribs, may also be used instead of chicken.

11. Even here, not everything is Chinese. Mung bean vermicelli (H. *tang hoon*) is not quite what it seems. The mung bean is of either Indian or Southeast Asian origin and was most likely introduced to China in the reign of the Emperor Chang-tsung (998–1022), which also saw the introduction of Champa rice (Anderson, 1988:63, 124–25).

12. The use of chillies in China is not, of course, unknown and Hunnanese and Sichuanese food have a well-earned reputation in this regard. In fact, chillies in dips (including *belacan*) can be found in Guangdong and Fujian. Dips similar to those found in Singapore and Malaysia are not unusual. This is because Chinese migrants who returned to these provinces brought back with them chilli-based dips and *belacan* concocted in the Nanyang or the South Seas (Anderson, 1988:143).

13. The term 'ketchup' raises a whole conundrum in hybridity in itself. The Oxford English Dictionary gives the meaning of the term as follows: "Sauce made from tomatoes, mushrooms, etc., with vinegar and other flavouring, used as a condiment [f. Chin. dial.koechiap pickled-fish brine]." Ketchup in the sense given here does not constitute any recognisable Chinese sauce or condiment and 'Pickled-fish brine' can only be 'fish sauce' or *hu to* in Hokkien. If the dialect term offered as an etymon by the OED is Hokkien, then the term is a compound term: *koe* (sometimes spelt as *kuay* or *kueh*) refers to wheat or rice flour based sweets (sometimes translated as 'cake'); *chap* (C. *chap*) refers to 'gravy' or 'sauce'. The compound term in fact refers to a dish consisting of pork leg, trotters (and other cuts with the skin on), pork offal, dried bean curd (H. *tau pok*) and hard-boiled eggs first simmered in soya sauce, ginger, and five-spice powder or variations thereof and served with broad flat rice-flour sheets in a soup of medium to thin consistency drawn from the simmering stock. The matter is further complicated by the fact that soya sauce is known in Malay (in Singapore and Malaysia) and in Indonesia as *kecap* or *kicap*. On the other hand, if the dialect term is Cantonese, then the term indeed refers to 'tomato sauce' from the Cantonese *koe* (Mn. *Chieh*; H. *kio* in short and *ang mo kio* in full, i.e. 'red-haired gourd' where 'red-haired' comes from 'red-haired devils' [*ang mo kuil*] or 'Europeans') for tomato — which originally designated indigenous eggplant. This, however, raises more problems than it solves because tomatoes are a New World crop and not a native species of the East. Anderson asserts that the Cantonese term cannot be regarded as the origin of ketchup or catsup in English. Citing David (1986), he notes that ketchup/catsup are 'cognate' with the French escaveche and Spanish escabeche ('food in sauce') which was long in use before the Cantonese had tomato sauce (1988:131). The solution to the terminological conundrum lies in the Malay/ Indonesian term which supports David's and Anderson's etymological attribution, though in a rather roundabout way. Chinese sauces that are produced without cooking such as fish sauce and soya sauce are described by terms such as *to* and *yu* (oil) in Hokkien or cognates in other Chinese dialects. It is only cooked sauces, often with a meat or bone-based stock, which are described as *chap*. This would suggest that the Cantonese *koe chap* for tomato sauce and other variants is actually derived from ketchup, which then entered into Malay/Indonesian languages where it came to refer to the most commonly-used Chinese sauce, i.e. soya sauce!

14. Given the multi-dialect environment of Singapore, noodles are known by different but cognate terms in various dialects; hence, different noodle dishes are identified and associated with different dialect groups by the terms used. Wheat noodles are known as *mien* in Cantonese, *mee* in Hokkien, both being variations of *mian* in Mandarin. Broad rice noodles are known as *horfun* in Cantonese (*hefen* in Mandarin) but as *kwaytiao* in Hokkien (*guotiao* in Mandarin).

15. In both cases, rice is served on individual plates while various items of food are placed on the table to which the diners help themselves. There are, however, significant differences in the way in which the food is prepared and in table manners that are wholly cultural (Geoffrey Benjamin, personal communication, 1 August 1996).

16. The Chinese dim sum is said to have had precisely this origin. The practice of serving tid-bits in small portions successively, thus taking a lengthy period of time to consume, was invented by imperial chefs to amuse and delight imperial concubines who otherwise had little to do apart from engaging in court intrigues and other diversions (Vivienne Wee, personal communication, 1976).

17. With the success of Islamisation, Malay hawkers have also invented different 'Chinese' food items that have no equivalent in the Chinese register itself. One such item is 'Hong Kong mee', which is a dish of noodles served in a beef, chicken or seafood stock. The noodles, however, are often instant egg noodles.

18. There has been no government policy to Islamise Chinese food in Chinese coffee shops in Malaysia. However, where Chinese food vendors have claimed to sell halal Chinese food (in response to the Islamic revival in Malaysia), the authorities have consequently implemented stricter checks on such shops. Chinese food establishments have always been free to sell pork and, indeed, some Chinese coffee-shops may include Malay side stalls (Tan Chee Beng, personal communication).

19. Still, a caveat needs to be entered here. These dishes are, not uncommonly, prepared by Malay street vendors. It should be kept in mind, however, that the crossing of culinary boundaries is paralleled by inter-marriages between Malays and Indian Muslims where Indian Muslims come to be considered or even socially classified as Malay by virtue of the process known as *masuk Melayu* (entering Malay-dom). The term also applies to anyone, whatever his or her ethnicity, who marries a Malay and becomes a Muslim.

20. The Merlion was in fact the creation of an Englishman who was director of the Van Kleef Aquarium, as a symbol or logo of the aquarium in the 1960s. The Merlion was subsequently appropriated by the Singapore Tourist Promotion Board. If anything, this must surely show that the creation of hybridised, phantasmagorical symbols in post-colonial states is not necessarily the sole prerogative of the native inhabitants or institutions of such states! It can include ex-colonisers who may in fact come to identify themselves with the post-colonial state.

Consumption Culture: Questions of Influence

7

Singaporeans Ingesting McDonald's

Globalisation of capitalism elicits two contradictory responses from managers of nation-states on the so-called periphery and semi-periphery. To prosper, indeed simply to survive, a nation must be able to insert itself as a node in the global network of capital flow. To this end the arrival of capital is to be enthusiastically embraced. On the other hand, one of the most apparent cultural effects of this arrival on local society is the expansion of material consumption and the development of consumerism as dominant cultural practice in everyday life. Global marketing of mass-produced objects broadcast through advertisements and popular culture media like TV and movies provide images to be emulated by consumers worldwide. Thus, it is imaginable that the expansion in consumption might lead to some level of global homogenisation of culture among consumers. Such an imaginary often gives rise to an exaggerated sense of 'panic' at cultural 'invasion' which, if left unchecked, will result in the demise of the local culture. This reduces enthusiasm. The embrace of capital is less than complete.

Understandably, local governments tend to regard negatively any possibility of global cultural homogenisation: It is antithetical to the idea of the 'uniqueness' in nationalist sentiments. It is potentially threatening to the nation-state's hold on its citizens. Emphasising the 'national' as 'local differences' is for the nation-state an act of self-preservation. Hence, alongside the active embrace of the arrival of capital there is a cultural/ moral critique of the 'cultural imperialisms' of the countries from which consumer goods originate. Conjoined but in tension, the material and cultural responses constitute an ideological disjuncture in almost all locations which respond positively to the penetration of globalised capital. This chapter examines this disjuncture at work in Singapore.

In Singapore the logic of capital operates unfettered, enshrined ideologically in a local version of pragmatism (to be discussed later). The result is a highly successful insertion into global capitalism, which has spawned domestic expansion of consumerism. Meanwhile, a critique of consumerism as cultural practice has emerged, framed by a larger public discourse of contestation between so-called 'Asian' and 'Western' values in the cultural sphere. The first are supposedly distilled from Chinese, Malay/Islamic and Indian traditional cultures; the latter from European and American sources (Ho, 1989; Mahbubani, 1994; Koh, 1993). This 'Asian-ness' is supposedly under siege by 'Westernisation/Americanisation', via consumption, among other factors. The most affected are said to be the young, the most avid consumers of all things 'foreign', whose bodies have become the foci of consumption in a city of relative affluence. The fear of Western cultural imperialism thus greets the arrival of almost all new consumer goods from the generic 'West'.

Symbolically, perhaps, no other consumer product carries a heavier ideological load of being 'American' than the McDonald's hamburger, which arrived in Singapore at the beginning of the 1980s. By 1995, the burger was sold in 65 outlets throughout the island. This makes Singaporeans among the largest consumers of McDonald's burgers per capita in the world. There is a McDonald's everywhere, sometimes two in larger public housing estates and shopping complexes. This extensive reach of McDonald's is indicative of its popularity with the population, making it an excellent representative site for the analysis of the material and cultural receptions of imported, 'foreign', consumer products.

Furthermore, 'McDonaldisation' has widely come to represent two separate processes in the discourse on late capitalism. First, from a production point of view, it stands for the continuing rationalisation of the process of mass production, a process that began with Taylorism. This involves progressive deskilling of workers through increasing simplification, standardisation and routination of job tasks (Ritzer, 1993; Leidner, 1993). Second, to cultural critics in both the US and locations invaded by McDonald's, the latter often stands as a US 'imperialist export' (Leidner, 1993: 471); reflecting the commonly-held thesis that 'homogenisation' of cultures which results from the globalisation of capitalism, is synonymous with 'Americanisation'. With this double representation, McDonald's as a consumption phenomenon contains within itself the analytic resources for examining the issues at hand.

McDonaldisation as Rationalisation

In *The McDonaldization of Society* (1993), George Ritzer suggests that the extreme automation of production, serving and consumption of hamburgers at McDonald's — hence, McDonaldisation as socioeconomic process — stands as the exemplar for the inevitable, logical outcome of the rationalisation of social life that began in the nineteenth century in the West. This trajectory of rationalisation has two loci; one in the bureaucratic management of society and the other in the breaking down of work into standardised routines in the mass production of industrial goods. The two processes have the same motivation and result: the increasingly efficient control of both people and production through standardisation, with its resulting predictability. Arguably, in broad outline, all contemporary capitalist nation-states must abide by the logic of these two sub-processes of rationalisation. Singapore is no exception.

From the very outset the PAP government decided that the only road to 'survival', in every sense of the word, as an island-nation, was to embrace global capitalism through export-oriented industrialisation fuelled by multinational companies and state-owned enterprises. The economic continues to be privileged, indeed hegemonic, over all other aspects of social life. The single-minded pursuit of continuous economic growth has become, at a minimum, the primary criterion for initiating and assessing all public policies. This instrumental rationality is ideologically crystallised into a version of 'pragmatism': that which aids economic development is deemed practical, any other arguments and criteria for or against a given policy are not entertained; for example, 'in principle' arguments are often trivialised as mere form or useless academicism.

To make the nation attractive to global capital, the necessary financial and physical infrastructure must be developed, and social conditions must be disciplined. Industrial peace is maintained through legislation and the efforts of the government-sponsored National Trades Union Congress; people are continuously developed by means of education and retraining into more valuable human resources; meritocracy is the criterion for allocation of social and material rewards, merit being measured by standardised performance criteria. In principle no sector of social life, however private, is exempted from state intervention to be harnessed for economic growth. These conditions translate into a generalised regime of social discipline under a highly-centralised rational public administration, governed by a single political party with a very high degree of continuity of both ideology and personnel.[1]

After more than 30 years of continuous economic expansion, the small labour force has become fully employed, creating a chronic shortage of labour. To save labour, social organisation and everyday life need to be further rationalised. In business, the Economic Development Board has become a one-stop facility to co-ordinate all relevant government agencies responsible for attracting foreign investments. In public administration, an ambitious information technology plan which will wire up the entire island has been implemented with the aim of enabling all transactions with government agencies to be conducted via computer (Kuo, 1988). In industrial production, computerisation, automation and robotisation are promoted with very substantial government grants-in-aid (Hing and Wong, 1995). Finally, in consumption, self-service is implemented whenever possible and a 'cashless' society is being promoted, where daily retail transactions are to be conducted through 'stored value smart cards'. All the above processes fit rather neatly into that trajectory of the idea of the McDonaldisation of everyday life.

The rapid economic transformation of Singapore has made the island-nation into something of a model for many Third World nations, especially for the Asian 'socialist' nations, such as China and Vietnam in which the respective Communist Parties hope to achieve rapid capitalist growth without having to share power with any political rivals. The result is that Singapore, an insignificant geographical space, has commanded a disproportionate space in neo-nationalist discourse on economic, social and political development. Economic success has led Singapore to champion so-called 'Asian Values' as a basis of organising all of society, including politics. It is at this level of values that McDonaldisation-as-cultural-imperialism raises its head.

As Singapore grew wealthy, the island-nation became increasingly inundated by American-produced mass cultural products and services, along with similar products from elsewhere in the world, notably Japan. The arrival and rapid spread of McDonald's can be readily evoked, ideologically, to 'represent' the increasing 'Americanisation' of Singaporeans. McDonald's stand as a sign(ifier) of a concept of 'American-ness' (Barthes, 1972), and Singapore stands as an example of the 'ineffable McDonaldisation of the world' (Appadurai, 1990). The consumption of McDonald's burgers is not, therefore, solely a nutritional concern, nor is it an economic one, for with current Singaporean wages, the food is inexpensive. Rather it may be of 'cultural' concern, seen contextually as part of the invasion and consumption of all 'icons' of America, such as blue jeans, sports shoes and other items of 'streetwear'. It is this cultural penetration of 'American-ness' into the supposedly 'Asian' values of Singaporeans that is being thematised in a cultural/ moral/political discourse of contestation between Asian and Western values. This 'Americanisation' thesis will be examined, first, in terms of the 'meanings' of McDonald's, both its food and its spaces, to the most avid consumers, Singaporean teenagers and, second, in the way McDonald's has advertised itself on local TV, the premier medium of popular culture and cultural penetration.

Familiarising McDonald's

As elsewhere in the contemporary world, there are no self-respecting Singapore teenagers who have not spent time in McDonald's. A basic mid-1990s survey (Ang, Low and Koo, 1995), of 200 youths aged between 12 and 24 who regularly hang out in groups at two McDonald's in Singapore — one in the prime shopping area and the other in the town centre of a public housing new town — found the following:

- the majority meet at McDonald's, chosen because of the convenient locations, before going out or going home;
- the mean length of time spent is about 24 minutes for all-male groups; 27 minutes for all-girl groups and 33 minutes for mixed groups (the larger the group the longer the time spent);
- about 70 per cent reported that they did not actually like the food.

It should be noted that the 'American-ness' of McDonald's, which makes it a place of 'cultural consumption', did not figure at all in the answers given for using the places, nor was it deemed significant for the teenage-researchers to pursue.[2] This is, perhaps, in contrast to the high level of awareness accorded to McDonald's 'American-ness' in other places outside the US.

To help document the reception and consumption of McDonald's in Singapore, it is instructive to examine ethnographic interpretation of how 'American/cultural' inscription of McDonald's is experienced in France and in the Netherlands. On the opening day of a new McDonald's in a small city in France, it was observed that:

> queuing behaviour differed substantially from the way the fast food ritual is practised in the United States. Customers would tend to gather all along the counter, with little respect for the integrity of the cash registers as line markers... Consequently the workers at the counter, for whom it was presumably their first active day on the job, spent a good deal of effort trying to lure customers over to their particular cash register 'station'.
>
> (Fantasia, 1995: 222)

> During the busier periods, an assistant manager placed herself about four or five yards in front of the counter to serve as a 'guide', answering occasional questions and directing traffic to available places at the counter. The fact that someone was assigned this task suggests that the company anticipated some initial difficulties for those unfamiliar with the ritual process and indeed there were occasional moments of chaos on the first day of business.
>
> (Fantasia, 1995: 222)

The same 'pandemonium' at the serving counter has been noted in the Netherlands. Anthropologist Peter Stephenson recounts the experience of his search for a cup of hot coffee, on a cold Sunday morning, in Leiden, where nothing was open, except for the church and McDonald's:

> Approaching the 'service area' I notice that there is considerable melee in front of the bank of cash registers where a swarm children and few lumbering adults are all trying to gain the recognition of small group of green uniformed and harried looking adolescent McDonald's employees.
>
> [A] voice lifts me out of my brief surreal reverie with. 'Excuse me, but is this a queue?' directed at Ms Junior Management Trainee... [whose] robotic smile fades a bit and a giggle escapes with the answer... 'Actually, I have never observed the Dutch to queue.' Several people in front of me begin to wave their order forms aloft, and when the 'service person' asks, 'Who is next?' they simultaneously yell, 'me!'. 'me!'.
>
> (Stephenson, 1989: 231, 232)

From this ethnographic account, Stephenson suggest that, 'there is kind of instant emigration that occurs the moment one walks through the doors, where Dutch rules rather obviously don't apply and where there are few adults around to enforce any that might' (1989: 237).

For Stephenson, the most unnerving behavioural demand that McDonald's imposes on the Dutch is queuing. It is a cultural practice that is in contrast to the type of loose ordering of Dutch customers awaiting service which is usually practised, in which one is responsible for noting one's position in the crowd and claiming the proper turn when it arrives. This difference in turn-taking 'marks' McDonald's as an 'American' space into which Dutch customers are transported and where an 'American form of presentation of self' is required. This reading was to be affirmed, for ethnographer Stephenson (1989: 237), by the mid-Western American couple complaining about the 'rudeness' of the Dutch at the same restaurant. Similarly, 'difficulties' of getting the French customers into queues behind the cash registers is used by Fantasia to mark one feature of the 'American-ness' of McDonald's.

Parenthetically, given that queuing is not a particular difficult exercise, one wonders whether the refusal of the Dutch to abide by McDonald's rules is not a form of cultural resistance in itself. As Leidner points out, in spite of McDonald's explicit scripting of the routines of interactions between staff and customers, it has to face some service-recipients who seem intent on thwarting the routines or on interfering with the workers' preferences about how to proceed (1993: 7).

However, the use of 'queuing' as representation of 'American-ness' is intelligible only contextually. Its indexical significance as the 'Americanisation' of the French and the Dutch is only remarkable with reference to the behaviours of the latter two. Its representation or symbolic efficacy for marking 'American-ness' fades, or disappears completely, in situations where queuing was already the norm even before the arrival of McDonald's, as is the case in Singapore.

Queuing was a non-issue in Singapore by the time McDonald's arrived in this island-nation. In keeping with a single-minded drive for economic success, every aspect of life is rationalised to increase orderliness, part of a 'totalising' strategy of government. Queuing 'naturally' falls into this strategy; unruly crowds at bus stations, ticketing outlets, department stores and supermarkets have all been disciplined into queues, defined by

128 CONSUMPTION CULTURE IN SINGAPORE

a space within guard-rails if necessary. That queuing has become a norm of everyday life is signalled by first, the appreciation of its efficiency; second, the psychological relief of not having to pay attention to who was before or after you nor of having to fight for your turn; third, the avoidance of others' anger when one inadvertently jumps the queue; and finally, the tinge of guilt one experiences in doing so purposely. Consequently, instead of being disoriented by or resisting the practice, Singaporean youth are undaunted by queues at McDonald's; queuing cannot be used as an index to signify 'American-ness'.

On the other hand, Singaporean youth appear to be appropriating McDonald's spaces for themselves.[3] The functional use of McDonald's as a 'meeting' place, mentioned above, may be explained contextually in terms of the characteristics of the friendship pattern of the youth themselves and the planning and allocation of public spaces in Singapore.

In Singapore's education system, schools are not assigned to secondary students by place of residence, as in community schools. Rather, assignment is according to the students' respective academic achievements in national examinations. Students are placed into a hierarchy of schools of descending 'quality', spread across the island. School-based friendship networks are correspondingly drawn from the entire island, and these networks are of great significance to young people because residential neighbourhoods have lost much of their function in generating contacts among residents.

During pre-industrial days, the 'urban village' environment was a prime site for simple, inexpensive, even free, recreational activities, which often amounted to little more than idling together in open spaces or local coffee shops. Friendships were prevalent among those who idled together, and they often cut across age groups (Chua, 1989b). The complete transformation of the island's residential landscape from urban villages to high-rise, high-density public housing estates has radically changed youth friendship patterns. Living in relative isolation in the air and surrounded by too many strangers at ground level, people find a high-rise, high-density living environment rather inhospitable for establishing acquaintances. Furthermore, a very significant improvement of comfort at home has encouraged individuals to stay at home rather than hang out in public spaces. These residential conditions combined with an increased affluence that enables them to purchase commercialised entertainment, and the desire to escape routine familial restraints and disciplines, all serve to drive youth away from the residential compound to seek entertainment in downtown areas, and to stay out as long as permissible, once they are away from the house.

Given the various distances which students must travel to and from home and school, a location which is convenient for everyone in a network must be found. McDonald's restaurants meet this need nicely. The business demand to capture the largest possible market slice dictates the spatial distribution of McDonald's outlets throughout the island: they are found in every public housing estate, home for approximately 85 per cent of Singaporeans. This ubiquity among the people normalises and reduces McDonald's presence to the quotidian. It is an important step towards the reduction of any sense of 'exclusivity' which may in turn impart to McDonald's a sense of the 'exotic', the 'foreign'/'American'. The same ubiquity also lends to McDonald's outlets a sense of convenience as meeting places: they are open for long hours, near mass rapid transit stations and in busy thoroughfares that offer visual pleasure for those waiting for friends.

McDonald's in Singapore is also particularly hospitable to upper-level secondary school students. At the outlets that are not within the central business district, local management tends to allow students to do their school assignments on the premises during non-peak business hours, in consideration of the fact that many of the students do not have the luxury of either study spaces and/or relative silence in the public housing flats that are their homes. This is in sharp contrast with the policy in the US itself of minimising the chances of outlets becoming 'teenage hangouts' (Leidner, 1993: 50). This generosity of McDonald's is especially appreciated during the annual national examination periods. Psychologically and symbolically, this particular use of McDonald's as a study space 'familiarises' it, in both senses of being familiar and familial. Such familiarisation displaces the sense of the space as 'exotic', a feature that is a necessary ingredient for a reading of McDonald's as an 'American' place in Singapore.[4] However this displacement does not erase the symbolic potential of representing McDonald's as an 'American' place, a point which I shall return to in the concluding section of this chapter.

Accommodating McDonald's

As a source of externally-introduced food, McDonald's is unavoidably inserted into local gastronomic practise of every location in which it sets up business. Marketing and consumption of McDonald's must, therefore, work within existing terrain in order to achieve desired results. Again, its reception in France is instructive to understanding its reception in Singapore.

Tobin, quoting various French writers, points out that cuisine is an arena of French cultural imperialism:

> Phileas Gilbert, writing in 1884, envisioned a French school of professional cookery... 'The products of our French restaurants and foodshops, which are exported all over Europe, would be represented on a vast scale, and the alimentary riches of the entire world would flood into the school, just as they once did into Rome. Our national culinary experts would, in their turn, imprint the seed of their genius upon these products, as they do with everything that passes through their hands, and redistribute them to the greater happiness of our modern gastronome'.
>
> (Tobin, 1992)

Against this totalising French culinary claim and ambition, American food has but a place in the extreme periphery. The insertion of McDonald's into France was, not surprisingly, met with cultural hostility. French sociologist Michel Crozier asserted, "for many French people there is an association that good food is French and fast food is American and foreign and bad" (Fantasia, 1995: 202). However, such scepticism did not prevent the subsequent penetration of McDonald's to become the largest fast food chain in France. Indeed Fantasia suggests that the popularity of McDonald's and other American fast-foods was one cause of the formation, in 1989, of the 'National Council of Culinary Art' by the French Ministry of Culture, charged with the duty of 'protecting the culinary patrimony'. According to the then Minister of Culture, Jack Lang, "France has developed the art of living which we all need to discover and safeguard" (Fantasia, 1995: 203).

It is against this proud French heritage that McDonald's defines itself. French cuisine requires for itself a certain decorum about how it is to be consumed; one has to have time for long meals with proper tableware and appropriate, if not exacting, manners. These culture entailments have apparently driven segments of the French urban population to fast foods. One example is the new breed of managers who are in a hurry and only stop long enough for disconcertingly simple lunches, consisting of a sandwich or an airline-style meal on a tray (Fantasia, 1995: 214).

'Old bourgeois' manners with their formal demands also turn away and turn off youth. It is here that the consumption of McDonald's is consuming 'American-ness' and is most clearly expressed as a form of 'resistance by ritual'. Self-served fast food is preferred by the young: "you can choose your own place to sit"; "each person orders direct from the cook"; "you simply pay individually, so you don't have to bother dividing up the check among everyone"; "the tables are not set, they are clear"; "no utensils and you can eat by hand"; "you can choose to eat one thing, one doesn't have to order several courses". In sum, "there are no rules".

The informality of McDonald's gets culturally 'essentialised' as essentially American: "You really feel the American atmosphere — the noise, the bright colours, the dress of the staff." This informality, 'loud' and 'gaudy' and 'disorderly', is marked as the difference against the 'sedate', 'subtle' and 'sophisticated' practices of the French. Hence, French adolescents' distinction between a 'cafe' and a fast food outlet: "you just wouldn't linger for a long time in a fast food restaurant like you would in a cafe" and, "No — its different, the cafe is more human — you can feel the presence of people; there's a warmer atmosphere there, people are not in hurry". Significantly and ironically, the consumed 'American' Other is not a valorised but a degenerate Other with reference to the French cultural self.[5]

The antipathy between French culinary establishments and practices and McDonald's, which is used as the basis of the 'hyper-real' representation of McDonald's as 'America(n)', is in turn appropriated by the latter in positioning itself in French society through advertisements.

For example, an ad running in 1994 consisted of a child's voice reciting proper table manners ("Don't put your elbows on the table"; "Don't play with your food"; "Don't eat with your fingers"; "Don't act like a clown"; "Don't make noise at the table"; etc.), with different images of people eating at McDonald's corresponding to each edict (i.e., people eating with their elbows on the table; playing with their french fries, or with their hands; joking around; etc.). The child's voice concludes the ad by announcing "that's how it goes at McDonald's" (Fantasia, 1995: 224). This intentional marking of differences between French gastronomic practices and those of McDonald's serve to intensify the symbolic representation of McDonald's as 'American' and the behaviours contained within as 'American' culture.

The insertion of McDonald's as fast food into the gastronomic terrain of Singapore is much less dramatic. 'Fast food' is a common phenomenon in Singapore, *avant la lettre*. Until recently, with extremely few exceptions, all food consumed outside Singaporean homes was 'hawker' food, purchased in a number of locations and modes: from itinerant hawkers, from stationary hawkers in markets in the morning or all day in local coffee-shops; from hawkers who gathered at open-air parking lots in downtown locations in the evening, when the cars of office workers had cleared. These various locations and modes were 'rationalised' by the government in its drive for orderliness and efficiency. Hawkers were herded, by the mid-1970s into purpose-built, 'hawker centres', which are little more than open shelters without walls.

In such centres, food is ordered individually and directly from the stalls. Consumers sit wherever there is a free table and the tables are numbered for ease of identification by hawker-assistants when they are delivering the food ordered. When hawkers are particularly busy customers often serve themselves. These practices are hardly any different from those of McDonald's.

McDonald's familiarity is further enhanced by the employment of middle-age or older Singaporean workers as frontline service staff because of the labour shortage and the reluctance of Singaporean youth to work during the school term. This removes the 'smiling' youth service that is the trade-mark of McDonald's in America.

Even the once significant exception of McDonald's being air conditioned, hence a more comfortable space is of decreasing relevance with the emergence of 'food courts', which are air-conditioned hawker centres in large commercial buildings. In sum, the practices which can be indexically identified as McDonald's essential 'American-ness' within and against French practices are, again, unremarkable in Singapore. They are devoid of the possibility of cultural thematisation and volarisation, and cannot, correspondingly be marketed as the Other to Singaporeans.

It should be noted, however, that hawker food in Singapore reflects the ethnic composition of the population, and is ethnically marked. One can get Chinese, Malay or Muslim and Indian food in every hawker centre; the same type of noodle may be cooked differently by different ethnic hawkers. While the hamburger has always been known to the English-educated Singaporeans, McDonald's contribution is to make it an 'everyday food', just another possible item of hawker food, available to everyone. Like all the other hawker foods, the hamburger is ethnically marked, in this case as 'Western' food, along with pork-chops, chicken-chops, hot-dogs and fish-and-chips, which together constitute the offerings of local hawkers who sell 'Western' food. However it bears no additional cultural significance to the rest of the equally ethnically-marked food; the consumption of the Western food materially is not tantamount to consuming the West culturally, it is merely a change of taste.[6]

Significantly, McDonald's further inserts itself into the local palate with deeper indigenisation of its offerings. Chicken McNuggets are served with curry or sweet-and-sour sauce. Chilli sauce, an essential ingredient for all hawker food in Singapore, is served with burgers along with ketchup. Finally, at the level of cultural signification, it introduces local emotive signs in the naming of some of its food items. For example, a chicken burger was marketed as a '*kampong*' burger; *kampong* refers to the villages in which most Singaporeans lived prior to being resettled into high-rise public estates. 'Kampong days' are a time which is remembered nostalgically as the 'good old days' when life was much more relaxed and the community more organic than in today's high-stress living in a globalised economy (Chua, 1995a). This level of use of local cultural signs is carried further into McDonald's advertising campaigns.

Inserting McDonald's into Singaporean-ness

In the absence of possibilities of marking behavioural differences, the selling of McDonald's in Singapore takes a completely opposite tack from that adopted in France. Instead of marketing itself against local culture, McDonald's seeks to insert itself into the latter. Furthermore, given the relatively short history of Singapore as a nation, and the fact that its national 'identity' and 'culture' remain a matter of active state promotion, McDonald's advertisements seek actively to partake in this constitution of a national identity and culture.

One of the repeatedly-used TV advertisements, especially during the run-up to National Day (August 9), begins with a morning assembly of primary school boys at a flag-raising ceremony, with the boys' choir singing, "when the sun shines over our land"; this is followed by an image of two eggs frying and piping hot coffee, suggesting that it is breakfast time; it then cuts to a middle-age Chinese lady in a shophouse, symbol of old Singapore architecture, opening a window to let the sunshine in; it next moves into a primary school classroom, with children sitting on the floor learning the alphabet, "b for boy", "g for girl" and "m for McDonald's"; the scene switches to a group of clean and fresh boys in McDonald's, one of them is attracted to a girl who flashes him a smile, he says "I will have whatever it is that she is having"; he is followed by a picture showing freshly-cooked French fries being poured onto a metal tray and a fishburger oozing with white creamy sauce; the next frame is of a young man driving a red convertible sports car — a very coveted possession in a land where cars can costs as much as public housing flats — singing to himself the McDonald's jingle in Mandarin, driving to pick up his hamburger; he is awakened from his self-contentedness, blushing slightly, by the applause and laughter of two McDonald's waitresses; the scene then cuts to the clock tower at the Victoria Memorial Hall, a monument to Singapore's colonial past, the time is 7 o'clock in the evening; the final shot is of an old Chinese gentleman in traditional clothes, no longer worn by anyone, sitting stiffly in a rosewood chair, in a very traditionally-appointed sitting room, playing the McDonald's refrain on a Chinese two-string musical instrument, the *erhu*.

That this ad aims to insert McDonald's into the daily life of Singaporeans is obvious. Rather than taking them out of Singapore and into an 'American' space, the ad takes viewers through a twelve-hour day of Singaporeans of all ages in less than a minute. In addition any Singaporean will readily recognise that the ad touches on various values (and their attendant activities) that continue to be actively promoted by the government as constitutive elements of a 'national' culture. Among these thematised values are; first, the restoration of the historic landscape of Chinatown and national monuments, such as the Victoria Memorial Hall. Restoration began in earnest around mid-1980s, when there was a serious decline in tourist arrivals because Singapore was becoming too much like any other big city, losing its 'exotic' Asian elements. Now four historic districts, namely, the civic district of colonial administrative buildings, Chinatown, Little India and the historical Muslim area of Kampong Glam (Kong and Yeoh, 1994), as well as individual buildings of significant architectural heritage, are being conserved.

A second key value, as mentioned earlier, is the emphasis on education as a human capital investment for individual social and economic mobility and national economic growth. This emphasis is also being ideologically transformed from its instrumental function into an 'Asian' essentialism. Education is promoted as a 'traditional' commitment of all three Asian ethnic groups that constitute the population, as signified by high levels of private financial investment devoted to children's education and by keen competition among students for scarce spaces in local universities. With reference to the US, the high achievement of Asian students in American academia is used as evidence of the 'Asian' commitment, relative to the others in multiracial America.

Another 'Asian' value promoted in the McDonald's ad is the veneration of the aged as part of the idea of 'family as the basic unit of society', which is legislatively enshrined as part of the national ideological system, known as 'Shared Values' (Lee, 1989). This veneration of the aged has also led to the promotion of three-generation family units through public housing policies. Such families are entitled to concessions in the form of cash grants, reduction of waiting time and preferential locations for flats. Pro-family advertisements which encourage marriage, childbirth and living in an extended family are constantly broadcast by the ministries responsible for different aspects of the overall pro-family policy. In public discourse the preservation of the 'Asian' family is ideologically contrasted with high divorce rates and ubiquitous senior citizen homes in the United States and elsewhere in the developed West.

Finally, the use of Mandarin as the language of all Chinese, reflected in the advertisement, has been promoted through an annual, month-long Speak Mandarin campaign for more than a decade. This policy was initiated by the then Prime Minister, Lee Kuan Yew, ostensibly as a means to bridge supposed communication gaps within the Chinese population, which was differentiated by often mutually incomprehensible 'dialects'. Since then, all Chinese students must obtain at least a passing grade in Mandarin, in order to secure a place in local universities; all dialect programmes on TV have been banned, and imported Cantonese or Hokkien programmes from Hong Kong and Taiwan, respectively, are dubbed into Mandarin. The result is that Mandarin has become the common language among Chinese, at the expense of cross-generational communication, especially between grandparents and grandchildren. However, the emotional appeal of dialects remains high among older and less-educated individuals (up to 50 per cent of the Singapore work-force has less than a primary education). This has resurfaced politically. For example, in the 1991 General Election, a successful opposition candidate made his mass rally speeches in the predominant dialect of that particular constituency. Furthermore, with the recent economic opening of the southern coastal areas of China, dialects are being rehabilitated in a limited manner and the use of dialects is less frowned upon.

The above set of values, actively sponsored by the state, are the recurring theme of annual national campaigns and of speeches by politicians and cabinet ministers, widely covered by the national newspapers. They constitute the ideological diet of Singaporeans, and are promoted as 'cultural ballast' against the excessive individualism of America or the West. Against this ideological background, any heavy selling of McDonald's as a sign(ifier) of 'American-ism' would be counter-hegemonic, positioning McDonald's as 'resistance culture', as is the case in France (but on a more political plane). What the government's response to a counter-hegemonic marketing of McDonald's might be will never be known. However, the response would undoubtedly be negative; this is a government which polices and censors images, including advertisements, that enter the national ideological space.

Conclusion

The motivation behind this analysis of McDonald's in Singapore is to counter any simplistic equation of product consumption with imaginary consumption of a culturally-desired Other. Whereas imported products potentially may be imprinted with the cultures of their respective places of origin, the consumption of the products is not automatically tantamount to the consumption of the culture of origin. With regard to the marketing and consumption of McDonald's in Singapore, it is apparent that the level of cultural consumption of a desired Other, of 'American-ness' in fantasy, is very low, if not completely absent.

The issue is not whether the potential of such imaginary or fantasy consumption of foreign products exists, for clearly it does, but the realisation of this potential is not a simple process. In spite of the relative ease with which McDonald's can be inserted into the Singaporean hawker food milieu, its potential for selling 'American-ness' is not absent. However, the realisation of this possibility depends on the cultural terrain in which the consumer item is inserted and against which it must act.

Within the political/ideological space of Singapore, arguably the space for the consumption of 'American-ness' is already provided by the state itself, as it is precisely against a concept of 'Americanisation' that the current 'Asianisation' and 'communitarianisation' of Singaporeans is being undertaken by the state. Against a reductionist version of 'individualism' as a proxy of liberal democracy in America is juxtaposed the reinvented 'communitarianism' of 'Asian' traditions to be inscribed on the Singaporean social and political body (Chua, 1995a). Thus, any version of 'American-ness' would in itself automatically constitute a powerful counter-discourse within contemporary ideological space in Singapore (cf. Lee Kuan Yew, 1995). It would be attractive to those who are critical of the constraints placed on political, cultural and social spaces by communitarian ideology, with its emphasis on the 'collective' over the individual. For them 'America' symbolises a space where individual rights and differences are valorised, and the consumption of any representation of America, through whatever medium — TV, movies, music and fashion — would constitute the imaginary inhabiting of that desired Other space.

The possibility of inserting McDonald's as a sign(ifier) of 'American-ness' is not pursued by the enterprise. This must be attributed to a profit motivation that avoids contesting the ideological sphere lest it incur the wrath of the managers of the state and be constrained in the market. In the selling of McDonald's, as of any imported goods, economic interest is strategic while the cultural representations used are always simply tactical.

Notes

1. Detailed discussion on pragmatism as national ideology in Singapore can be found in Chua (1995a: 57–78). For a discussion of the very intrusive reach of the 'survival' ideology see Devan and Heng (1992).
2. The researchers for this project were three secondary school students in the gifted education programme under the mentorship of a lecturer at the National University of Singapore.
3. Given the generalised 'rationalisation' of social life in Singapore, both the idea that McDonaldisation stands as a trope, for the 'rationalisation' — namely, efficiency,

calculability, predictability and control of society (Ritzer, 1993) — and that fast-food production and service stand as exemplar for the standardisation of service work in late capitalist societies (Leidner, 1991) would readily apply to this very successful bastion of multinational capitalism. It should be noted, however, that these processes of production rationalisation are the consequences of the logic of capital, which in being globalised has its own homogenising effects on cultures of different locations. This homogenisation of cultures should not be read simplistically in 'Americanisation'; indeed, Ritzer could be said to implicitly disavow such a culturalist reading of the process.

4. Secondary school students are particularly inventive in their search for places to study, and everything else besides, in groups. One of the favourite sites is the Changi International Airport, which has large, secluded but well-lit spaces that are available to all 24 hours a day.

5. All quotations from French youth are to be found in Fantasia (1995: 222–5a).

6. In his analysis of the penetration of Japanese mass consumer goods in Taiwan, an ex-Japanese colony, Leo Ching (1994) has raised similar reservations regarding any simple attempt to equate popular material consumption, even technological consumption, with simultaneous consumption culture of the Other.

8

Japanese Influence in Singapore: "Where Got?"

Consumerism has been expanding rapidly in Singapore, a consequence of the relative affluence of the population. A very large part of the frenetic rate of consumption among Singaporeans is the consequence of the releasing of frustrated desires imposed by decades of under-development. Consumption is one of the many avenues of catching-up with the modern world, symbolised by the owning of all conceivable forms of household and personal commodities: televisions, video recorders, refrigerators, telephones, cars and fashionable clothes. Like other successful Asian economies, Singapore is driven by exporting as much of its industrial production as possible; however, unlike most of them, Singapore produces few of its own consumption goods, all are imported from elsewhere in Asia, Europe and America.

If, as is often theorised, consumer goods are highly inscribed by the cultural context of their production, then imported goods are accordingly stamped with the cultures of the locations of their origins, and consumption of such goods carries with it the consumption of the attendant cultures. Such an argument undergirds the idea and the fear of 'cultural imperialism' in consumption and consumerism. It is within this argument that the question of possible Japanese 'influence' in Singaporean everyday life may be posed because Singaporeans consume a significant amount of imported Japanese goods. My response to the question is unambiguous: There is no 'Japanisation' of Singaporeans, by which I mean that there is no significant 'Japanese-ness' in Singaporean consumer culture, in spite of the hype in local and international mass media.

Such a categorical position obviously requires some qualification. The central issue here is the idea of influence. It would be nonsensical to argue that consumption of 'Japanese-ness' — the selective consumption of cultural products because they represent the idea of 'being Japanese' — is entirely absent. There are small pockets of highly-committed consumers of certain Japanese cultural products, like those who stay up late or stay home on weekend mornings to watch Japanese soap-operas, those who spend substantial amounts of money and time reading Japanese manga and those young primary school female students who collect 'cutesy' Japanese stationeries. If one were to study these groups, one would undoubtedly discover their careers as 'Japanophiles'.[1] In my view, these small but highly-committed groups of consumers cannot be said to represent the 'popular'.

I would like to suggest that the term 'popular' be used to denote, minimally, highly-visible phenomena which dominate the imagination, if not reality. A conceptual clarification is necessary here. In the conventional usage, the term 'popular' can denote two phenomena; first, the sense that something is consumed by a very large number of people and second, that although consumed by a relatively smaller number of people, the products and the rituals of consumption are highly visible to any passing audience. For example, it is a common worry among adult Singaporeans that Western fast-food will replace local hawker food for future generations. Such a view trades on a substitution of the high visibility of fast-food outlets for the actual quantum of sales and volume of food consumed. In actuality, there are at any one time more pounds of noodles of different flavours and cooking styles consumed by Singaporeans than Big Macs, Whoppers and various 'American' style fried chicken combined. There should be no fear of the former being replaced completely. Such instances of equating 'high visibility' with actual consumption would be consistent with the second sense of being popular. Both senses of the popular should be deployed in the analysis of consumer culture, without dismissing the 'highly visible' as falsely popular.

With the above caveat and the adoption of two senses of the popular, I will reiterate my conclusion that there is no 'Japanisation' of Singaporeans; a conclusion that the rest of this chapter will attempt to substantiate.

Some Immediate Impressions

First, a young Japanese anthropologist/sociologist who had spent one month in Singapore researching consumerism, once declared in my office that "Singaporeans are very immature in their fashion!", quite unaware that this might be an affront to a Singaporean like me. In the course of the conversation, the unsaid part of his declaration emerged. To him, Singaporeans' fashion sense appears immature, "in comparison with Japanese fashion practices". The difference is indicative of the absence of influence of the latter in the practices of Singaporean dress codes.

Second, a visitor reading through the advertisements in the daily newspaper will be impressed by the presence of Japanese departmental stores in Singapore; Takashimaya, Isetan and Seiyu/Parco, in addition to the now defunct Daimaru, Tokyu and Sogo. These department stores are the biggest in the country, with no local or other foreign competitors of similar scale. Their prominence in the city-scape is unchallenged in the retail sector. Yet, if one should go to any of these stores in search of Japanese goods, one would be greatly disappointed. Certainly, there would be spaces allocated for Japanese consumer products, but these are distinctively confined to Japanese goods 'corners', particularly for food. This has not always been so. In the early 1970s, when the first of these stores, Yaohan, made its entrance, Japanese goods featured extensively. They have since then been diminishing and Yaohan went out of business in 1997. In the words of a Japanese cultural studies scholar, "Isetan in Singapore is not a Japanese store, nor is Takashimaya."

Third, Singapore is culturally a rather defensive space, constantly vigilant against 'polluting' influences from the 'constitutive' outside. This vigilance is raised generally against the 'West/US', against 'Westernisation/ Americanisation', but there is no equivalent anxiety regarding 'Japanisation'. Ironically, there is not a single big American department store in Singapore. The joint venture between local enterprise Metro and American chain K-mart folded after about three years of operation. Indeed, Metro had up to four big stores in the prime tourist-shopping belt of Orchard Road, but it was progressively edged out of business in this district by the earlier-mentioned Japanese stores.

In spite of these impressions, there is no doubt that Japan, via its transnational corporations, has massive economic presence in the Singaporean consumer sector. Japanese products are ubiquitous; witness the cars on the road, the electrical appliances in the homes, the personal electronic gadgets on strolling bodies along Singaporean streets. Furthermore, in both these sectors, Japanese products are preferred over products from other, particularly Asian, nations; for example, Japanese cars and televisions are preferred over Korean ones. The superior technology of Japanese products is readily recognised. However, technological superiority is embedded in culturally 'neutral' commodities, or what Koichi Iwabuchi called 'no smell' Japanese products (personal communication).

The general observation that can be drawn here is that the cultural 'influence' of Japan or the Japanese on Singaporeans, via consumerism, is far less than economic power would suggest. In this chapter, I will examine three different areas of popular culture consumption in Singapore to substantiate this. The three areas examined are fashion, food and mass media entertainment.

Fashion

In a city-state where the population is relatively young,[2] and prices of both houses and cars are prohibitively high, much of the discretionary expenditure of those who are outside the clutches of family responsibilities is spent on self-adornment, on fashion and accessories. Besides, as mentioned in Chapter 1, a successful local designer has suggested that in a country where political freedoms are heavily circumscribed, "the only protest you can make is how you look, short of taking off your clothes. So people make a statement with what they wear" (Peter Teo, *The Straits Times*, 8 June 1997). This is especially so for teenagers and 20-somethings who spend freely on diffusion-line designer clothes: casual wear in jeans and t-shirts from European and American designers such as Armani, Versace, Gaultier, Paul Smith, Dolce & Gabbana and Calvin Klein. This market has also been penetrated by Australian 'surf wear' companies, like Billabong, Rip Curl and Quicksilver. A jeans and t-shirt ensemble is the common attire of the young, signifying the informality which typifies the Singaporean dress code. The young may buy similar items and accessories from no less expensive Japanese sources, from shops such as those in the Heeren Building, but will not 'programme' these items on their bodies in the same way as a Japanese youth might; Singaporean youth decidedly do not use Japanese configurations as models to emulate. In general, the readiness of the young to part with their money for such 'branded' goods has caused much public consternation, mild 'moral panic' and some 'teenage bashing'. This is because of the fear, expressed by elders and the moral gatekeepers of society, including journalists, that the young are not acquiring the habits of frugality and savings, exemplified by the old in a nation where savings rates reach 40 per cent of monthly income.

If at the street level Japanese influence is not present, and if present is often negatively represented as an Other, the possible influence at the high end of the market in formal wear is equally limited. Kenzo, Issey Miyake and Hanae Mori each has their respective boutiques in international hotel arcades, but they are seldom visited by Singaporeans.[3] In the case of women's formal wear, it is not the absence of Japanese designer influence that is significant but, as analysed in Chapter 4, the observable, relative disappearance of 'Western' formal wear in the 1990s, replaced by 'national' or 'ethnic' clothes. Women's formal wear has undergone a very significant change. It has been 'ethnicised'. This was a reflection of the rise of capital in Asia throughout the 1990s which has affected Singapore's cultural terrain, giving Singaporeans a sense of cultural confidence.

Through the 1990s, this cultural confidence had been culturally productive in generating a sense of pride in things 'Asian' among many Singaporeans. This pride is almost obligatory among those who are in the public arena and nowhere is this more clearly expressed than in the ethnicisation of women's dress codes at formal, especially televised, gatherings. The 'traditional' clothes of the three major ethnic groups (updated in expensive fabric and contemporary tastes) have made a return on the bodies of women with power or close to power; Indian *sari*, Chinese *cheongsam* and Malay *baju* are now 'power' clothes, their bright colours and floral prints contesting the understated, formal black of Western/modern dress. In this ethnicisation, all overt cultural influences from outside have been excluded. The sustainability of this ethnicisation and possible trickle down to the younger generation and trickle out into the mass market became doubtful after the 1997 Asian regional crisis, followed by sustained downturn in the global economies in the early years of the twenty-first century.

In the area of fashion, therefore, Japanese influence is not significant. Japanese fashion and fashion designers do not figure significantly among 'brand' conscious young Singapore consumers. The informality of Singaporean fashion is antithetical to the formality of the Japanese fashion code, including street clothes. It is this contrasting informality that had caused the earlier-mentioned Japanese urban anthropologist to comment on the 'immaturity' of the Singaporean fashion sense. Against the Japanese practice of a strong sense of 'co-ordination', even when (s)he is attired unconventionally in street-wear, the Singaporean practice of seeming randomness of mixing-and-matching is decidedly 'unacceptable', thus 'immature'.

The differences in fashion practices are also noticed by Singaporeans. During the euphoric days of the bubble economy, which brought Japanese tourists by the plane load, the dress code of female Japanese tourists seen in the streets of Singapore was itself a code distinct from local practices. It became a cliché and sometimes a target of ridicule and derision. The Japanese dress code of the time was identified in stylised manner as such: very-pale-close-to-white facial make-up, small floral print, light weight dress in light pastel shades, white nylons or socks, comfortable walking shoes and, occasionally, a hat. To young Singaporeans, this dress code exemplifies the Japanese 'culture of cuteness' (Clammer, 1995). In Singapore, 'cute' may be a term of endearment, but 'cuteness' in behaviour and configured appearances — signalling immaturity — is decidedly 'not cool'. Thus, the 'Japanese' code is seen as an unedifying caricature, which no Singapore teenager, male or female, will emulate.

Before closing this section, it is opportune to raise a fundamental issue of cultural influence/inscription. In the case of fashion, it must be said that there is by now an 'international' uniformity which has its origin in Western clothes. For men, this consists of different combinations of suits, trousers, shirts and neck-ties. For women, in addition to the same items of clothes as men, there are dresses and skirts. The rate of internationalisation in a location depends partly on its contact with global economic and cultural transactions. Generally, the rate is slower for women than men as ethnic codes are usually kept alive by women rather than men, as in the case of Singapore. The Western origin of the internationalised uniform code is all but unremarkable, until it is placed in a context, usually on ritual occasions, where the participants revert to their ethnic clothes.

Inserted into the sartorial space of the international code are individual designers. A designer may be inspired by his or her own cultural sources, or may borrow from other sources, in creating globally marketable items.

To be so marketable, the ethnic/cultural inspiration has to be relaxed and reworked into the international code, thus diluting the cultural inscription on the clothes and its consumers. For the consumer, the identification is with the designer rather than the latter's cultural inspirations. Particular cultural inscriptions are thus refracted through the signature of the designer and the imprint of the international market. Paralleling architecture as a practice, international fashion design is thus a 'star' system rather than a vernacular/cultural system without designers. This is, of course, true of 'Japanese' fashion designers.

Mass Media

Almost every household in Singapore owns a television; indeed, this fact is often used by the government as an indicator of its success in bringing material richness to the nation, which in turn, legitimises its right to govern. Until early 2000 there were four broadcasting stations, two under the Television Corporation of Singapore (TCS) and two under Television 12 (TV12), all government owned. One of the TCS channels continues to be dedicated exclusively to English programmes, the other to Mandarin programmes. One of the TV12 stations was dedicated to Malay and Tamil/Hindi programmes, the languages of the two minority ethnic groups, Malay and Indians, respectively. The other is the 'arts' channel, which showcase nature/wild life, opera of different languages, art films from around the world and global sports competitions. TCS broadcasts 24 hours, TV12 airs for 12 hours a day.

In 2000, only the Chinese channel on TCS broadcast regular Japanese programmes, dubbed in Mandarin, for up to nine hours per week. None of the programmes were on prime time. The most concentrated broadcast period was on Saturdays; two one-hour drama series, at eleven in the morning and at half-past-five in the afternoon. The rest were half-hour cartoons or animated drama programmes. The scheduling of these programmes was as follows: in the mornings, Mondays at six o'clock; in late week nights at half-past one and at four to five o'clock in the morning. The highest ratings were for the Saturday and Sunday afternoon programmes, six and seven per cent respectively of an estimated audience of approximately three million. The ratings for the other shows ranged from three to zero per cent.

TV12 had three hours of regular Japanese programmes. All three hours were broadcast in late prime time between ten to half-past-twelve in the evenings. The one-hour documentary on contemporary Japan, *The Japan Hour*, was divided into two halves; the first half a news magazine broadcast exclusively in the Japanese language and the second carrying English subtitles and covering wide ranging cultural practices in Japan — for example, regional cuisine, the fishes consumed by Japanese, where to repair broken home appliances and personal items in cities. (Some television sets can receive the programmes simulcast in English.) *Japan Hour* had an audience rating of three per cent. The other two one-hour programmes were drama series, broadcast in Japanese with English subtitles, both with ratings of two per cent. In addition to these regular programmes, there were occasional programmes of Japanese films and cultural documentaries in the 'foreign language' programmes on the same channel.

The non-prime or graveyard hours of much of the broadcast in the main Chinese channel, and the low ratings of prime time programmes on TV12 were indicative of the absence of popular support, signalling the absence of Japanese cultural in-roads into the most popular entertainment medium for Singaporeans. Indeed, the prime time programmes were there on TV12 only because of substantial Japanese corporate sponsorship.

The last truly popular Japanese drama series was *Oshin*, screened in the 1980s, first in Mandarin and again in English. The 'familialism' of this series had tremendous appeal and most young Singaporeans can still recall their weeping mothers and grandmothers in front of the television; indeed, *Oshin* has a singular place in the representation of the best of Japanese television drama or the worst cliché soap opera, depending on the age and gender of the audience in question. The space for similar genres of 'family' drama in Chinese broadcasts has been usurped by a seemingly endless supply of Taiwanese series which dramatise the excesses of Confucian ethics in Chinese families, broadcast every Saturday and Sunday in the early evenings, between six to eight o'clock, with high audience ratings.

The popular music scene in Singapore may be divided into Chinese and English pop, entirely dominated by foreign imports, despite the laments of local musicians. The former is carried by Hong Kong and Taiwan artistes and the latter by US and British musicians. Until the mid-1980s, Singapore was a relatively small market for Chinese pop music. The scene was seriously affected by the government's banning of the use of Chinese dialects in the broadcast media of television and radio. This was part of the government's strategy to 'integrate' the Chinese population, which were supposedly divided by their different mutually incomprehensible dialects, through a common language, Mandarin. In the process, the dominant presence of Cantonese pop music, or Canto pop, was replaced by Mandarin songs from Taiwanese singers.

By the late 1980s, saturation of the Hong Kong market and the opening up of the massive mainland China market induced many Canto pop singers to sing in Mandarin. This enabled them to sell their records and to perform on stage in Singapore, which was by then swelling with affluent youth with substantial spending power. Fan clubs of artistes from Hong Kong and Taiwan are now formed regularly and the entertainment columns of both Chinese and English newspapers cover the gossips about these singers (Soh, 1995). With these developments, Mandarin and Cantonese pop music are now part of an integrated market of Taiwan, Hong Kong and Singapore. Singers and song-writers co-operate freely across borders; for example, EMI signed on Singapore song writers for its stable of singers in Hong Kong and Taiwan (*The Straits Times*, 10 February 1996).

The expansion of Chinese pop music drastically reduced the potential pool of Japanese pop music consumers from among Mandarin-speaking students and young adults. The air-waves of local radio stations are by now almost completely devoid of Japanese popular music. This absence is largely because Japanese is not a common tongue in Singapore, although many of those who ply the tourist trade do possess the rudimentary skills necessary for their work. Judging by the display in local music shops, Japanese pop is consumed by both the expatriate resident Japanese population and a small group of Singaporean aficionados. However, there remains one nagging question: To what extent do Singaporeans realise that Taiwanese music is heavily influenced by Japanese music? Does the fact figure in their appreciation of Taiwanese music? These are questions that have to be resolved by further empirical research.

Any discussion of possible Japanese influence in mass media entertainment would not be complete without mention of the Fuji Television-TCS co-produced television talentime programme, *Asia Bagus* ('Asia is Good' in Malay). The weekly programme showcased contestants from different parts of Singapore, Malaysia, Indonesia, Taiwan and Japan. Winners were awarded with 'mini-compo' radio sets from Japanese manufacturers. The show was fronted by a Singaporean DJ/actor/ comedian, the zany Najib Ali. He completely dominated the show with his antics. He was assisted by a female Japanese compere and a male Mandarin compere from Singapore or Taiwan. The programme was staged and taped in Singapore and broadcast locally and in Japan. Contestants sang in any language they chose, from English to their national languages. Those who did not know English would not comprehend each other on the show. The Japanese content was limited to the female compere, who played second string to Najib, and contestants from Japan. Rather than conceptualising this show as an attempt to exert Japanese 'influence' on the rest of Asia, it would be more fruitful to think of it as Fuji Television's desire to promote a 'pan-Asianism' into Japan. However, given that the show was broadcast in Tokyo at one o'clock in the morning, its influence on the mainstream television audience was likely to be limited, so too its cultural effects.[4]

Food

If there were one area in which 'Japanese-ness' is visibly present in Singapore's public spaces, it is Japanese food. Indeed, counter to trends in other spheres of popular consumption, Japanese food is gaining in popularity, especially *teppanyaki* and *sushi*. There are several reasons for this. First, with the exception of *sushi* and other raw seafood, popular Japanese food items bear close resemblance to Singaporean-Chinese food. For example, *teppanyaki* is similar to Chinese stir-fried cooking, the only difference is that the former is fried on an open flat grill and the latter in a *wok*; *shabu-shabu* is similar to 'steamboat', where fresh food are cooked in a pot of boiling stock, at the table, by the diners themselves[5]; and finally, *yakitori* is similar to the Malay and Chinese *satay*, where bite-size morsels of meat are skewered on a stick and grilled. Given these similarities, Singaporeans often conceive of such Japanese food items as variations of their familiar palette rather than foreign; an instance of the indigenisation of the Japanese. The 'quotient' of consumption of 'Japanese-ness' is not high here although not entirely absent or it would defeat the purpose of eating Japanese food.

There is a significant shift in tastes, however in the consumption of raw food, *sushi* and *sashimi*, as seafood is very seldom eaten raw in Chinese, Malay or Indian practices. *Sushi* is now sold in convenient see-through plastic boxes in small shoplets, in small stalls at shopping centres and in the most ubiquitous supermarket chain. Quietly and seemingly suddenly, *sushi* has become street food, consumed as snacks particularly by the young and 20-somethings. These snack stands are owned and operated by Singaporeans and the *sushi* they sell uses local seafood, with a very short shelf-life of a few hours in the tropical heat. Hence, the quality and prices are in sharp contrast to those available at five-star hotel restaurants which use only imported Japanese ingredients, air-flown daily to Singapore and destroyed daily if not used.

The age of the consumers of what may be called 'street sushi' is significant. It is a generation which spends more time outside than at home and eats more meals, at irregular intervals and with varied contents. Not surprisingly, in Singapore, as elsewhere globally, the popularisation of *sushi* is part and parcel of the sprouting of Italian pasta outlets, French croissanteries and restaurants hewn from the cuisines of other Southeast Asian nations, such as Thailand and Vietnam. This expansion signifies the consumption of food as part of leisure and recreational activities. As these restaurants tend to be informal in character they are conducive to 'hanging out' for the young, which explains their popularity. This internationalisation of food has seldom, if ever, been incorporated and domesticated into the family kitchens and dining tables of Singaporeans. At home, the meal remains largely unaffected by internationalisation. Only where one or more adult members of the family has spent extensive amounts of time sojourning in another country is there a limited incorporation of food from the familiar country into the daily meal. Here, the incorporation of Japanese food is decidedly rare because Japan has not been a popular destination for either Singapore students or expatriate workers.

In the absence of domestication, consuming Japanese *sushi* remains the ingestion of the 'exotic'. It is a brief entry "into an existence far removed from the humdrum of everyday life" where "a safe but fulfilled return to everyday life" is guaranteed (Cooper, 1994:144). Eating *sushi* and *sashimi* is thus the briefest experience of an 'exoticised' Japan, particularly for those who have never physically been to Japan. This exoticism is intensified by the food's rawness, in contrast to Chinese, Indian and Malay foods, particularly overcooked stews and curries. So exoticised, 'Japan' and 'Japanese-ness', via *sushi* and *sashimi*, remain outside the 'cultural-self' of Singaporeans, to be visited at will and when convenient, ever so briefly.

Concepts and Tools

The above instances notwithstanding, the very visible Japanese economic presence in the retail sector and Singapore's status as a market for Japanese consumer products, must certainly have some influence on Singaporean everyday life. Indeed, there are such influences. However, in such instances Japan provides the concept but not the cultural substance in practice. There are two notable and illustrative examples in the consumption sphere.

First, with the arrival of Japanese supermarkets and department stores came the concept of 'one-stop' shopping centre; that is, a centre that provides services including post office facilities, ticketing services for cultural performances and restaurants, cafés and a food court. Until the arrival of the now defunct Yaohan in the early 1970s, the few supermarkets in Singapore, like Cold Storage and the defunct Fritzpatricks, had no facilities for any of these services on their premises or as extensions. Yaohan was the first to establish an extensive cooked food court in the basement level of its premises on Orchard Road, Singapore's premier shopping strip. Significantly, this food court initially sold only Japanese food items. Slowly and steadily these were replaced by local fast-foods, until there was no trace of Japanese food left at all. In turn, food courts are now not only essential service in all new shopping malls but are also found in large office complexes. *Sushi* and *teppanyaki* stalls are commonly found in these new food courts along with local foods; they have been recontextualised and embraced by interiorised Singaporean hawker centres, brought indoors.

Parenthetically, the ability to adjust quickly to local market conditions and Singaporean tastes is testimony to the Japanese companies' business acumen. The same adjustments to local tastes account for the earlier noted absence of Japanese contents in large Japanese department stores. Indeed the tastes of Singaporeans have sunk many foreign companies which were over-committed to their own cultural and consumer preferences. These include French companies, Printemps and Galleries Lafayette, the up-market Hong Kong department store Lane Crawford and the earlier-mentioned down-market American chain K-Mart. It appears that for Japanese companies, as for other successfully internationalised retail businesses, profit is always strategic and essential while selling 'culture' is always tactical and incidental.

Perhaps the Japanese concept with the greatest reach into the mass culture of Singapore is 'karaoke'. This trend has spawned a range of entertainment outlets from private homes to karaoke lounges and bars and cabarets. As family entertainment, karaoke has become a 'machine' for generating greater family sharing and integration; a family that sings together stays together, maybe. As commercial recreation, Chinese restaurants provide large open stages for all and sundry to perform to an audience formed largely of strangers, often unappreciative ones. In contrast, karaoke lounges provide private rooms for small parties who prefer to share either the celebration or the embarrassment of their voices or, in other cases, the physical presence of paid hostesses as well. Again, in this case, the Japanese are to be credited with the hardware of the karaoke machine and, perhaps, with promoting the practice of singing in 'public'. But karaoke discs and music are almost totally devoid of Japanese songs. Instead the discs used are often cheaply produced in Taiwan, Thailand and locally and the music ranges from Western pop to those of different Chinese languages, namely, Mandarin, Cantonese and Hokkien. If there can be said to be a substantive cultural influence from karaoke, it is the re-emergence of Hokkien music into Singapore from Taiwan. This dialect, like others, had been suppressed in state-owned broadcast media by the Singapore government under the campaign to 'encourage' all Chinese to speak Mandarin. Karaoke as 'private' entertainment, even when sung in restaurants, may escape official sanction. As the proverbial 'forbidden fruit', singing in dialects is popular because it provides the additional pleasure of transgression of government edict, an issue which will be analysed in relations to the consumption of movies in the next chapter.

At the conceptual level, in addition to serving the function of encouraging and assisting individuals to sing, as it does everywhere, karaoke has in a sense extended a common Singaporean street entertainment[6], called colloquially *getai* (Singing Stage). In this form, troupes of untrained amateur singers perform on a large temporary stage set up for the specific purpose in front of a street audience. Such performances were often a substitute for more traditional street opera and are staged generally during the anniversary celebrations of local deities of particular temples, *in situ*. Formally, karaoke is similar to *getai* and its popularity among some Singaporeans is reflected in the fact that individuals will practise specific songs at home until their delivery is polished and then find every opportunity to perform the same tunes in public. *Getai*, already in its throes of extinction in the 1980s, has been revived in part by the popularity of karaoke, as enjoying others singing is the flip side of performing oneself. Another factor may be the attraction of local television artistes performing at these events, as fees have become substantial enough to entice them to compete with, and edge out, the amateur singers.

In both instances, the concepts were derived from Japanese cultural practices and inserted into Singaporean everyday life. And in both instances the cultural substances that realise these concepts are non-Japanese. This distinction between conceptual and cultural influence is particularly useful in conceptualising the effects of Japanese technological exports, the 'no smell' Japanese goods, which are readily found in many spheres of Singaporean life. This distinction makes clear the possibility of consuming Japanese goods and concepts without 'consuming cultural Japan' (Ching, 1994).

Conclusion

It is apparent that in spite of its very observable presence in the economy of Singapore, not only in manufacturing but also retailing, Japanese cultural influence on Singaporeans is minimal. The cultural 'mainstream' of Singapore is visibly different from that of urban Japan. There is no equivalent of Harajuku in Singapore. There is no green or orange coloured hair among youth, partly because it is proscribed by strict school discipline. Among the 20-somethings, hair is tinted in shades of brown or copper. There are few who would dress in the layered fashion or highly individualistic styles of Tokyo youth who can be found every Sunday at Yoyogi Park. On the contrary, as analysed in Chapter 4, youth in Singapore are differentiated and divided by class lines, from middle-class English-educated to lowly-educated, working-class Chinese 'Ah Bengs and Ah Lians', and Mat Rockers, their Malay equivalent. Each group has its own fashion sense that is anything but Japanese. Both televisual and radio air-waves are dominated by American, British, Hong Kong and Taiwan imports; Japanese soap-operas were broadcast on the minor television stations from ten o'clock till midnight weekday evenings, competing with the very popular locally-produced Chinese drama series, nightly news and the best American sitcoms and crime series. They have usually received very low viewership. By early 2000, their viewers were likely to have switched over to Korean urban stories and Taiwanese youth romance series. In a country where movie going is very popular, Japanese movies are rarely found on the screens of the multiplexes. The only place where consuming 'Japanese-ness' is evident is the popularising of *sushi* as fast-food.

There are several possible reasons for the absence of Japanese cultural consumption. First, and most importantly, Japanese is not a common language in Singapore. Some facility may be found among those who are in contact with Japanese tourists, who have taken up the language for occupational reasons. Without language facility, the ability of Japanese culture to penetrate the daily life of Singaporeans and the latter's ability to absorb the influence remain very limited.

Secondly, the absence can be made even more apparent when compared to the success of American cultural influence on Singaporeans, in part facilitated by the ubiquity of English as one of the common languages among Singaporeans. More significantly, however, I believe that the relative success of American influence lies in the very presentation of American culture and products. In general, 'American-ness', whether it is New York sophistication, southern California casual or northern Seattle grunge, is sold as a way of life for the 'modern' individual. In this sense, 'American-ness' is ironically unethnically, unexotically and unremarkably 'marked' or 'unmarked' because it is the 'universal' modern. In emphasising the generalised 'modern individual', 'American-ness' is able to interpellate everyone who comes into contact with American cultural products. This ability enables 'American-ness' to be internationalised and American cultural products to form the core of much of life-style consumption around the world. On the other hand, 'Japanese-ness', like all other consciously 'ethnicised' cultures, can and will be consumed only by non-Japanese who explicitly identify with it and thus a desire to be assimilated by it. Others may treat 'Japanese-ness' as a liminal consumption, as in a theme party for only a brief moment of celebration, with depthless cultural appreciation.

Finally, specific to Singapore, the consumption of 'Japanese-ness' is increasingly reframed into a discourse of 'Asian-ness'. Japan has been mythologically transformed, by the ideological machine of the Singaporean government, into a space that is able to economically and technologically modernise itself without losing its 'traditions'; that is, without being 'Westernised/Americanised'.[7] In this ideological transformation, it is the cultural conservatism of Japan that is being eulogised. This conservatism is re-wrapped in Confucian terms and themes. It is the presumed depth of Japan's cultural resistance to the 'West' and its ability to maintain its cultural 'uniqueness' in the contemporary globalised cultural space that the Singapore government would like Singaporeans to emulate. Ironically, at this level, it is again 'Japan' as a concept that is to be consumed, not the uniqueness of Japanese culture, which by definition cannot cross cultural borders.

In conclusion, as a Singaporean colleague writes, "Japan remains a foreign and hard-to-understand country in Singapore, and is more so than many Western societies; the historical British colonial connection created an interactive relationship in cultural terms with the West — pre-existing global connections that are now part of the 'local' — that does not exist with Japan" (Wee, 1997).

Notes

1. An example of such focused analysis on Taiwanese youth can be found in Lii and Chen (1998).
2. The possible problems associated with 'ageing' population will not be a concern until 2030 or so.
3. Of the three, Issey Miyake has a small but dedicated following. For ethnographic studies of fashion shopping in Singapore, see Chua (1990, 1992).
4. For a detailed discussion of *Asia Bagus*, see Iwabuchi (1994). I have omitted here the popularity in Japan of Singaporean singer and song writer Dick Lee. Apparently, his popularity was precisely the appeal to the Japanese of his self-avowed, 'Westernised yet Asian' identity and his use of 'pan Asian' casts in his musicals; see Wee (1997).
5. Along similar lines, the Korean 'steamboat' has become popular with some Singaporeans. In this version, the pot for the boiling stock is made out of copper, and its surfaces can be used to grill meat, thus combining two modes of cooking in

one utensil. Some restaurants now serve both the local and the Korean versions without any additional effort, as the ingredients for cooking are the same.

6. It has been suggested that karaoke's role of abetting individuals to perform is similar to that of the 'geisha', whose task is not to perform but to provide the excuse for the guests to sing along; hence, karaoke has been referred to as the 'electric geisha' (Ueda, 1994).

7. For detailed discussion of Singapore and Malaysian governments' use of Japan as a model of Asian modernisation, see Wee (1997).

9

Taiwan's Future/Singapore's Past:
Hokkien Films in Between

Introduction

The rise of capital in East and Southeast Asia has generated a very large body of comparative work in economics and politics but little comparative analysis of contemporary cultures. Furthermore, while there is constant public discussion of the cultural implications of economic development, particularly the question, indeed fear, of 'Western' influence,[1] very little attention is paid to the very substantial cultural traffic and exchange between locations within East and Southeast Asia. This is perhaps because, as in Singapore, the cultural products that cross national boundaries in the region are subsumed under the sign of the 'same', i.e. similarly Asian, and thus do not warrant analysis. That is, of course, a delusion. The present chapter aims to disclose the differences in cultural formations within this presumed sameness through one instance of cultural exchanges between Singapore and Taiwan,[2] movies that use a language that the two locations share, namely Hokkien.

Owing to the process of migration from China to Taiwan that began in the early seventeenth century (Chen, 1980), the 'local' language of Taiwan, excluding the aboriginal population, is that of Fujian province, in the southeast of present People's Republic of China. The language spoken in this region is known as Minnan 'dialect' in Mandarin. However, in their own phonic terms, both the province and the language are known as Hokkien. In Taiwan, the language has come to be known as Taiwanese (*Tai yu*), signifying the overwhelming majority of Hokkien speakers on the island.[3] Again, significant numbers of the waves of migrants from

156

southern China to Southeast Asia, in the early nineteenth century hailed from Fujian province. They formed the majority of Chinese immigrant population in Singapore, Penang in Malaysia and Manila in the Philippines. A Hokkien-speaking person, from either the PRC or any of the Southeast Asian Chinese communities, will have few problems, other than local accents and idioms, in conversation with a local Taiwanese. There is thus a common spoken language between the Hokkiens in Singapore and the majority of Taiwanese. This shared language situation makes possible a comparison of the different receptions of Hokkien cultural products in these two locations and provides an opportunity to challenge the earlier-mentioned delusion of similarity within Asian-ness and recover cultural differences in national boundary crossings.

Taking the shared language as the starting point, I am concerned in this chapter with the political positioning of Hokkien as a representation of and vehicle for the national politics in Taiwan and Singapore in the films produced in the respective locations. Two films, one from each location, will be subject to detailed analysis. A synopsis of the two films is thus necessary before the analysis.

The Hokkien Films: A Synopsis

For the purpose at hand, the Singaporean film selected is the financially very successful 'Money No Enough', a 'Singlish' — hence intentionally clumsy — translation into English of the Mandarin title (*qian bu gou yon*). The Taiwan film that is the focus here is 'Kingdom of Peace', the literal translation from Mandarin (*tai pin tian guo*), which was screened to a full house during the 1998 Singapore International Film Festival under its English title 'Buddha Bless America'.[4] I will consider the Singapore film first.

The narrative of 'Money' is a straightforward one about the trials and eventual financial success of three men, all good friends. One is Mandarin educated or, in the Singapore colloquialism, 'Chinese' educated (as opposed to 'English' educated). The other two lack formal education, and are illiterate, monolingual Hokkien speakers, with some facility in Mandarin, presumably picked up during primary school days, before they failed or dropped out. Like 85 per cent of contemporary Singaporeans, they live in public housing estates. When the film begins, the Mandarin speaker has a white-collar job, gambles and makes gains in the stock market, and confidently buys a large number of consumer durables, including a car (a most prized possession because of its exorbitant cost), all on monthly instalment payments. As the film unfolds, he loses his job to a younger man who is English-educated and studied overseas, his stock holdings collapse, vendors re-possess all his hire-purchase goods and his wife leaves with their only child. His successive attempts to secure a new job fail for want of an English education and other 'certified' skills, or in Singaporean parlance, 'no paper qualification'. He is left with an empty flat; fortunately for him the public housing authority, unlike private financial institutions, does not repossess flats on account of financial difficulties of the lessees.

Meanwhile, one of his two friends, who is a building renovation contractor, is cheated of his working capital, which he had borrowed from a loan-shark. Predictably, he cannot pay the high interest on the loan and is reduced to being a fugitive from the debt collectors, whose only means of recovering unpaid loans is violence. The third and least able man works as a lowly 'waiter' at the local coffee shop and in spite of his advanced years still lives with his mother. His sole ambition is to have a girlfriend. At their most destitute, they pool their meagre means to set up a car-wash business, after hearing of a friend's success in this trade. One thing leads to another, they became successful in that business, which extends to owning an exclusive dealership for car-care products. With success, the educated one is reunited with his family, but the other two simply spend lavishly on women in karaoke lounges.

The Taiwanese film, 'Peace Kingdom', centers on the events that transform and rupture the moral basis of life in a farming village when it is commandeered for a military exercise by the US Army stationed in Taiwan. Throughout the entire episode, the villagers' disposition is one of incomprehension. The adults do not understand the point of the exercise, as they watched their tilled land being destroyed by tanks and bombs. Their attempt at protest is thrown into disarray by warning shots from the US soldiers. The only person who stands up against the destruction is a village widow who owns a cabbage patch. Determined to protect her vegetables, she camps out at her patch and literally stands in the way of the traffic of tanks and other military vehicles. The American military, out of frustrated incomprehension, diverts the tanks away from her patch. The other villagers, herded into the village school building and kept away from their daily routine of work, spend their days idling, gambling and drinking. The children, let off from attending school, do not realize the danger of the mock battlefield and run around freely amongst the soldiers, the tanks and the guns. This reduction to idleness leads to the corruption of the villagers. The adults are seduced into stealing everything they can from the military, from canned goods to army uniforms, by an outside Taiwanese agent who promises to buy the loot. They end up stealing things for which they have no use, such as a box of condoms stolen by an old man. The children hang out at the army camp looking for handouts from the soldiers, peer into a bar staffed with prostitutes brought in from the city, see disco dancing and hear rock and roll music for the first time, and fight over bullet and bomb casings, which they sell for cash.

A central narrative thread is built around an unemployed village teacher, apparently the only literate person in the village. He is fascinated by everything about the United States; its politics, its wealth, and particularly its science and technology, the 'knowledge' of which he obtains from newspapers. His younger brother has returned from the city after having lost some fingers (number unspecified) in an industrial accident. The severed fingers are soaked in liquid and kept in glass jar, and the unemployed teacher believes they can be sewn back in place someday. The arrival of the US military is just the opportunity he has been waiting for. So, one evening, the young man shows up at the entrance of the bar with his fingers-in-the-jar and tries to get the US soldiers to look at his hand and fingers. The soldier and a prostitute who meet him at the door thought that the fingers are props for begging and stuff some US dollars into his hand, to his consternation. The same happens when his 'knowledgeable' brother accompanies him to the military camp; however, this time, the brother feels insulted, screams that they are not beggars and throws the money back at the US soldier, to the latter's puzzlement.

The moral corruption of the villagers reaches its highest point when the wife of the unemployed village teacher begins to despise her husband's refusal to steal from the US military, reading his moral integrity as cowardice. In anger, he takes off with his brother to steal the 'biggest' loot the village will ever see. As night falls, they pull into the village two huge black metal boxes on a cart, to the great admiration of all.

The villagers open the boxes after much difficulty, only to discover two dead American soldiers, one black and one white. Admiration turns instantly into criticism of the brothers for bringing bad luck to the village. Bowls of rice and incense are immediately prepared to propitiate the spirits of the two dead soldiers. The possibility of burying the corpses in the village is rejected by the villagers for fear that the spirits will not make it back to the US and will thus visit the villagers in future. Thus, without any assistance from the others, the two brothers tow the coffins to the side of a road to be picked up by the military, which was by then shutting down its exercise, leaving the village. As the film draws towards its close, the village slowly returns to its previous life.

Positioning Hokkien

Both are in the main Hokkien films. However, in both films, Mandarin and English make appearances as appropriate through the characters in the films. It is the relative positioning of these three languages that is the concern of this analysis.

In 'Money', the dialogue between the three main characters throughout the film and most of their social encounters are in Hokkien. English makes a brief appearance on two occasions: First, when the Mandarin-speaking main character is fired from his job and second, after becoming successful, when he has to use English in his dealings with the manager of the car-care products company and in his public relations appearance in front of the media. The brevity of these scenes emphatically enhances the privileged position of the English language in the working life of Singaporeans. Mandarin appears in conversations at the coffee shop among and with friends of the main characters. Significantly, the hierarchy of social, cultural and economic power of the three languages varies inversely with the predominance of the languages in the film. English is hegemonic; this is signified by its dominance in the economic life of Singaporeans, as when the Mandarin-speaking character loses his job and is unable to get re-employment for want of competence in English. The significance of facility in Mandarin is less explicit and becomes apparent only after it is juxtaposed with Hokkien in the film.

The political position and representation of Hokkien is immediately manifested in the very genre of the film: a comedy. Laughter from the audience is in part a response to the slapstick antics of the characters. However, more significantly for the present analysis, laughter is also drawn from puns in Hokkien. An example is the repeated scene in which one of the regular female customers of the coffee shop orders her usual 'tea with milk', *nai chai* in Mandarin. The waiter character consistently shouts out the order to the counter, which is a common practice in Chinese coffee shops in Singapore but in this instance more for the amusement of everyone present (including the film audience, of course): "This lady wants *teh nee*", which in Hokkien could mean, "This lady wants her breast squeezed", since in Hokkien, as in other Chinese languages, milk and breast are the same word, and a slight shift in tone will change the sound for 'tea' to the sound for 'squeeze'. In addition to the puns, the 'pathetic' character of the Hokkien speakers is further portrayed in the scene featuring the funeral of the waiter's mother, in which his shameless sisters began to quarrel about the funeral costs through their (hilarious, laughable) false wailings and crocodile tears. Finally, Hokkien being the language of the low-life is driven home by the swearing and cursing of gangsters, their bodies covered with tattoos, who are the henchmen of the loan-shark. In these and other instances throughout the film, the use of Hokkien is crude, uncouth and bawdy, that is, intentionally 'low-class'.

A similar positioning of Hokkien as the language of the lowest social class, the marginally employed, the unemployed and the unemployable, can be found in all films produced in Singapore and released in the 1990s. In the film 'Mee Pok Man' (noodle vendor in Hokkien), which was very successful on the international film festival circuit, the noodle vendor lives on the furthest edge of the underbelly of Singapore, surrounded by Hokkien-speaking pimps and prostitutes. He is himself without voice. A similar situation applies in a film that was released in December 1999 and selected for showing at Locarno and other international film festivals, 'Eating Air'. The title is a clumsy translation of the Hokkien colloquial *chiak hong* (*chi feng*), which should be translated as 'Eating Wind', meaning 'enjoying leisure', particularly involving road travel, when one can feel the wind on the face. In this film, Hokkien-speaking youth get up late, stay out of their homes all night and in between ride around on flashy motorcycles and hang out in electronic games arcades. These youth are more irrelevant to than alienated from Singapore society.

It should be noted that in contrast with this positioning of Hokkien speakers as low-life, there have also been attempts in the entertainment media to 'romance' them in the generic character of what is locally called the 'Ah Beng'. Ah Beng and his female counterpart, Ah Lian are two caricatures of the Singlish-speaking Singaporeans who are 'adoringly' laughable to the middle-class English-educated writers and audience, for whom switching code from standard English to Singlish is a marker of 'authentic' Singaporean identity. The most successful construction of such characters is found in the very popular family sitcom, *Phua Chu Kang*, which features the comedy of everyday life in the family of a poorly-educated building renovation contractor, similar to the character in 'Money'. Not surprisingly, the show's popularity is based on the 'silliness' of the Phua and his 'Lian' wife, even as they triumph repeatedly over their commonsense-deficient, university-educated architect brother and his Westernised pretentious wife. Significantly, this romancing of the adorable and guileless main character has been disrupted by the behaviour of 'real' Ah Bengs in the movie house. A young lawyer who was watching a movie with his girlfriend was beaten up by four youths after the movie because he had told one of them to stop talking on a mobile phone during the show. This incident immediately led two English-medium columnists to remind their readers of the 'reality' of the Ah Bengs' fists (Tan Tarn How, *The Straits Times*, 8 January 2000 and Susan Long, *The Straits Times*, 9 January 2000).

In a country where 40 years of continuous economic growth has engendered a substantial middle class, and where individuals' social and economic positions are dependent on academic and professional achievements, Hokkien is being positioned, in representations and in social reality, as the language of those who have been left behind by the economic and cultural development of Singapore, laughably low-class and not a serious language for civil community. The use of Hokkien as the voice, and thus the representation, of low-class Singaporeans in 'Money' and other films, is therefore an exercise in artistic 'social realism'.

'Peace Kingdom' is also a Hokkien film in which American English and Mandarin also make their appearance through the appropriate characters on screen. However, in contrast to the Singapore film, in which the characters are able to conduct low-level communication in all three languages, in 'Peace Kingdom', the incomprehension of the villagers about all that has befallen them is intensified by the mutually incomprehensible languages of the villagers' Hokkien, the heavily northern-accented Mandarin of the Taiwanese military men and the English of the US Army personnel. The villagers, young and old, cannot make themselves understood because they neither speak nor comprehend American-English. The Taiwanese military personnel, representing the KMT army which retreated from mainland China, who act/intervene as translators/go-betweens between the villagers and the US army, are inept in both American-English and Hokkien and their Mandarin accent is incomprehensible to the villagers. The impossibility of crossing language barriers is the root cause of all the misunderstandings between the three different parties and the consequences are often rather humorous.

This mutual incomprehension is an interesting structuring of the politics among the speakers of the three languages; it allows all three to be placed on the same plane, without apparently privileging any one over the others in spite of obvious differences in power and influence. The mutual incomprehension enables the powerless villagers to subvert the intentions of the powerful US military machine; for example, the incomprehensible Hokkien protestations of the middle-aged village woman in the face of the tanks and soldiers forced the military machine to divert its progress and not only spared the life of the woman but also saved her lowly cabbage patch. The bewilderment of the US soldiers in this confrontation is quite humorously portrayed (a humorous version of the unknown man in front of the tank that rolled into Tiananmen in 1989). In another instance, US military personnel, upon discovering the thefts by the villagers, chase them into their school house, but find no evidence after ransacking the make-shift rooms in the building. The US military officer's statement of apology to the villagers is (mis)translated by the Taiwan military officer into a thorough scolding of the villagers for disgracing the Taiwan nation. Future infractions — they are warned — will be punishable by military court. It is not clear to the audience whether the Taiwan officer's mistranslation is intentional or for lack of understanding of the US officer's speech. The US military officer has no idea at all of what has happened to his apology, nor more importantly, of the feelings his mistranslated 'speech' have generated among the villagers towards the US military and US-Taiwan relations. (The US soldiers are supposed to be friends of Taiwan, in Cold War rhetoric.)

Finally, the US soldiers' exclamation of 'Hey you!' directed at villagers is misused by the villagers as a way of swearing at each other. In each of these instances, the mutual incomprehension of the three languages acts to frustrate the powerful US and Taiwan military officers, and ironically provides the avenue for the villagers' resistance to the former's power and oppression.

It is apparent that the political positioning of Hokkien, the common language among a majority of Chinese in Singapore and the overwhelming majority of Taiwanese, is different in its representation and hence, the representation of its speakers, in the social constructions of the two countries. This difference can be explained by the trajectory of Hokkien in the political histories of language in the two countries.

Hokkien: The Suppressed Language

Comparatively, the history of the politics of language in Taiwan is perhaps less complex than that of Singapore. In 1949, the Kuomintang (KMT) Republican Army of China, under Chiang Kai Shek, retreated to Taiwan after having lost the mainland to the People's Liberation Army of the Chinese Communist Party. Taiwan was seen as a province of China, and the link between the two traced to the seventeenth century, when the island was within the territory of the Q'ing dynasty before its colonisation by Japan. From the Taiwanese point of view, however, the retreating army was an invading army from the outside, specifically from the 'outside provinces' of China. Until today, Taiwan residents who are either members or descendants of members of the retreating KMT military, or who followed the KMT retreat to Taiwan are still known/labelled as 'people from outside provinces'.

Upon arriving in Taiwan, the KMT set out to continue the legacy of the 1911 Revolution, which overthrew the Q'ing dynasty and ended imperialism in China. According to Chun, the KMT "invoked, resuscitated and reinvented tradition; for the purpose of legitimatising its own vision of modern [Nationalist] society" and "felt compelled to define national identity in terms of race, language and history" (1994:51); namely, a 'Chinese' nation. Citing the works of Ernest Gellner (1983) and Benedict Andersen (1993), Chun suggests that, as in all nation-state building projects, a central prerequisite is universal literacy for the realisation of a 'national' culture through a "common colloquial language" (1994:50). In this case, Mandarin is the language for the realisation of a 'Chinese' culture in Taiwan. From 1949, Mandarin became the 'national' language (*guo yu*), the language of government and public administration, of state-supported education and of 'national' representation in general. Yet, as Chun argues, the KMT government's exercise in constructing a Chinese nation in Taiwan is an "attempt to *nationalize* Chinese culture (by making the latter a metaphor or allegory of that imagined community called the nation-state) where no such culture (of the nation) previously existed" (1994:54, emphasis in the original). As contemporary political agitation for Taiwan independence shows, this attempt has had at best limited success, despite lasting more than 50 years.

From the point of view of the Hokkien-speaking Taiwanese, the imposition of Mandarin is an act of political violence and repression, inextricably tied up not only with the colonisation of Taiwan by the KMT but also with the ongoing claim of the PRC to Taiwan. Against this history of colonisation, the Hokkien language is an emotive rallying icon around which anti-KMT sentiments can be organised and harnessed. It is a political resource that can be invoked as the 'ethno-national' language of Taiwan and used to confer upon its speakers the status of Taiwan nationalists, in opposition to Mandarin, Chinese nationalism and the KMT. Arguably, according to the logic of nation-state building discussed above, invoking Hokkien as Taiwan's national language would appear to be less artificial than promoting Mandarin. Thus in contemporary Taiwan political parlance, Hokkien is symbolically elevated as *Tai yu* (Taiwanese language), and the most vehement Taiwan nationalists will speak no other language, although those who aspire to state power have little choice but to compromise and speak a mixed code language in their public presentations that contains both Mandarin and Hokkien. The possibility of invoking Hokkien as representative of Taiwan nationalism draws on the fact that at street level and at home, given its demographic dominance, Hokkien has never been under any threat of erasure. Instead, it has accommodated itself to Mandarin, leading many Taiwanese to switch and mix codes between the two languages in their everyday life, as well as in the mass media and in political campaign speeches. What this means is that 50 years of instituting the 'Chinese' nationalist programme is not without effects; the result is that both Mandarin and

Hokkien, as Taiwanese, have achieved common usage among residents in Taiwan.

Besides Mandarin and Hokkien, one needs to also mention the place of English in Taiwan. The language was introduced by and is thus associated with US military personnel, who were stationed in Taiwan in support of the KMT immediately after the Second World War and throughout the Cold War period. The English language is also taught in secondary schools. However, it is a language that does not feature significantly in Taiwanese everyday life. With the exception of those who have studied in tertiary institutions in Britain or the US, even university students who can read English competently are reluctant to speak the language. Indeed, it is a language less used in Taiwan than the Japanese language (as a consequence of the legacy of 50 years of Japanese colonialism). Many older, or elderly, Taiwanese can still speak Japanese fluently. Furthermore, some Japanese lexical items are mixed into Taiwanese conversational practice. However, one almost never encounters two Taiwanese conducting a conversation in Japanese. Both English and Japanese are present only at the margins of the Taiwanese public sphere and of daily life.

Given this history, the contemporary linguistic situation in Taiwan is thus one of equal predominance of Hokkien and Mandarin, in exclusive or mixed codes. In the daily life of the Taiwanese, English is specialised knowledge, for those with reasons to know it, but largely incomprehensible to a majority of the population.

The dismal fate of Hokkien in Singapore is also politically determined, in this case by the single-party dominant state of the People's Action Party (PAP). As mentioned earlier, the majority of Chinese migrants from southern China to Singapore were Hokkien speaking, with smaller groups of Cantonese and Teochiu speakers among others; 13 dialects were officially listed in the 1957 census of the British colonial government (Purushotam, 1997:32).[5] With British colonial neglect, the languages of instruction in the early schools set up within the Chinese immigrant community tended to follow the respective Chinese languages of their financers. However, in the early decades of the twentieth century, in response to the modernist movement in China, the language of instruction of Chinese schools in Singapore, and other parts of Southeast Asia, switched to Mandarin. Nevertheless, the different Chinese languages remained the languages of the streets and the homes. The importance of Chinese languages, particularly Hokkien, was driven home to then would-be Prime Minister, Lee Kuan Yew, in the early years of political mobilisation towards independence from British colonial rule. According to Lee,

> When I made my first speech in *Hokkien* in 1961 during the Hong Lim by-elections, the children in China Street hooted with derision and contempt. I was unintelligible. I was talking gibberish. They laughed and jeered at me. I was in no mood for laughter. I could not give up. I just had to make myself understood.
>
> (Purushotam, 1997:54)

However, as we have seen from the analysis of 'Money', Hokkien has clearly lost its political position and been relegated to the margin. Its displacement from the centrality of everyday life of the Chinese in Singapore involves a complex politics of language in the formation of a multiracial post-colonial state, a process not unique to Singapore but found elsewhere in Southeast Asia as well.

Immediately after World War II, Britain began to prepare Malaya, of which Singapore was a part, for political independence. After a series of protracted negotiations, Singapore was excluded from the Federation of Malaya, which became independent in 1957. However, it remained inconceivable for the emerging political leaders of all political leanings to imagine Singapore as an independent island nation. The uncertainty was 'resolved' when, in the face of possible electoral victory on the island by the political left, the Malayan government initiated the formation of Malaysia, which would include Malaya and Singapore, along with Sabah and Sarawak, the two British territories in the island of Borneo. Malaysia became an independent nation in 1963. However, in a brief two years, Singapore would leave and became the independent island state that had been until then inconceivable; *realpolitik* had triumphed over political imagination.

During this period of entry into nationhood, the political positioning of the different languages of the resident population was a constant source of concern in the imagining of a new nation. The desire to be part of Malaya and later the reality of becoming part of Malaysia led to the adoption of Malay as the 'national' language. Within the Chinese community, the positions of the different languages was resolved in 1956 by the first elected assembly, which agreed to adopt Mandarin as the language of Chinese education, as was already the common practice in Chinese schools, regardless of the languages spoken at home. With separation from Malaysia, and a demographic dominance of more than 70 per cent, the possibility of adopting Mandarin as the 'national' language for Singapore was mooted by various segments of the Chinese population. This was resisted by the newly-independent government, in spite of its dependence on Chinese electoral support, because of the perceived hostile geopolitical environment in Southeast Asia, which would not accept the establishment of a 'Chinese' state with equanimity. Instead, a system of four official languages was instituted; namely, Mandarin, Malay, Tamil, the south Indian language prevalent among Indian residents, and English.

English continued to be dominant in the business of government and public administration and was further entrenched by political independence. Singapore, without any natural resources, would have to make its way in the global economy where facility with English would be a necessity. Economic realism was evident in the continuous expansion of enrolment in English-medium schools at the expense of those using the other three languages. For example, in 1965, the year of independence 61 per cent of Chinese children registering for entry to primary education chose English-medium schools (Purushotam, 1997:65). To allay the apprehension of the different racial groups and to gain political support for the government, a second-language policy was introduced, in which all students were compelled to take their respective 'ethnic' language, which meant Mandarin for the Chinese students. This 'bilingual' education policy had evolved from a multilingual education system into the present 'national' system in which the primary medium of instruction is English, with the other three languages as compulsory school subjects for their respective students. The dominance of English is complete, disadvantaging all who are not fluent in it with (irregardless of their facility in the other languages). In this way Mandarin, along with other second languages, has been displaced. Learning Mandarin has come to be treated by some students and their parents as an inconvenience, if not an obstacle, to educational achievement.

Ironically, difficulties with instituting the learning of Mandarin in school became the direct cause of further displacement, and subsequent suppression, of other Chinese languages, including Hokkien. In 1978, a study by the Ministry of Education discovered that the bilingual education system was not working among Chinese students because their competence in either language remained seriously deficient after completion of primary education, creating great wastage of money and human resources. It was discovered that learning Mandarin was like learning a new language to Chinese students, who were overwhelmingly speaking other Chinese languages at home. Thus, in practice, Chinese students entering school were coping with three languages — home Chinese, Mandarin and English. It was argued that the learning of Mandarin in school would be greatly facilitated if it were spoken at home. The government, with the support of the Chinese organisations, initiated the 'Speak Mandarin' campaign in 1979. One month every year was designated Speak Mandarin Month, and during this time the city was bombarded with posters and other public messages promoting Mandarin. Furthermore, other Chinese languages, marginalised as 'dialects', were banned from all public broadcast media; all imported programmes from Hong Kong and Taiwan have since been dubbed into Mandarin from Cantonese and Hokkien, respectively. The consequence, after 20 years, is that Hokkien, along with all other Chinese languages, has become a language spoken by those who have never received a formal education and/or those who did not make the grade in the highly-competitive bilingual education system. It is thus reduced to a language of the lowest-educated section of the working class and the illiterate. The linguistic hierarchy, in order of economic and political advantages, is thus English, Mandarin and Hokkien, as depicted in the film, 'Money'.

The different trajectories of state formation in Singapore and Taiwan display two different political displacements of Hokkien by Mandarin as the language of the 'Chinese'. The displacement of Hokkien in Taiwan has not been altogether successful. One sees this in the ubiquitous use of Hokkien in every sphere of social life, including politics, where Hokkien idioms and popular songs are adopted as campaign slogans and theme songs. Hokkien is even being revived and elevated to the status of a national language, in the name of Taiwan nationalism against the PRC. This tying of the language to a Taiwan-nation, instead of a Chinese-nation, guarantees the continuing relevance of the language in Taiwan. In contrast, in Singapore, without any educational infrastructure support, Hokkien is a dying language.

Among Singaporeans who are below 25 years of age, the Chinese language used is Mandarin while facility in Hokkien is either non-existent or very rudimentary, reduced to occasional words for emphatic expression. At home children are increasingly unable to converse with grandparents who are exclusively Hokkien speaking, and the aged are being coerced into speaking Mandarin rather than the young learning Hokkien, reversing any Confucian notion of venerating the elder.

Consumption of Hokkien Films in Singapore

The fateful trajectories of the Hokkien language obviously determine the different political positioning of the language in films produced in Taiwan and in Singapore, as demonstrated above. One would expect, therefore, that as Hokkien films cross national boundaries from Taiwan to Singapore and vice versa, the reception and consumption of these films would be significantly determined by local political history and the contemporary cultural configuration of the audience. The respective receptions of films exchanged between the two locations are issues that warrant cultural analysis. For this occasion, I will restrict myself to the reception/reading of Taiwanese films in Singapore.

After a lapse of about 20 years when not a single movie was made in Singapore, movie making began to emerge again in the early 1990s. One common element of films made during this period is the depiction of the under-belly of what is commonly viewed as the most successful economies in Asia; almost all the films made during the decade feature marginal, poor, working class and alienated Singaporeans, individually or in groups, a situation that will be discussed in the next chapter. Among the more commercially successful films are those that use Hokkien predominantly in the dialogue; among the most successful of these is the film 'Money'. At the time of its release, it was the highest grossing film ever made in Singapore, even edging out the box office take of the Hollywood blockbuster, 'Titanic'. It drew large audience attendances in cineplexes in public housing estates, including individuals who seldom go to movies. One of the reasons is that the film depicts and reflects the daily life of the lower-middle income housing estate residents themselves.

It was one of the very first occasions that Hokkien speakers could see their 'self-representation' on the big screen, since the 1977 ban of Chinese dialects from mass media. Indeed, many Singaporeans were openly amazed by the fact that a made-in-Singapore Hokkien film was allowed to be screened in movie houses. Politically, the significance of this film in bringing the banned Hokkien language to the big screen was arguably greater than the obvious critical theme of emerging class inequalities. It staged a 'return of the repressed' that brought pleasure to Hokkien speakers; the viewing pleasure was the more intense because it was done in the suppressed language, their language. However, this pleasure was, ironically, also at their own expense because of the depictions of the 'crudeness' of illiterate Hokkien speakers and their generally being the butt of slapstick antics and jokes. Such doubled pleasure constitutes a frame within which Singaporean audiences view Hokkien films, a frame that can be shown to be at work in their viewing of Hokkien films imported from Taiwan or elsewhere.

Taking the film 'Peace Kingdom', what comes through to the audience is a 'comedy' of errors that arise out of (i) the mutual incomprehension of the three languages, Hokkien, northern-accented Mandarin and American-English, and (ii) the 'ignorance' of the monolingual Hokkien-speaking villagers. In Singaporean colloquial terms, the villagers would be 'hill tortoises' (*suanh goo; san kwui* in Mandarin). Thus, the widow who successfully diverts the tanks and soldiers is hilarious with her screaming and stubbornness; the severed fingers in a jar are laughable because they display such ignorance of scientific knowledge; the dragging home of the refrigerated metal-coffins is funny because of ignorance and the subsequent attempt to propitiate the spirits of the US soldiers is laughable for its superstitious nonsense; and the adoption by the boys of 'Hey you!' as 'swear' words is laughable to anyone who understands English. Such are the ways of the illiterate monolingual Hokkien speakers who inhabit the margin of a highly-competitive, highly-skilled and highly-professionalised urban economy that is well integrated into global capitalism.

Undoubtedly, there are Taiwanese who see the 'comedy' in these scenes. However, the episodes are more likely to be seen as 'tragic-comic', with greater empathy for the multiple ways in which the moral life of the village is invaded and trampled upon by the US-KMT military machinery, within the complex politics of contemporary Taiwan nationalism and the KMT 'Chinese' nation. The highly urban perceptual horizon of Singaporeans has no purchase on life in a rural community. The very stable political condition, laced with rhetorical anti-Westernism, itself a refracted contemporary expression of a colonialism that is externalised, offers Singaporeans no access to the sentiments of internal colonisation of the Hokkien villagers by the KMT mainlanders and their US allies. The vehicle by which this politics is carried, namely the juxtaposition of the mutual incomprehensibility of the three languages, is likely to be lost upon the Singaporean audience. The nuances of these laughable scenes as reflections of resistance, rural innocence and sympathy for Taiwan independence have little resonance with the Singapore audience.

Yet ironically, in a country in which the educated and successful speak only English and Mandarin in all social transactions, including at home, the marginalisation and suppression of Hokkien and its speakers is a process of internal colonisation that is even more violent than the suppression in Taiwan under the KMT. For whereas it is possible to raise Hokkien to the status of a language of political protest and subversion, to the status of the language of ethno-nationalism in Taiwan, Hokkien speakers in Singapore are condemned to a slow but certain silencing. Their absence of voice and speech ensures an eventual erasure of their histories from the collective memory of the Singapore nation because their past and participation in local history can no longer be communicated fully, as each successive generation of the young becomes progressively more incompetent in the language. The return of the repressed language through an occasional Hokkien film marks its demise as all the more tragic, as fewer and fewer Singaporeans are able to understand the films in their totality for want of language competence, no matter where the film is produced.

Conclusion

This essay attempts to initiate a direction of comparative cultural analysis among East and Southeast Asian countries, beyond the dominance of comparative studies of the economy and formal political processes. The shared presence of Hokkien as the language of the Chinese majority in Taiwan and Singapore provides a privileged opportunity to demonstrate the fruitfulness of the comparative analysis of the cultural traffic between these locations via various media, of which film is one. The difference in the current position of Hokkien in the two places tells us much about cultural politics in their respective histories and the future trajectories of the state formation process. If it is possible still to address Hokkien-speaking Taiwanese as 'Chinese', then the different fates of Hokkien in the two locations are manifestations of the different ways of 'doing' Chineseness, giving the lie to claims of a single 'Cultural China', an idea fashionable among some in the globally-dispersed overseas Chinese communities.

Notes

1. The most comprehensive series of work assessing the different aspects of the rise of capital in Asia is the six volume *New Rich in Asia Series*, published by Routledge.
2. In the case of Taiwan, due to its Japanese colonial past, the influence of Japanese culture on Taiwan has been a focus of interest among cultural studies writers, see for example Ching (1994), Lii (1998) and Chen (2000).
3. I have left out for this particular discussion the language of the Hakka, who constitute a substantial proportion of the Taiwan population.
4. Many of the films from Taiwan are not released in the commercial movie houses, although they are frequently included as 'art' films during Singapore's annual film festival and are usually among the films that have sold-out attendance. Commercial outlets will pick up such films for popular release based on their sales record during the festival.
5. To date, Purushotam has provided the most comprehensive analysis of the politics of language in Singapore. This section is highly indebted to her analysis even when specific references are not provided.

REPRESENTING SINGAPORE

10

Cinematic Critique from the Margins and the Mainstream
(with Yeo Wei Wei)

Perhaps as a consequence of their living in a very small island-nation, Singaporeans often perceive that the People's Action Party government, which has ruled interminably since 1959, maintains its power in part through its intrusive presence in every aspect of social and cultural life. Its interventions in the minutiae of everyday Singapore create a sense of the state being literally everywhere; in any serious conversation about anything Singaporean, the government will creep in within a few turns of the conversation. It is therefore not surprising that, as in all authoritarian regimes, artists have a tendency to embed their work within quite explicit critiques of politics. Political criticism is common in the artistic spaces of Singapore, most explicitly in theatre performances. Indeed, it may be argued that it is precisely because conventional expectations of the mass media and organisations of professionals to play the role of public watchdogs of government cannot be met (since these institutions are stringently regulated by constraining legislation), that the artistic sphere, which includes theatre, literature, and films, has emerged as a 'privileged' space for critical reflection on society. And, one might add that the all-pervasive presence of the PAP government makes itself a relatively easy target for critique. Indeed, it is almost too good to pass up. This is true of the films of both Eric Khoo and Jack Neo.

Eric Khoo's debut feature *Mee Pok Man* was first screened at the 8th Singapore International Film Festival (SIFF) in 1995. *12 Storeys* premiered at the 10th SIFF in 1997. In 1994 at the 8th SIFF Khoo's short film *Pain* was shown and won awards for best director and special achievement in the Short Film Competition. But it was then banned from public screening.

It was at the 3rd SIFF in 1990 that Khoo was discovered as his short films came to the attention of festival programmer Philip Cheah.[1] Khoo's association with the SIFF bears notice for it provides a sense of the kind of director Khoo set out to be: not mainstream, not conventional, not commercialised. It seems apt that the festival that aims to expose local audiences to new and independent films, particularly those from Asia, should be the launching place of Singapore's most high-profile independent filmmaker. In a 1991 interview he did for *BigO*, an alternative magazine covering made-in-Singapore music and pop culture, Khoo reveals that from the outset he was self-conscious about where his art should be placed, or rather, of its displacement in the Singaporean mainstream: "What does have a place in Singapore? Commercialism? I don't know... If I went ahead and made a feature film, it will run for two or three days and that's it. No one is going to care. Maybe with the right ingredients, it will work. But not with the stories in my head. It won't with the public here."[2] Khoo's critique of society in his films is informed by this raw sense of marginality, of his art's place in the margins. The subjects in his films share the predicament of marginality with their director: even when their experiences seem extraordinary, the films in which these are represented leave the audience in no doubt that the characters and their lives belong to the fringe of society's concerns. In *Mee Pok Man*, Khoo's intention was to "steer away from the usual antiseptic type drama that is common here and inject a fragment of real life — dirty, grimy and gritty, yet ultimately beautiful".[3] His protagonists are socially misunderstood or outcast: a slow-witted young man, a *mee pok* seller in a *kopitiam*, infatuated with Bunny, an attractive prostitute in Geylang, Singapore's red-light district. The story takes a macabre turn when Bunny dies in the noodle seller's flat after he brings her there to recover from a road accident. The *mee pok* man's obsession with Bunny continues after her death and the film becomes a portrait of necrophilia.

Khoo's critique is oblique. No mention is made of any repressive administrative policies and thus no direct presence of the state is represented, except on the snowy television screen in the *mee pok* man's tiny flat, broadcasting the government's elitist policies on education. The public housing flat in which he resides inevitably points to the presence of the government, which takes much pride in its efficiency and efficacy in housing the nation — 85 per cent of the resident population lives in comprehensively planned high-rise, public housing estates. Public housing is the literally concrete reminder of the pervasive presence of the government. In a public housing estate landscape that suggests the omniscience of the state, and in a flat that is itself a part of that landscape, Khoo foregrounds a situation in which an unusual state of affairs is played out: Without seeking the permission of anyone or any authority, the *mee pok* man continues to love the dead Bunny. Individuality is possible even when the space that we inhabit is so tightly monitored and owned by the state, the film seems to say, driving its point across through extremes in characterisation and plot development.

The bleak landscapes in *Mee Pok Man* silently evoke a critique of certain aspects of Singapore's governance. Apart from the *mee pok* man's public housing flat, the film is set largely in Geylang, where Bunny and her pimp work. One of the ironies of the Singapore cultural and physical landscape is the fact that prostitution is very public, on parade even, in Geylang, an area of small roads and lanes running off both sides of the main trunk, Geylang Road itself. In this nest of lanes are rows and rows of low-rise terrace houses, many sporting the proverbial 'red lattern' every evening, signaling that they are open for business. Commercialisation of the sex trade beyond small brothels has also taken place. The area now has high-rise hotels that rent rooms by the hour, the hourly rates posted prominently at the entrances of these edifices. In contrast to the often understated presence of five star hotels, the better to suggest comfort and rest, if not prestige, the hotels in Geylang announce their presence with neon lights that trace the outlines of the buildings; the cold hue of the purple neon lights may suggest 'death' to the semiotically sophisticated but must signify something else to the hotel customers. In contrast, the main street, Geylang Road, is a very popular eating area for Singaporeans; cars double-park illegally on each side, groups of consumers, including families with young children, descend on the food stalls, and could not care less about (but are not oblivious to) the goings on in the lanes. The coexistence of businesses that satisfy different appetites, all in the same locale, is an implicit jibe in the film, present in the camera's shifts between *kopitiam* and *mee pok* stall to hotel bed and pimp's car. The point is resonant too in the relationship that forms between the food seller and the prostitute. The combination of food and sex brings to mind two aspects of Singaporean culture, one allowed freedom of expression and the other repressed and outlawed.

Singaporeans' love of good food is ubiquitous: the subject of sex is taboo (*Cosmopolitan* and *Sex in the City* were banned for many years, ostensibly for their overuse of the prohibited word). The Geylang setting in *Mee Pok Man* is obviously a very selective 'representation', perhaps embodying the director's questioning of certain double standards.

To the Singaporean eye, the apartment to which the *mee pok* man brings Bunny after the latter is hit by a car is obviously a one-room flat, the smallest built by the public housing authority. Such flats are intended for rental to the poorest segment of economy, very often the single, destitute, and aged. The general emptiness and the dilapidated condition of the surroundings of the block suggest that the building is largely vacated, very likely to be the case in reality. Such blocks of one-room flats are being progressively demolished; having existed past their use-by date, they are deemed dispensable by a nation that has economically arrived at First World status. This economic growth is almost always the backdrop of both international and local constructions of the Singapore Story as synonymous with Success. Analyses on Singapore by local writers often have success in their titles: *Struggle for Success* (Drysdale, 1984), *Management of Success* (Sandhu and Wheatley, 1995) and *From Third World to the First* (Lee, 2000). Against this triumphal discourse of independent Singapore, the intentional choice of combining various elements of the marginalised and the ready-to-be-discarded — the old flat, and all the characters in the film — is an intentional act of subversion, deflating the triumphalism by pointing to the underbelly of the nation where failures are too well hidden under the new affluence.

Khoo's next film *12 Storeys* follows the lives of several persons who live in the same twelve-storey block of public housing flats. The community consists of an assortment of types who jar, in varying degrees and forms of banality, failure, and indifference, with the state's triumphal self-projections, particularly in the 1990s, of global economic wealth, material success, and social well-being. The attraction of Khoo's vision is understandable — all the more so for audiences who do not have any visual knowledge of Singapore beyond what they see in tourist promotion materials, and this is perhaps one of the reasons for Khoo's winning accolades at international film festivals.

Like *Mee Pok Man*, *12 Storeys* suggests that Khoo has some sympathy for the lower classes, for failures in an increasingly class-stratified

Singapore. Again, the film is set in the physically and visually unavoidable Singaporean landscape of public housing estates, where all but the very wealthy live. Again, it is set in an older and poorer estate with flats of smaller size than the newer yuppie-oriented executive condominiums. The characters are all failures in one measure or another: among others, a group of middle-aged men who are apparently not gainfully-employed, collectively idling at the neighbourhood coffee-shop — a cultural continuity from pre-development days in the urban squatter *kampongs* (Malay for village); a bucktoothed Chinese hawker (played by Jack Neo with a set of false front teeth) who presumably could not find a Singaporean mate but married a mainland PRC woman who was lured to Singapore by his lies about his success in business and his Mercedes Benz; a family of three siblings, in which the eldest brother is a sexually-repressed school teacher who speaks proper English and interferes with the lives of his two younger siblings, one sexually-charged younger sister and a somewhat delinquent younger brother. The characters are representative types of Singaporeans who have fallen out of step with the Singapore Success Story.

However, the director's treatment of his subject seems more voyeuristic than sympathetic. The characters in *12 Storeys* are watched impassively by the camera, filmed with detachment to such a degree that the audience is given no entry to their thoughts, reflections and/or daily struggles. Instead, frame after frame delivers surface upon surface of impressions, showing nothing beyond the characters' manifest behaviours. Their stories are not told from the inside but represented in the most superficial ethnography. This absence of entry into their miserable lives, the absence of sympathy for their miseries, is most manifest in one of the characters in the film. A traditionally-dressed old woman sits in her flat, close to the ground on a very low stool, and does nothing throughout the film except to scold and curse her sullen and obese daughter, pushing the latter to contemplate suicide. The film generates in the audience a hatred for the meanness of this pathetic figure, without much sympathy for her bitterness, so much so that one is relieved when she dies even though her death leaves a gap in the life of her surviving daughter, reducing her already empty life even further into nothingness. The other characters in the film are presented with the same cold detachment. This absence of entry into the inner lives of the marginal people is, perhaps, the consequence of Khoo's own upper class background. Perhaps his fascination with the poor stems from a fascination with the Other rather than empathy for the Other, making his cinema disturbingly voyeuristic.

Although the title suggests an entry into the lives of the people living in those 12 storeys (through its pun on stories), the film provides a detached and objective view of the goings-on in the block, seeming to proclaim its value as documentary as opposed to feature film. The film's self-conscious representation of recognisable or distinctive Singaporean situations *for* Singaporeans is often painful to watch. 'Singlish' (the vernacular form of ungrammatical English mixed with Malay and Chinese dialect spoken by most Singaporeans but not acceptable in official public discourse) is exaggerated and *kopitiam* discussions seem stilted. The screenplay and the acting seem to relentlessly foreground the camera's representations as representation. Although this is probably unintentional, the lack of verisimilitude in the speech and the interactions of characters adds to the audience's detachment from their stories. Apart from his work in film, Khoo has also freelanced as a comics artist for *BigO* since the early 1990s.[4] Marvel comics have been an influence for Khoo since his childhood. The flatness of the characters in *12 Storeys* and the romanticisation of the outcast and the misfit in *Mee Pok Man* are features drawn from the world of comic-strips; the kind of sympathy between readers and characters that this medium avails is generated through the laying on of surfaces in which actions take place in quick succession and cause-and-effect appears as a linear sequence. The medium cannot achieve the representation of embodied psychological dramas. Its influence in Khoo's films is stark once recognised.

In contrast to Khoo's objectification of Singaporean lives, Jack Neo's filmic depictions of the same subject are attentive to subjectivities in the archetypal Singaporean struggle to make it into the world of wealth and status. Rather than ritualistically go through the routines of 'failed' lives, his characters strive to be part of the Singapore Success Story. The audience is not only given insights into the life-as-lived experiences of the marginalised in Singapore but also into the obstacles that are in their way as a result of explicit government policies. In the characters' confrontations with these policies, Neo presents a direct critique of the government; the popularity of his films, *Money No Enough* (1998) and *I Not Stupid* (2002), shows the resonance of his representations with the

Singapore audience who see their lives played out and their grouses voiced on screen.[5]

Widespread unhappiness with the government's wage increases for high-ranking civil servants and ministers is reflected, for instance, in *I Not Stupid* when a father tells his young son to study hard so that when he grows up he will be able to find a job in the civil service and earn a high wage. The boy's mother quips, "Better still, be a minister", meaning that he could earn even more as a politician in government. The government's policy of praise and perks for 'foreign talent', a phrase coined by the government in reference to expatriate executives from abroad, typically the United States and Europe, is satirised in the film when the Caucasian artistic director of an advertising company confuses the Hokkien term for his client's product, *bah kua* (barbecued pork slices), with *ah kua* (Hokkien for transvestites). Neo's films also contain jokes that make the audience recognise their flaws as a society and laugh at themselves. For instance, in *I Not Stupid* Jack Neo in his role as a copywriter poses a riddle to his colleagues: why is it difficult to catch fish in Singapore? The answer — "because fish in Singapore are like Singaporeans, they never open their mouths" — is both humorous and incisive in the way it points to a fundamental problem and trait of Singaporean culture: self-censorship. Humour with a social conscience is a basic ingredient in Neo's films *I Not Stupid* and *Money No Enough*. Neo has made it clear in interviews that his films are meant to provide more than entertainment for Singaporeans. He seeks to represent the real concerns of Singaporeans in their everyday lives: "As a director, I like real. Everything in my movies is real."[6] By reality, Neo means the problematic aspects of Singaporean social reality: "The problems have always been there and did not suddenly appear, for example, in our education system. However, people only take notice infrequently. I had hoped that *I Not Stupid*, by creating mass awareness, would get everyone, including the authorities, to take notice of current issues, talk about them more regularly and address them for the good of society. It was not my intention to poke fun at anyone. I just wanted to show reality as it is."[7]

The contrast between Khoo and Neo can be illustrated through a comparison of the theme of suicide in *12 Storeys* and *I Not Stupid*. The first story in *12 Storeys* introduces a young man who commits suicide; up to the point of his suicide and beyond, he remains a mystery, an unknown to the audience apart from the visual details of his person and his belongings, all randomly shown by the camera: a smoker, he throws up blood in the toilet and goes on to down a glass of vodka; he has a tattoo on one arm, and a room with empty hooch bottles and a bin full of crushed beer cans; he is asthmatic, using an inhaler at one point; he has a large CD collection, at least three G. I. Joe toy figurines, a Sony video camera, some comic books, and an Astroboy t-shirt that he wears when he leaves his flat to jump off the block. The suicide is a surprise to the audience — nothing in the preceding moments prepares us for this act. In fact, the man had left his flat and taken the lift up to the 12th storey with another character in the film, the overweight woman who lives with her endlessly nagging old mother. He had observed her putting down her shopping, looking over the parapet at the cars below, putting one leg over, then deciding against it, climbing back on to the corridor, and turning around to see him. He then walked away quickly. Nothing prepares the audience for what he does next — walking to the end of the corridor, he hurls himself over the parapet and lands at ground level, a sprawling body with a pool of blood under his head. A couple of frames later, the audience sees the spirit of the young man returning to gaze at his dead body. The spirit will continue to appear at various points of the film, all involving the large woman with whom the man had shared the lift moments before he died. These are instances where the spirit seems to empathise with the suffering of the woman, appearing by her side as she continues to bear her mother's barrage of verbal abuse; how or why this happens is left unexplained, as if it were but a cursory detail that the audience should take note of and then simply dismiss. These appearances are as random and banal as the event of the young man's suicide.

Suicide is not treated as a random happening in *I Not Stupid*; the contemplation of suicide as an option for escape by a child in the film reflects a specific problem of Singaporean society, driven for too long by rigid ways of evaluating achievement and indifferent for too long to the plight of those who cannot survive the unforgiving education system. *I Not Stupid* follows the lives of three primary school boys who have been streamed into the lowest academic ability class of EM3. Kok Pin is one of the boys, driven to consider killing himself after he is caught cheating in a mathematics test, a backfired attempt to get a higher grade to please his mother. All his efforts to master the subject leave him floundering and in despair. His mother, like many a worried parent in Singapore, is anxious about him, perceiving his lack of aptitude for the subject as laziness and lack of effort. Depressed by the thought of having to face his mother, and her anger and disappointment with him, Kok Pin wanders around until he sees a television news report about an eleven-year-old boy who jumped off a building because of his poor academic results. A defeated and determined look on his face tells the audience that he has decided to follow the poor boy's example. He goes to a block of flats, takes the lift to a high floor, takes off his shoes and prepares to climb over the parapet. Suddenly a group of teenagers chased by policemen run past him, one of them colliding into him and pushing him to the floor. A policeman mistakes him for one of the gang. When Kok Pin denies this he is questioned, "What are you doing here, so late at night in your school uniform?" To which Kok Pin replies in a small voice: "I came here to kill myself."

The sequence of events builds up suspense and tension in the audience who are sympathetic to Kok Pin, having seen how he tries hard to become a better student but fails every time, and having seen how his mother, taking the advice of her colleagues, canes him each time he cannot answer a mathematics question. Eventually Kok Pin's problems are solved when his form teacher sends one of his drawings to an international art competition and his artistic talent is acknowledged when the drawing wins a top prize. His parents are advised to send him to an art school in America where his talent can be properly nurtured — a plot development that serves to remind parents in the audience to value their children's individual gifts, and not measure them only in terms of academic results. The social context for the suicide scene is not the only reason for its relevance to the audience. It is also a comment on the expression of love between parents and children in Asian families. In Neo's own words: "What many *I Not Stupid* movie-goers might not realize, is that love is also a very important theme throughout the entire movie. When we scold our children, they feel unwanted and unloved, and this can be very damaging for their self-esteem. Kok Pin tried to end his life because he felt his rattan-wielding mother did not love him. Yet, it was love that drove Mrs Liu to cane her son, and she would feel terrible each time after she did it."[8] The attempted suicide scene foregrounds the need for better communication and understanding between parents and their children through the example of Kok Pin and his parents. The young man's suicide in *12 Storeys* seems to make a similar point at a later stage in the film when the dead man's parents speak to the camera about how they were unaware he had any problems. This is related to the audience in an interview-like segment; but with no prior knowledge of the young man's relationship with his family, or any actual acquaintance with him beyond his possessions in the flat, the audience remains indifferent to his death, and no wider implication or commentary can be drawn.

Unlike Khoo, Neo was famous before he made his foray into directing films. A comedian familiar to many for his impersonation of an old woman by the name of *Liang Po Po* (Granny Liang) on television since the late 1980s, he is a household name on Channel 8, the Mandarin television channel. In contrast to Khoo's self-conscious marginality, Neo keeps his foothold firmly in the mainstream. The target audience for his films is the Chinese Mandarin-speaking masses, primarily the same audience who follow his antics on television. Neo's two most successful films in terms of box office sales, *Money No Enough* and *I Not Stupid*, are both family-oriented comedy-dramas in which several of the male characters belong to the type of the man of the house who struggles to give his family a better life in material terms. These characters, typically middle-aged and married, are non-English-educated Chinese whose careers are either stalled or destroyed by English-educated competitors. In *Money No Enough*, the character played by Jack Neo is a Chinese-educated non-graduate who loses his job of many years to a younger man who has just returned from the West with a university degree; in *I Not Stupid*, the company that the character played by Jack Neo works for loses a major advertising contract to a firm headed up by a newly-appointed Caucasian artistic director. In the first instance, the economic and political dominance of English is disclosed, the result of intentional national language and education policies, along with the marginalisation of the non-English speaking. In the second film, in addition to the domination of English, the government's explicit statements that 'foreign talents' are needed to fuel the local economy is clearly the target of criticism. "*Angmoh*'s [Caucasian] idea is always very special", says the client of the advertising firm in the film, echoing what many Singaporeans have been told by the government in justification of its policy of using higher wages to attract foreign talent.

I Not Stupid raises the question of prioritising English not only through the pressures upon the Chinese-educated at the workplace, but more centrally, through the stresses of the education system and its evaluation of children based on their results in English and mathematics. Children who cannot master two languages — English plus the language of the student's father's ethnic group — and other substantive subjects such as mathematics are considered to be 'gone cases' to use a colloquial expression, as they will most likely end up in industrial training for low-end blue collar work at the Institute of Technical Education, its acronym ITE colloquially spelt out as signifying 'It's The End'. The criticisms of existing systems and institutions of political and social life in Neo's films are commonplace to Singaporeans. Consequently, when such criticisms are screened, the audience's pleasure is understandable; a significant part of the comedy in both films rides on the audience's familiarity with the cuts against the government on the screen.

An additional critical commentary is embedded in the intentionally poor translation of the titles of the films from Mandarin Chinese into English: *Money No Enough*, is an ungrammatical translation of the Mandarin Chinese title, *Qian bu gou yong* (literally translated it says: "the money I/we have is insufficient for expenses") and *I Not Stupid* is a translation of the Mandarin title, *Xiao hai bu ben* (literally translated it says: "Children are not stupid"). The translated titles would be readily recognised by locals as Singlish. This is a political act in itself as there is explicit government injunction against the use of Singlish in the mass media.

In addition to the use of Singlish, Hokkien is extensively used in the dialogue of both films. This again defies the ban on the use of Chinese dialects, which has been in place since the early 1970s. The ill-conceived government policy to 'Mandarinise' the local Chinese population by erasing the use of Chinese dialects in mass media, with no concern at all for the fact that a significant proportion of the older population have had no formal education and are incapable of understanding or speaking Mandarin, has resulted in the severing of intergenerational communication and the marginalising of dialect speakers. The extensive use of Hokkien in the film not only discloses the continuing presence of dialect speakers but also allows them to have a voice in mass media for the first time in almost 30 years. The politics of suppression of Hokkien and other Chinese languages and the exclusive promotion of Mandarin has already been commented on in the previous chapter. So too was the place of *Money No Enough* in breaking the ban and the viewing pleasures it generated; the jokes on the government and its policies told in dialect double the audience's pleasure, showing once again Neo's ability to strike a chord with Singaporeans.

We have therefore two critical takes in the filmic representation of Singapore to Singaporeans. One uses a cold and objective, perhaps analytic, lens, distant and unsympathetic to those who have fallen out of the 'success net'; the other is an almost insider's view, with heart, eliciting sympathies from the audience for the obstacles which the characters have to overcome in their struggle to join the economically successful. In the first case, the 'reality' of the marginalised is portrayed without any letting up, but also with a certain degree of romanticisation; in the latter, the struggling individuals find happy endings in relative wealth and success. In this sense, Neo is unable to sustain the trajectory of his criticisms and can be said to have appropriated himself into a version of the 'success' myth — striving and hard work will produce results eventually — thereby letting the government and its administrative structures off the hook; while Khoo is more unrelenting in his portrayals of the marginalised, refusing entry into the system for them as perhaps he himself is determined to remain 'alternative' as a director.

That Neo has let the system off the hook was made apparent when the politicians of the ruling party appropriated *I Not Stupid* by endorsing its supposed message regarding children's education. The Minister of Education endorsed the film on the basis of its criticism of parents who put excessive pressure on their children to perform well at school. The Prime Minister, in his most important annual speech to the nation, the National Day Rally of 2002, jokingly said that his wife saw the film three times and that Neo should be given a national cultural medallion, an honour reserved for individuals with a track record of extraordinary artistic achievements. In a political and cultural context where the ruling government is desperately trying to engender 'creativity' — supposedly a much needed quality in the so-called knowledge-based economies of high-technology, high-finance and bioscience — Neo has become the national icon of creativity and success. For he is someone who was Mandarin Chinese speaking, never went to university, learned his drama and acting skills during his stint in compulsory military service and despite all odds has emerged as a leading comedian and film director. This iconic status is affirmed by his apparently bankable image in advertisements: he endorses a brand of air-conditioners on television saying "I not stupid — that is why I use this brand" and the same image has appeared on posters printed on the sides of taxis and buses. The success of the film has also led to the creation of a spin-off television series (also called *I Not Stupid*) shown in a primetime slot on Saturday evenings. Although Neo merely acts in the series with the television station responsible for directing and scriptwriting, the repetition of dialogue and scenes from the film creates a sense of *déjà vu* in the audience, not to mention an ever-increasing sense of disappointment with Neo for allowing the essence of his film to be diluted in this fashion.

Notes

1. It was the first time that Singaporean short films were shown alongside short films from Japan, Korea, and the Philippines. Since then the screening of local short films has become an integral and important part of the SIFF. See Jan Uhde and Yvonne Ng Uhde (2000).
2. "Eric Khoo: Dude in Toyland", *BigO*, no. 63 (March 1991): 29.
3. The 8th SIFF catalogue, p. 25.
4. Khoo (1989) is also the author of a graphic novel.
5. Jack Neo acted in and co-wrote the screenplay of *Money No Enough*, directed by Tay Teck Lock. He also did not direct his next film *Liang Po Po — The Movie* (1999), directed by Teng Bee Leng. Spurred on by the success of these two films, Jack Neo took on the mantle of director in his next film project, *That One No Enough* (1999), a box-office flop.
6. *Time Magazine* (8 April 2002), Vol. 159(13).
7. *SMA News* (April 2002), Vol. 34(4).
8. *Ibid.*

References

Amies, H. (1973), 'What makes fashion?' in G. Willis and D. Midgley (eds.), *Fashion Marketing.* London: Allen and Unwin, pp.341–56.

Anderson, B.O'G. (1993), *Imagined Communities: Reflections on the Origin and Spread of Nationalism.* London: Verso.

Anderson, E.N. (1988), *The Food of China.* New Haven: Yale University Press.

Ang, Fu Sheng, Ian Low Chin Narn & Jason Koo Kiat Whye (1995), 'Youth at McDonald's', in Lily Kong & Doreen Goh (eds.), *Social Compass.* Faculty of Arts and Social Sciences, National University of Singapore, pp.69–74.

Ang, I. and Stratton, J. (1995), 'The Singapore way of multiculturalism: Western concepts/Eastern cultures', *Sojourn* 10: 65–89.

Appadurai, A. (1988), 'How to Make a National Cuisine: Cookbooks in Contemporary India', *Comparative Studies in Society and History* 30: 3–24.

——— (1990), 'Disjuncture and Difference in the Global Cultural Economy', *Public Culture* 2: 1–24.

Barthes, Roland (1972), *Mythologies.* New York: Hill and Wang.

Baudrillard, Jean (1981), *Towards a Critique of the Political Economy of the Sign.* St. Louis: Telos Books.

Belk, R.W., J.F. Sherry Jr. and M. Wallendorf (1988), 'A naturalistic inquiry into buyer and seller behaviour at a swap meet', *Journal of Consumer Research* 14: 449–70.

Benjamin, G. (1976), 'The Cultural Logic of Singapore's 'Multiracialism', in R. Hassan (ed.), *Singapore: Society in Transition.* Kuala Lumpur: Oxford University Press.

Bhaba, H. (1983), 'Difference, discrimination and the discourse of colonialism', in F. Barakerr *et al.* (eds.), *The Politics of Theory.* Colchester: University of Essex Press, pp.194–211.

Bloodworth, D. (1986), *The Tiger and the Trojan Horse.* Singapore: Times International Press.

Bourdieu, P. (1977), *Outline of a Theory of Practice.* Translated by Richard Nice. Cambridge: Cambridge University Press.

Brissenden, R. (1996), *South East Asian Food,* revised edition. Ringwood, Victoria: Penguin Books Australia Ltd.

Carroll & Brown Limited (1994), *Le Cordon Bleu Classic French Cookbook*. London: Dorling Kindersley Limited.

Castells, M., Goh, L. and Kwok, R. Y.-W. (1990), *The Shek Kip Mei Syndrome*. London: Pion.

Chan, H.-C. (1992), 'Democracy, human rights and social justice: which comes first?', *The Straits Times*, 22 November.

Chaney, David (1983), 'The department store as a cultural form', *Theory, Culture and Society* 1: 22–31.

Chen, Chi-Nan (1980), *Taiwan's Traditional Chinese Society* (in Chinese). Taipei: Asian Culture Company.

Chen, Kuan-Hsing (2000), 'The formation and consumption of KTV in Taiwan', in Chua Beng-Huat (ed.), *Consumption in Asia: lifestyle and identity*. London: Routledge.

Chia, Felix (1980), *The Babas*. Singapore: Times Books International.

Ching, Leo (1994), 'Imaginings in the Empire of the Sun: Japanese Mass Culture in Asia', *Boundaries* 2, 21: 198–219.

Chiu, S.W.K., Ho, K.C. and Lui, T.-L. (1997), *City-States in the Global Economy: Industrial Restructuring in Hong Kong and Singapore*. Boulder, CO: Westview Press.

Chua, B.-H. (1989a), *The Golden Shoe Building: Singapore's Financial District*. Singapore: Urban Redevelopment Authority.

_____ (1989b), 'The Business of Making a Living in Singapore', in K.S. Sandhu and Paul Wheatley (eds.), *Management of Success: Moulding of Modern Singapore*. Singapore: Institute of Southeast Asian Studies.

_____ (1990), 'Steps to becoming a fashion consumer in Singapore', *Asia Pacific Journal of Management* 7: 31–47.

_____ (1992), 'Shopping for women's fashion in Singapore', in Rob Shields (ed.), *Lifestyle Shopping: The Subject of Consumption*. London: Routledge.

_____ (1995a), *Communitarian Ideology and Democracy in Singapore*. London: Routledge.

_____ (1995b), 'That Imagined Space: Nostalgia for the Kampungs', in Brenda S.A. Yeoh & Lily Kong (eds.), *Portraits of Places: History, Community and Identity in Singapore*. Singapore Times Editions, pp.222–41.

_____ (1996), 'Culturalisation of economy and politics in Singapore', in R. Robison (ed.), *Pathways to Asia*. Sydney: Allen and Unwin, pp.87–107.

_____ (1997), *Housing and Political Legitimacy: Stakeholding in Singapore*. London: Routledge.

_____ (1999), '"Asian Values" discourse and the resurrection of the social', *Positions: east asian cultural critique* 7: 297–316.

Chua, B.-H. and Tan, J.E. (1995), *Singapore: new configuration of a socially stratified culture*. Working Paper No. 127, Department of Sociology, National University of Singapore.

Chun, Allen (1995), 'From nationalism to nationalizing: cultural imagination and state formation in postwar Taiwan', *The Australian Journal of Chinese Affairs* 31: 49–69.

Clammer, John (1980), *Straits Chinese Society: Studies in the Sociology of the Straits Chinese in Malaysia and Singapore*. Singapore: Singapore University Press.

——— (1995), *Difference and Modernity: Social Theory and Contemporary Japanese Society*. London: Kegan Paul International.

Classen, C. and Howes, D. (1996), 'Epilogue: the dynamics and ethics of cross-cultural consumption', in D. Howes (ed.), *Cross-cultural Consumption*. London: Routledge, pp.178–94.

Cooper, Dave (1994), 'Portraits of paradise: themes and images of the tourist industry', *Southeast Asian Journal of Social Science*, theme issue: Cultural Studies in the Asia Pacific, 22: 144–60.

Crawford, Margaret (1992), 'The world in a shopping mall', in Michael Sorkin (ed.), *Variations on a Theme Park*. New York: Hill and Wang, pp.3–30.

D. Howes (ed.), *Cross-cultural Consumption*. London: Routledge,

David, E. (1986), *Spices, Salt and Aromatics in the English Kitchen*. Harmondsworth: Penguin.

Devan, Janadas & Geraldine Heng (1992), 'State Fatherhood: the Politics of Nationalism, Sexuality and Race in Singapore', in Andrew Parker *et al.* (ed.), *Nationalism and Sexuality*. New York: Routledge, pp.343–64.

Dicken, P. and Kirkpatrick, C. (1991), 'Services led development in ASEAN: transnational regional headquarters in Singapore', *Pacific Review* 4: 174–84.

Douglas, Mary (1984), 'Introduction: Standard Social Uses of Food', in M. Douglas (ed.), *Food in the Social Order: Studies of Food and Festivities in Three American Communities*. New York: Russell Sage Foundation.

Drysdale, J. (1984), *Singapore: Struggle for Success*. Singapore: Times Books International.

Ewen, S. (1976), *Captains of Consciousness*. New York: McGraw Hill.

Ewen, Stuart and Elizabeth Ewen (1982), *Channels of Desire: Mass Image and the Shaping of America*. New York: McGraw-Hill.

Fairservis, Walter A. (1971), *Costumes of the East*. Riverside, Conn.: The Chatham Press/The American Museum of Natural History.

Falk, Pasi and Colin Campbell (eds.) (1997), *The Shopping Experience*. London: Sage Publications.

Fantasia, Rick (1995), 'Fast food in France', *Theory and Society* 24: 201–243.

Featherstone, Mike (1987), 'Lifestyles and consumer culture', *Theory, Culture and Society* 4: 55–70.

———— (1995), *Undoing Culture: Globalization, Postmodernism and Identity.* London: Sage.

———— (1998), 'The *Flaneur*, the city and virtual public life', *Urban Studies* 35: 909–926.

Ferguson, Harvie (1992), 'Watching the world go round: atrium culture and the psychology of shopping', in Rob Shields (ed.), *Lifestyle Shopping.* London: Routledge, pp.21–39.

Finkelstein, J. (1996), *After a Fashion.* Melbourne: Melbourne University Press.

Foo, S.M. (1995), *Paradox of affluence.* Unpublished exercise, Department of Sociology, National University of Singapore.

Foucault, Michel (1988), 'Technologies of the self', in L. Martin, H. Gutman and P. Hutton (eds.), *Technologies of the Self: A seminar with Michel Foucault.* Amherst, Mass: University of Massachusetts Press.

Friedman, J. (1995), 'Where we stand: a decade of world city research', in P. L. Knox and P.J. Taylor (eds.), *World Cities in a World System.* Cambridge: Cambridge University Press, pp.21–47.

Gellner, Ernest (1983), *Nations and nationalism.* Oxford: Basil Blackwell.

Gerke, S. (1995), *Symbolic consumption and the Indonesian middle class.* Working Paper No. 233, Sociology of Development Research Centre, Bielefield University.

Goffman, Erving (1959), *The Presentation of Self in Everyday Life.* New York: Doubleday Anchor.

———— (1971), *Relations in Public.* New York: Colphon Books.

Goss, J. (1993), 'The "magic of the Mall": an analysis of form, function and meaning in the contemporary retail build environment', *Annals of the Association of Geographers* 83:18–47.

Hall, S. (1991), 'The local and the global: globalization and ethnicity', in A.D. Icing (ed.), *Culture, Globalization and the World System.* London: Macmillan, pp.19–39.

Hart, D.M. (1993), 'Class formation and industrialization of culture: the case of South Korea's emerging middle class, *Korean Journal* 33: 42–57.

Haug, W.F. (1986), *Commodity Aesthetics.* Minneapolis: University of Minnesota Press.

Hing, Ai-Yun and Wong, Poh-Kam (1995), 'Impact of Industrial Automation on the Workforce in Singapore', in Hing, Wong & Schmidt (eds.), *Cross Cultural Perspective of Automation.* Berlin: Ed. Sigma, pp.285–31.

Ho, K.C. and Chua, B.-H. (1995), *Cultural, social and leisure activities in Singapore.* Monograph No. 3. Singapore: Department of Statistics, Census of Population 1990.

Ho, Wing Meng (1989), 'Values Premises Underlying the Transformation of Singapore', in K.S. Sandhu & Paul Wheatley (eds.), *Management of Success: Moulding of Modern Singapore*. Singapore: Institute of Southeast Asian Studies, pp.671–91.

Howes, D. (1996a) (ed.), *Cross-cultural Consumption: Global Markets, Local Realities*. London: Routledge.

—— (1996b), 'Introduction: commodities and cultural borders', in D. Howes (ed.), *Cross-cultural Consumption*. London: Routledge, pp. 1–18.

Huff, W. (1994), *The Economic Growth of Singapore: Trade and Development in the Twentieth Century*. Cambridge: Cambridge University Press.

Ibrahim, A. (1997), *Asian Renaissance*. Singapore: Times International Press.

Iwabuchi, Koichi (1994), 'Return to Asia? Japan in the global audio-visual market', *Sojourn* 9: 226–45.

Kahn, J. (1996), 'Growth, economic transformation, culture and the middle classes in Malaysia', in R. Ronison & D.S.G. Good Man (eds.), *The New Rich in Asia*. London: Routledge, pp.49–78.

Khoo, Eric (1989), *Unfortunate Lives: Urban Stories and Uncertain Tales*. Singapore: Times Books International.

Kim, S.-K. (1996), *The changing lifestyle and consumption patterns of Korean middle class*. Paper presented in the Workshop on 'Patterns Consumption of Asia's New Rich'. Asia Research Centre, Murdoch University, Western Australia, 9–10 September.

Kinsella, S. (1995), 'Cuties in Japan', in Lisa Skov and Brian Moeran (eds.), *Women, Media and Consumption in Japan*. London: Curzon Press, pp.220–54.

Koh, G. and Ooi, G.L. (1996), *Public policy and the Singapore Dream*. Paper presented at the Conference on 'The Singapore Dream: Private Property, Social Expectations and Public Policy'. The School of Architecture and Estate Management, National University of Singapore, 6 September.

Koh, Tommy T.B. (1993), 'Ten Values that Help East Asia's Economic Progress; Prosperity', *The Straits Times*, 14 December.

Kong, Lily & Brenda S.A. Yeoh (1994), 'Urban Conservation in Singapore: a Survey of State Policies and Popular Attitudes', *Urban Studies* 31: 247–65.

Konig, Rene (1973), *The Restless Image*. London: Allen and Unwin.

Kuo, Eddie C.Y. (1988), 'Policies and Strategies of IT Development in Singapore', in Dorothy I. Riddle (ed.), *Information Economy and Development*. Bonn: Friedrich-Ebert-Stiftung, pp.120–34.

Lai, Ah Eng (1995), *Meanings of Multiethnicity: a case study of ethnicity and ethnic relations in Singapore*. Singapore: Oxford University Press.

Lai, T.C. (1984), *At the Chinese Table*. Hong Kong: Oxford University Press.

Lam, Wai Ning (1991), *Fashion: Chinese ethnic clothing*. Unpublished academic exercise, Department of Sociology, National University of Singapore.

Lee, Chin-koon (1974), *Mrs. Lee's Cookbook: Nyonya Recipes and Other Favourite Recipes*. Singapore: Eurasia Press.

Lee, Hsien Loong (1989), 'The National Identity — a Direction and Identity for Singapore', *Speeches*, no. 13: 26–38. Ministry of Information and the Arts, Singapore.

Lee, Kuan Yew (1995), 'Need for Governments to Draw Lines between Right and Wrong', *The Straits Times*, 6 October.

_____ (2000), *The Singapore Story. Volume 2: From Third World to First World*. Singapore: Times Publishers.

Lee, N.P. (1994), 'Money culture and higher education', *Korea Journal* 34: 48–56.

Leidner, Robin (1993), *Fast Food, Fast Talk: Service work and the routinization of every day life*. Berkeley: University of California Press.

Leong, Wai-teng (1995), 'Consuming the Nation: National Day Parades in Singapore'. Paper presented at the Second ASEAN Inter-University Seminar on Social Development, 28–30 November 1995, Cebu City, The Philippines.

Levi-Strauss, C. (1973), *Tristes Tropiques*. Translated by John and Doreen Weightman. London: Jonathan Cape.

Lewis, G.H. (1990), 'Community through exclusion and inclusion: the creation of social world in an American shopping mall', *Journal of Popular Culture* 24: 121–36.

Lii, Ding-Tzann & Chen Zhao-Yong, 'Satellite TV and national imaginary: Japanese melodrama on Star TV as an example', *Mass Communication Research* 56: 9–34 (Chinese).

Lii, Ding-Zhang (1998), 'A colonized empire: reflections on the expansion of Hong Kong films in Asian countries', in Kuan-Hsing Chen (ed.), *Trajectories: inter-Asia cultural studies*. London: Routledge, pp.122–41.

Lincoln, Y.S. and E.G. Fuba (1985), *Naturalistic Inquiry*. Beverly Hills: Sage Publications.

Long, Susan (2000), 'Where Mr Cosmopolitan clashes with Mr Heartland', *The Straits Times*, 9 January.

Ma, Eric Kit-wai (1999), *Culture, Politics and Television in Hong Kong*. London: Routledge.

Mahbubani, K. (1998), *Can Asians Think?* Singapore: Times Books International.

—— (1993), 'The dangers of decadence', *Foreign Affairs* 72: 10–14.

—— (1994), 'Pacific Community: Fusion of East and West', *The Straits Times*, 17 September.

Mak, Lau-fong (1995), *The Dynamics of Chinese Dialect Groups in Early Malaya.* Singapore: Singapore Society of Asian Studies.

Mansfield, E. (1994), *Microeconomics.* New York: W.W. Norton and Company.

Mariam Mohamed Ali (1989), *Uniformity and Diversity among Muslims in Singapore.* Unpublished Masters of Art thesis, Department of Sociology, National University of Singapore.

McCracken, G. (1986), 'Culture and consumption: a theoretical account of the structure and movement of the meaning of consumer goods', *Journal of Consumer Research* 13: 71–84.

Mercer, K. (1988), 'Diaspora Culture and the Dialogic Imagination: The Aesthetics of Black Independent Film in Britain', in Mbye B. Cham & Claire Andrade-Watkins, *Blackframes: Critical Perspectives on Black Independent Cinema.* Cambridge, Mass.: MIT Press.

Miller, David (1998), 'Could shopping ever really matter?', in Falk & Campbell (eds.), *The Shopping Experience.* London: Routledge, pp.31–55.

Ministry of Labour (1995), *Profile of the Labour Force of Singapore 1983–1994.* Singapore: Ministry of Labour.

Ministry of Trade and Industry (1986), *Economic Committee Report*, Republic of Singapore.

Mizra, H. (1986), *Multinationals and the Growth of Singapore's Economy.* London: Croom Helm.

Morawetz, D. (1981), *Why the Emperor's New Clothes Are Not Made in Columbia.* New York: Oxford University Press.

Morris, Meaghan (1989), 'Things to do with shopping centres', in Susan Sheridan (ed.), *Grafts: Feminist Cultural Critique.* London and New York: Verso, pp.193–225.

Nagata, Judith (1984), *The Reflowering of Malaysian Islam: modern religious radicals and their roots.* Vancouver: University of British Columbia Press.

Oldenberg, R. and D.Bissett (1982), 'The third place', *Qualitative Sociology* 5: 256–84.

Oon, Violet (1978), *Her World Peranakan Cookbook.* Singapore: Times Periodicals.

Peretz, Henri (1995), 'Negotiating clothing identities on the sales floor', *Symbolic Interaction* 18:19–37.

Perry, M. (1992), 'Promoting corporate control in Singapore', *Regional Studies* 26: 289–94.

Prus, Robert (1987), 'Developing loyalties', *Urban Life* 15: 331–36.

Purushotam, Nirmala S. (1998), *Negotiating Language, Constructing Race: Disciplining difference in Singapore*. Berlin: Mouton de Gruyter.

Rahim Ishak, Lily Z. (1994), 'The paradox of ethnic-based self-help groups', in Derek Da Cunha (ed.), *Debating Singapore*. Singapore: Institute of Southeast Asian Studies.

Rajah, A. (1984), 'Au Ma Xae: Domestic Ritual and the Ideology of Kinship Among the Sgaw Karen of Palokhi, Northern Thailand', in P. Cohen & G. Wijeyewardene, *Spirit Cults and the Position of Women in Northern Thailand*. Special Issue 3. *Mankind* 14(4): 348–56.

_____ (1989), 'Commensalism as Practical Symbol and Symbolic Practice among the Sgaw Karen of Northern Thailand', *Southeast Asian Journal of Social Science* 17(1): 70–87.

_____ (1990), 'Orientalism, Commensurability, and the Construction of Identity: A Comment on the Notion of Lao Identity', *Sojourn: Social Issues in Southeast Asia* 5(2): 308–333.

_____ (1992), 'Transformations of Karen Myths of Origin and Relations of Power', in G. Wijeyewardene & E. C. Chapman, *Patterns and Illusions: Thai History and Thought*. Canberra: The Richard Davis Fund and the Department of Anthropology, Research School of Pacific Studies, The Australian National University, pp.237–76.

Rajah, A. and V. Sinha (1994), 'The Myth and Management of Tradition'. Paper presented at 'Our Place in Time', a conference on *Heritage in Singapore* organized by The Singapore Heritage Society and The Substation, 17–18 September 1994, Guinness Theatre, The Substation, Singapore.

Rajaratnam, S. (1987), 'Singapore: global city', in Chan Heng Chee & Obaid ul Haq (eds.), *The Prophetic and the Political: selected speeches of S. Rajaratnam*. Singapore: Graham Brash.

Reekie, J. (1975), *Traditional French Cooking*. London: MacMillan London Limited.

Ritzer, George (1993), *The McDonaldization of Society*. Newbury Park, Calif.: Pine Forge Press.

Rodan, G. and Hewison, K. (1996), 'A 'clash of cultures' of the convergence of political ideology?', in R. Robison (ed.), *Pathways to Asia*. Sydney: Allen and Unwin, pp.29–55.

Rodan, Garry (1989), *The Political Economy of Singapore's Industrialization*. London: Macmillan.

Rokiah, T. (1995), 'Credit and consumer culture in Malaysia', in T. Rokiah & C.B. Tan (eds.), *Dimensions of Tradition and Development in Malaysia*. Kuala Lumpur: Pelanduk Publishers, pp.203–236.

Rudolph, Jurgen (n.d.), 'Reconstructing Identities: A Social History of the Babas in Singapore'. Unpublished inaugural dissertation, Friedrich-Alexander University Germany.

Said, E. (1979), *Orientalism*. New York: Vintage Books.

Sandhu, K.S. and Paul Wheatley (eds.) (1995), *Management of Success: the Moulding of Modern Singapore*. Singapore: Institute of Southeast Asian Studies.

Sassen, S. (1991), *The Global City: New York, London and Tokyo*. Princeton, NJ: Princeton University Press.

Scruton, Roger (1984), 'Public space and the classical vernacular', *The Public Interest* 74:5–16.

Shields, Rob (1992), *Lifestyle Shopping: the subject of consumption*. London: Routledge.

Shun Lu and Gary Alan Fine (1995), 'The Presentation of Ethnic Authenticity: Chinese Food as a Social Accomplishment', *The Sociological Quarterly* 36(3): 535–53.

Simmel, G. (1950), 'Metropolis and mental life', in Kurt Wolff (ed.), *The Sociology of Georg Simmel*. New York: Free Press.

Sklair, L. (1995), *Sociology of the Global System*. London: Prentice Hall Harvester Wheatsheaf.

Sofer, C. (1965), 'Buying and selling: a study in sociology of distribution', *Sociological Review* 13: 183–209.

Soh, Seok Hoon (1995) *Fandom in Singapore*. Unpublished academic exercise, Department of Sociology, National University of Singapore.

Steele, Valerie (1996), *Fetish Fashion, Sex and Power*. New York: Oxford University Press.

Stephenson, Peter H. (1989), 'Going to McDonald's in Leiden: Reflections on the Concept of Self and Society in the Netherlands', *Ethos: Journal of the Society for Psychological Anthropology* 17: 226–47.

Stone, G. (1962), 'Appearance and the self', in Arnold Rose (ed.), *Human Behaviour and Social Process*. London: Routledge and Kegan Paul.

Suziela Yassin (1999), *Alcohol Use by Female Muslim Youth*. Unpublished academic exercise, Department of Sociology, National University of Singapore.

Tan Tarn How (2000), 'Come, so you want to fight?' *The Straits Times*, 8 January.

Tan, A.H.H. (1986), 'Singapore's economy: growth and structural change', in *Southeast Asian Affairs 1986*. Singapore: Institute of Southeast Asian Studies, pp.271–95.

Tan, Chee-beng (1988), *The Baba of Melaka: Culture and Identity of a Chinese Peranakan Community in Malaysia*. Kuala Lumpur: Pelanduk Publications.

Tan, Terry (1981), *Straits Chinese Cookbook*. Singapore: Times Books International.

Tester, Keith (ed.), *The Flaneur*. London: Routledge.

Tobin, Jeffrey (1992), 'A Japanese-French Restaurant in Hawaii', in Joseph J. Tobin (ed.), *Re-Made in Japan*. New Haven: Yale University Press, pp.159–75.

Ueda, Atsushi (1994), *The Electric Geisha: Exploring Japan's Popular Culture*. Translated by Miriam Eguchi. New York: Kodansha International.

Uhde, Jan and Yvonne Ng Uhde (2000), *Latent Images: Films in Singapore*. Singapore: Oxford University Press.

van den Berghe, Pierre L. (1984), 'Ethnic Cuisine: Culture in Nature'. *Ethnic and Racial Studies* 7(3): 387–97.

Vasil, Raj (1995), *Asianising Singapore: the PAP's management of ethnicity*. Singapore: Heinemann.

Wee, C. J. W.-L. (1995), *Buying Japan: Singapore, Japan and an "East Asian" Modernity*. Paper presented at the Second Symposium on 'From the Americanization to the Japanization of East Asia?'. Rikkyo University and the International House of Japan, Tokyo, 26–28 June.

_____ (1996), 'Staging the "new" East Asia: Singapore's Dick Lee, pop music and a counter-modernity', *Public Culture* 8: 489–510.

_____ (1997), 'Buying Japan: Singapore, Japan and an "East Asian" modernity', *The Journal of Pacific Asia* 4: 21–46.

Wernick, Andrew (1991), *Promotional Culture: Advertising, Ideology and Symbolic Expression*. London: Sage Publications.

Wheatley, Paul (1961), *The Golden Khersonese*. Kuala Lumpur: University of Malaysia Press.

Williams, Rosaline (1982), *Dream Worlds: Mass Consumption in Late Nineteenth Century France*. Berkeley: University of California Press.

Wilson, Elizabeth (1985), *Adorned in Dreams*. Berkeley, California: University of California Press.

Yohanna Abdullah (1990), *Beyond the Veil: The case of Muslim women in Singapore*. Unpublished academic exercise, Department of Sociology, National University of Singapore.

Young, R.J.C. (1995), *Colonial Desire: Hybridity in Theory, Culture and Race*. London: Routledge.

Zakaria, Fareed (1994), 'Culture Is Destiny: A Conversation with Lee Kuan Yew', *Foreign Affairs* 73: 109–126.

Index